NEWTON SOLNEY

BY

MICHAEL DAY
&
MAXWELL CRAVEN

MMIX

First published in Great Britain by
Newton Park Publishing
Primavera,
Trent Lane,
Newton Solney,
Derbyshire

*

*

ISBN: 978-0-9566646-0-0

*

Printed in Great Britain by
Glenwood Printing Ltd.,
Unit 4, Baines Industrial Park
Woods Lane, Derby DE22 3UD

*

CONTENTS

****

Pedigree Tables in the text

****

AUTHOR'S NOTE

I have always enjoyed visiting Newton Solney. There is something outrageously memorable about the great folly (or was it?) on the hill, and the memorably eclectic group of Regency buildings clustered around the former Newton Park House. I first came with my friend Michael Stanley in 1980 to write about Bladon Castle and Newton Park (when we took John Farey at face value concerning its possible architect) for the second volume of *The Derbyshire Country House*. Indeed, Volume II was launched at the hotel in May 1984.

I returned following the marriage of my friends Susan and Norman Ellis, to visit the latter's strikingly modern home, *Primavera*, and to be introduced to the sequestered charm of the Newton Park estate, where Susan's amiable brother Michael lived, having been one of the pioneer purchasers of the houses there.

It was Michael Day's ambition to chronicle the park at Newton, although he was a trained engineer rather than an historian, and his researches led him inevitably to encompass the story of the entire village. After his tragic death in 2008, after much research but before he had a chance actually to begin the text, I was exceedingly flattered to be asked to complete his project, when I suspected that others may perhaps have been in some ways better qualified. I was entrusted with numerous boxes of notes and photocopies of source material. From these I saw that he envisaged one of the more comprehensive village histories to have been attempted and that the work he and Susan had been doing on the Newton Solney portion of the recently resumed *Victoria County History* had whetted his appetite to make a thorough job of it.

Thus I have tried to build on the work that that he had done and to bring in more sources, re-evaluate all of them, scrutinise more closely the eccentric architecture of the place and make more of the characters who had lived in the village, for a built environment is nothing without the people who lived in it and the threads that brought them together.

I have tried to give each era equal weight, for many village histories tend to concentrate heavily on the twentieth century, especially those compiled collaboratively. Such an approach certainly guarantees sales, as every settlement still (mercifully) has a solid base of people whose roots go deep into their village's past and who can be relied on to enjoy the setting-out and illustration of living and recent memory. Yet the history of the later 19th and 20th centuries cannot fully explain why a village is like it is, nor reveal the hidden things which, even if not of pivotal importance, are invariably matters worthy of record. Fortunately, the excellent Newton WI millennium history, *Newton Solney Remembered*, tells the more recent story most excellently, leaving the field clear for Mr. Day's somewhat more ambitious concept.

Michael Day also hoped to set the history of the village in a comprehensive global context, which I have been obliged to scale back, and hope that the reader will have enough basic knowledge of the milestones of British history to be able to read what follows without it becoming meaningless. He had (as have I) also to cast our net widely for sources, and I have tried to avoid saying anything that I cannot support. Footnotes have been essential, but have been rationed to a maximum of one per paragraph and corralled at the end of each chapter so as not to interrupt the flow of the text. Where authoritative sources have been lacking I have tried to reconstruct events – especially Abraham Hoskins' creation of his estate – using what little evidence there is, both written and architectural, combined with the application of common sense. In other words, I have tried to put myself in Hoskins' place in order to understand the reasons why he may have done what he did. Not everyone will agree with my assessments, but any further debate can only hope to illuminate matters further and the mere act of publication may well flush out information that has not been available beforehand.

I can only hope that what has finally rolled off the press is an adequate attempt to complete Mike's ambitious vision and does sufficient justice to a most delightful and notable village.

FOREWORD

by

Sir Henry Every

It is a great pleasure to be asked to write a foreword to this remarkably thorough village history. It is all the more pleasurable when the book concerned conveys matters of particular personal interest and put together with style and considerable scholarship.

The story of Newton Solney is quite a complex tale containing, as it does, the changing ownerships which mirrored the changing fortunes of local families – my own amongst them - and the coming of the new generation of industrial land owners, each in their way creating parts of the delightful village and landscape we can see today.

Perhaps it is surprising we have waited so long for this story to be told. It's been well worth the wait. In Max Craven we have an author with a huge interest in and wide knowledge of Derbyshire history. Throughout he has sought to enlighten us (gently) with the facts and to provide the background and context to promote a wider understanding of the way our countryside and communities have evolved. That he has been able to build on the original vision and research of the late Mike Day is much to his credit. Our thanks are due to Mike Day's sister, Sue Ellis, who selected Max to realise Mike's enterprise.

It is also a happy co-incidence that this book is published on the two hundredth anniversary of Abraham Hoskins' renewed programme of building and improvements at Newton Park.

I believe this book will be of great interest to many, not just those who live in or near to Newton Solney but also those who are interested in following the changing nature and times of living in the countryside: a fast disappearing phenomenon.

Sir Henry Every 13th Bt. DL
Egginton, Derbyshire
High Sheriff of the County 2009/2010   27th July 2009

MICHAEL DAY

Michael Day was born in Richmond , Surrey and was brought up in the North London suburb of Winchmore Hill and educated at Highgate School. He took an engineering degree at Imperial College, London University, and moved up to Derby to take up a graduate apprenticeship at Rolls Royce in the early '50s. Always interested in modern art and architecture, he firstly built a modern split level house near Darley Park. Later, seeking a more rural ambiance and having an acquaintance with the village of Newton Solney through visiting the annual produce show in the Village Hall, he heard about the proposed development in Newton Park. He wished to provide a pleasant home for his newly widowed mother and was attracted by the proposed single storied modern houses to be built around the lake. After studying carefully each proposed plot, he chose one with a view of the lake to one side and lovely countryside views to the South. He contributed extensively to the design of the house and it became his very attractive new home, full of light, with large floor to ceiling windows, a built-in conservatory and an internal courtyard. As more people moved in, the development became a very sociable community of like-minded enthusiasts, and he and his mother settled in very happily.

Taking early retirement from Rolls Royce, Mike busied himself with the Residents' Association, latterly taking care of the delightful grounds. Becoming fascinated by the surrounding landscape, he enthusiastically took up the job of finding out how it all came about. Meticulously researching the Hoskins' role in the village, he became so absorbed with its overall history that he spent many months, if not years, researching the de Solney family after whom the village was named and whose monuments lie in its church to this day. His primary intention then was to distribute his findings to all the home owners of the estate in pamphlet form, whilst simultaneously preparing a complete history of the settlement from the earliest times.

Sadly Michael died unexpectedly before he could bring this idea to fruition He left behind such extensive notes that his executors thought it would be worthwhile putting them together into a book, and Max Craven, who had assisted him in some of his research, kindly agreed to write it using the material he had assembled as a basis.

Thus what has been produced stands as a memorial to a person who truly loved the village of Newton Solney.

SE

*

iv

ACKNOWLEDGEMENTS

Without Michael Day this project would never have been started, and his preliminary industry was prodigious and his vision a commendable one to which I have tried throughout to adhere. And without his sister, Susan Ellis, the matter would probably have died with Michael, so her vision and energy in bringing the matter to publication redounds to her great credit, the more so from the untiring assistance she has rendered.

Many others have been helpful beyond all expectations. Sir Henry Every, Bt. has been kind enough to allow me access to the material relating to his family and former estate still in his possession and he and Lady Every have kindly kept us refreshed on our several visits. Sir Henry has also made available a number of pictures and has kindly written a foreword.

I would also like to pay tribute to Norman Ellis, for colossal amount of hospitality, and sharing his memories of building *Primavera*; to Dinah & Noel Freer, Alan Gifford, Philip Heath (heritage officer for South Derbyshire District Council), Jonathan Marshall, Derrick Pounds, Philip Riden (the County Editor of the Victoria County History), Jennifer Thorp and David Rymill, Lord Carnarvon's archivists at Highclere, the management of the Newton Park Hotel and numerous local people who have helped in various ways, not to mention those who have been kind enough to invite us into their homes, especially my friends Tony Ratcliffe, and Peter McManus. Also I owe a debt of gratitude to the staff of Derby Local Studies Library, those of the Derbyshire Record Office, Staffordshire Archives (both at Stafford and Lichfield), and others upon whose material I have been able to draw.

This work is also heavily in the debt of Brian Appleby who was far-sighted enough to bid successfully for an apparently unconsidered album of old photographs at the sale of Olive Ratcliff's effects in 1972 when he was a memorable landlord of the *Unicorn*. In so doing he saved the younger Richard Keene's momentous record of the Newton Park estate as it was in 1878 or thereabouts, when it was offered for sale by Lord Carnarvon's agents, atmospherically run-down and virtually untouched since 1837 when sold by Abraham Hoskins. Most of the best pictures in the album have been used where appropriate, although the interpretation of one or two is open to question.

I am also grateful to Chris Bond for his excellent pictures of the estate, to the committee of the Newton WI for the use of some of the illustrations from their book, and to *Derbyshire Life* and the Magic Attic at Swadlincote for permission to use photographs from their collection. I must also pay tribute to my wife, Carole, for her tolerance and help, and to my 14-year-old-daughter Cornelia for allowing me to use my computer occasionally!

To all those others whom I have failed to mention, and one or two others who wanted to help anonymously, my heartfelt thanks for their assistance and forbearance.

MC

*

PARISH OF NEWTON SOLNEY AFTER 1894

EGGINTON

STRETTON

REPTON

Ford .....

Waterside

Trent Fm.

Poplars Fm.

Rock .Ho.

Grange Fm.

Cliffe Ho.

Newton Park

Brickyard Fm.

Dale Fm.

Bladon Castle

Newton Park Fm.

Bladon House

Bacon Lodge

Bladon Hill

Bladon Fm.

Hawfield La.

Newton Lane Fm.

Common Fm.

Newton Mount

WINSHILL

One mile

I

ORIGINS

One of the great strengths of the English countryside until well into the twentieth century was self-sufficiency; another, much less easy to spot to the outsider, has been continuity. Although topography changes hand in hand with changes in the practices of husbandry, there has been a continuous thread, a timelessness, in the countryside and in the human beings who people the landscape.

Academic research over the last forty years has established that boundaries are very much older than used to be thought. The late Professor H. P. R. Finberg's classic analysis of the parish of Withington, Gloucestershire convincingly established that the Roman villa estate there was closely co-terminous with the boundaries of the early parish as set out in an early Saxon charter, and numerous other examples have emerged subsequently in Britain and in even more convincing detail in France. In Derbyshire, too, Hazel Wheeler's major excavation at Willington in the 1980s, established that there property boundaries had remained largely unchanged from the late Bronze *Age* until the settlement had died out and migrated to the site of the present village in the middle Saxon period. It has been suggested since that many Midland counties of England represent the *pagi*, or rural sub-regions of the Romano-British *civitates*, or tribal areas. Hence, it is possible to argue - but not yet, unfortunately, to prove - that Derbyshire's boundaries, when being fixed in the wake of the defeat of the Viking occupation of the area in the early tenth century, represented a well-known unit, once the north western *pagus* of the *civitas* of the *Corieltauvi*, centred on Leicester, originally Roman *Ratae Corieltauvorum*[1].

Likewise, a continuity of blood, as it were, may well exist in any given settlement which could indeed be as ancient as the average parish boundary. A recent DNA analysis of the oldest complete human skeleton ever found in Britain, recovered from a site in Gogh's Cave, in Cheddar Gorge, Somerset, found a match in a group of local families still living south of the Mendips, the most positive sample of all coming from a teacher at a local school![2] Again, this particular example, which has yet to be matched quite as spectacularly elsewhere, gives us a truly stupendous thread of continuity lasting from the Neolithic to the present, some 9,000 years. Had records survived better, there is little doubt that such continuity would have been long ago taken for granted instead of standing out, as at present, as something wholly remarkable.

With this in mind, it is worth being reminded that the Trent is one of Britain's great rivers, and that its valley, long one of the only corridors of communication through middle England, was thickly settled by ancient man, with well established sites from the Neolithic onwards. In the Bronze Age, with numerous settlements, barrows, tumuli, settlement features at least one henge and *cursi* – highly elongated parallel earthworks about which almost nothing is known - it seems to have been particularly thickly settled, with concentrations at Aston-on-Trent, Findern, Twyford, Swarkestone Lows, Stenson and Shardlow[3].

Such impressive continuity cannot, however, be demonstrated quite so arrestingly at Newton Solney, yet the parish without doubt had a place in the events of prehistory and the Roman period, even though no artefact nor topographical clue from those periods has yet come to light. Yet Newton Solney, immediately west of the important parish of Repton, itself once one of the capitals of the Kingdom of Mercia and the burial place of its kings, occupies a position that must have involved it in the events of those bygone eras. The village sits on the inside of the river as it curves south westwards toward Burton-on-Trent, on the gravels of the wide vale of the Trent and, opposite the confluence with the Dove, an important tributary. In view of the fact that both rivers must have formed essential arteries of communication, the settlement's position must have accorded it some prominence, and the low gravelly beach quarter of a mile east of the church might well mark an ancient disembarkation point, prior to the more important and acknowledged ones of Repton and, to the SW, Burton. The topography is further marked by the low eminence of Bladon Hill and by rising ground stretching southwards towards the boundary with Bretby.

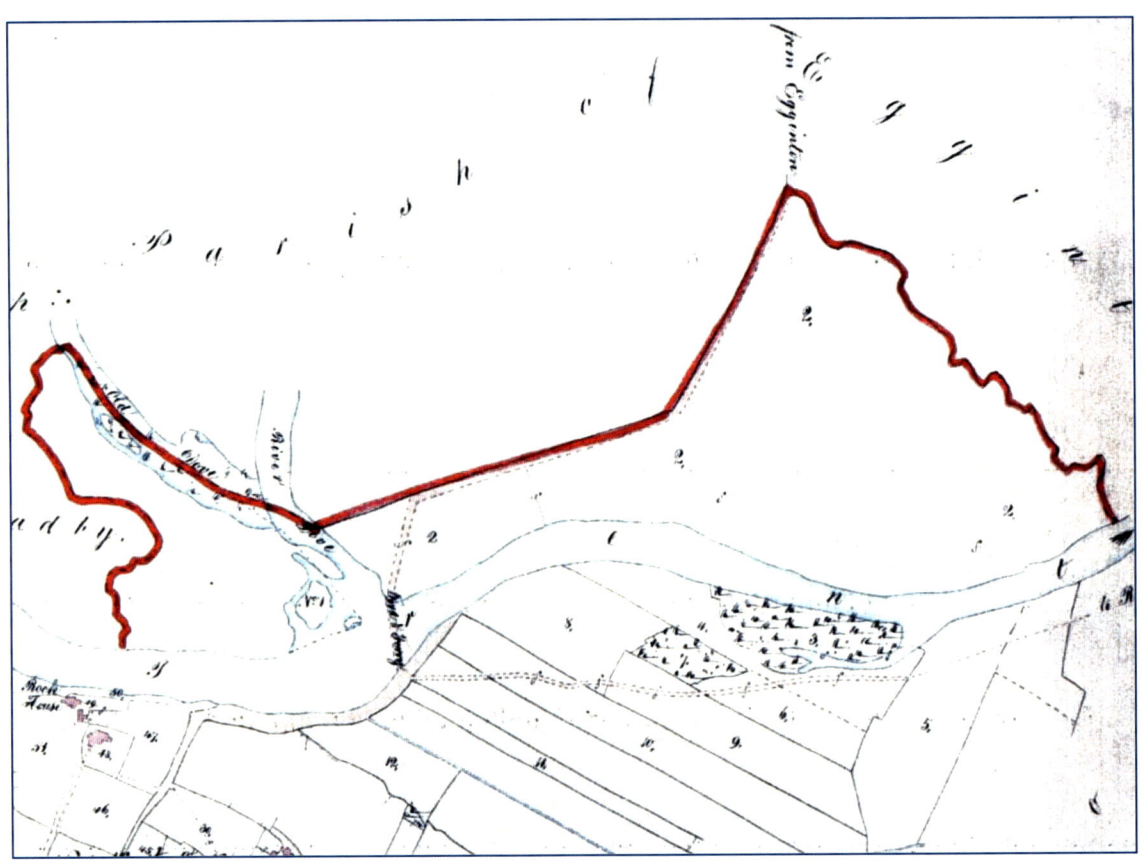

Newton Solney northern parish boundary (marked in red), 1851. The Dove joins from the north.

If there can be any facet of Newton Solney that might hark back to an early period, it might well be the boundary of the settlement, the parish boundary, both ecclesiastical and later, civil. An attestation of its antiquity lies in an anomaly on its northern edge. Instead of following the course of the Trent, as one might expect, it does nothing of the sort, and meanders north over part of the west (Staffordshire) bank of the mouth of the Dove and then across the fields of Egginton, north of the Trent. The present boundary clearly indicates that, since it was fixed at some unknown point in the past, the course, not only of the Trent, but also of the Dove, has changed considerably, leaving a substantial portion of the parish on the north side of the river and some either side of the mouth of the Dove. This anomaly is shown on the 1767 map of P. P. Burdett as much as on modern maps, and the time when the Trent flowed slightly further north and the Dove a little further to the west (where the Staffordshire-Derbyshire county boundary still lies) might well take us back as much as 2,000 years. That the Trent is still moving south at this point is supported by the still eroding scarp on which the village stands, well clear of floods.

Yet even if one could convincingly argue that the parish boundary crossed the river *ab initio*, one could hardly imagine that the County boundary with Staffordshire would not have originally followed the Dove from its mouth. And as the County itself appears to have come into being in the wake of the Saxon *reconquista* of the Norse occupied portion of Mercia in the earlier tenth century, this would at least suggest that the river has migrated since c. 925 AD. If, on the other hand we accept that the boundary may go back through the Saxon settlements to one drawn in Roman times (or long before) to separate the *civitates* of the *Corieltauvi* and the *Cornovii*, or indeed two separate sub-groups of the *Corieltauvi*, then we could argue that the boundary might be two millennia old and that the movement of the river – quite a drastic and complex one, being at a confluence – could have happened at any time between the Roman period and the Norman Conquest.

It follows from all this, that the road from Egginton village to a ford across the river to Newton – today barely visible in the water meadows – must be of considerable antiquity, too, for the northern boundary between Newton Solney and Egginton actually follows its course; the likelihood is that it was once a littoral path along the northern bank of the Trent for its southern portion, at least. A field name, now lost, quoted by William Fraser's 1947 work on South Derbyshire field names, also adds to our knowledge of the early topography. He noted the toponym or locality name Scarsey in the 1758 Every terrier (estate property list), which occurs earlier in a 14th century Every charter as *Scaruseye,* from old Norse *scar* ('precipitous') and *ey* ('island' or 'islet'), clearly an island in the Trent, probably detached from the confluence by erosion with its banks made steep by the seasonal action of the river. Since 1758, and before the 1767 map of Burdett, however, it seems to have disappeared.

A Saxon origin

The lack of ancient artefacts at Newton Solney means that we have to assume that the settlement was a Saxon foundation, although that of Bretby, two miles to the south, might be a Saxon settlement on a much older site, for the Norse name means 'farm or place of the British' - just as nearby Ingleby in contrast means 'place of the English' – suggesting a surviving enclave of Romano-British population, unassimilated by the incoming Anglo-Saxons, who reached the area – from the North Sea via the Trent of course - in the mid-sixth century. Although some recent commentators have assumed that the name derives from the settlement here of a unit of Britons from NW Britain, brought into the area as a mercenary part of the Danish Great Army of 873/4, the most likely explanation still must be that they were a surviving group of indigenous folk

As something of an aside, it is worth considering two of the arguments against the British having been settled at Bretby since the Anglo-Saxon settlements in the mid-sixth century: that the British would have been assimilated long before the Vikings could have arrived to coin the name of Bretby, and that there are no other Celtic-derived place names in the area. The British population was treated with a form of *apartheid* by the Anglo-Saxons, as is established by the Laws the Kingdom of Kent and those of King Ine of Wessex relating to them nearly two centuries after these regions were settled. Even if this legacy had begun to break down in the ninth century, nearly three hundred years after the settlement of Mercia, the social and demographic affects of it must have endured for the Vikings to pick up on. Furthermore, there are several Waltons, place names many of which are acknowledged as Anglo-Saxon ones indicating an enclave of indigenous Britons – *Weala-tune*, the 'place of the Welsh' - in the vicinity, to attest to the survival of groups of second class British-descended citizens: Walton-on-Trent, Walton-by-Chesterfield, Walton-by Stone and Walton-by-Stafford on the other side of the Trent as well as three in Leicestershire and another near Rugby. Nor is the southern half of Derbyshire completely bereft of surviving names with Celtic elements – like Crich, Pentrich, and so on - although as with other parts of lowland Britain, they are indeed, rare.

Another interesting argument for its having been long an enclave of Britons is that, unlike Newton Solney, Bretby has even today no real focal point: it is not, strictly speaking, a nucleated village but one of dispersed groups of buildings and farmsteads. In this it strongly resembles Welsh villages, or villages long settled by the descendants of Britons, un-diluted with Anglian incomers, like Orcop or Kentchurch in Herefordshire, once in the proto-Welsh Kingdom of *Erging* (Archenfield) , and free from Anglian admixtures until the fall of this part of what later became the Kingdom of Gwent in the later tenth century. The supposed foundation of a Celtic monastery at or very near Repton in the later sixth century by St. David could, if accepted, offer further support for this supposition[4].

We also know, from the *Domesday Book* of 1086, that Bretby and Newton Solney were then linked, so the two settlements might have grown up in the Dark Ages as parallel British and Anglian ones, set in a shared landscape.

Following the Anglo-Saxon settlement of the Trent Valley, the establishment of Repton must have happened fairly hard on its heels. The Mercians were a large confederation of many Anglian tribes and, from the place name of Repton, we can confidently assert that one of them was called the *Hreope,* Repton meaning 'the hill or place of the *Hreope'*. This grouping is thought to have had a fairly wide settlement area, especially as the place name of Ripon, 120 miles to the north has the same origin. It could be that elements of the *Hreope* entered Britain in two separate waves under different leaders to explain another group of the tribe having established themselves in what later became Northumbria. Thus we can safely assume that Newton, the 'new place, or farm', was founded by elements of the *Hreope* sometime after the mid-6th century. The most recent historian of the county, Gladwyn Turbutt, goes on to make the further suggestion that the later dependent chapels pertaining to the Anglo Saxon mother church (and double religious house) of Repton, which by the time of the Norman settlement included Bretby, Foremark, Ingleby, Measham, Newton Solney, Smisby, and Ticknall. He further suggests that this swathe of territory also originally included Melbourne, detached at a very early post-Conquest date and given to the Bishops of Carlisle. Added to this, the *Domesday Book* berewicks (outliers) and sokeland (dependant free territory) of Repton should be included as well, which would add to the total area. These were Milton, Ticknall, Ingleby, along with Willesley, Thringstone and Measham (now in Leicestershire) as well as Chilcote (now in Staffordshire): a substantial portion of Derbyshire south of the Trent, and of course, at the time of settlement, it may have included other settlements which, by 1086, had been detached by royal grant from the core tribal area

This large chunk of land in its earliest extent probably also represents a major *territorium* or *pagus* of the *Corieltauvian* tribal area of Roman times, and probably survived intact as a unit through the dark ages, perhaps under the sway of the shadowy Celtic kings of *Luitcoit*, formerly Roman *Letocetum*, present day Wall, Staffordshire. As Repton held a central place in the development of the Mercian Kingdom, the territory the *Hreope* had settled, possibly therefore by direct take-over from its previous Romano-British overlords, was clearly important, too. But after the conversion of its kings to Christianity from Northumbria after the death of Mercia's first great king, Penda in 655, came the Viking age. From 873/4 until Queen Aethelflaeda of Mercia threw them out of the area in 917 most, but not all, of Mercia was part of a Viking polity which embraced most of Northern and Middle England.[5] In its recovery, however, the process of the dismemberment of the tribal lands of the *Hreope* may have begun. Yet it was not until after that upheaval that Newton Solney makes its first appearance on the pages of history.

A debut on the pages of history

In a charter of 956, forty years after King Edward the Elder of Wessex had forged the Kingdom of All England from the Danish held parts of England recovered during the *reconquista*, King Edwig granted five hides there to his *karus* ('most treasured friend') Aethelgeard.[6] The place is called *Niwantune* or Newton, thus, 'new farm' or 'new settlement'. Five hides amounts, in our region, to between 600/750 acres, which compares interestingly with the acreage of Newton in the early nineteenth century of 1401.[7] A hide, or carucate (the term most often used in parts of England like Derbyshire which had been under Danish domination) was the amount of land that could be kept under cultivation for a year using a team of eight oxen - sufficient to support a family. By the tenth century, it had also become a unit of tax assessment, too. Thus, Aethelgeard's grant was not for the *whole* settlement, assuming its boundaries were approximately as they were in later centuries, but quite possibly for the entire cleared and cultivable area, for the assarting, or clearing of woodland to create pasture was then still a necessary adjunct to settlement, as population expanded.

Aethelgeard is the first named person to be associated with the village, too, so anything we can say to flesh out a person who at first glance is merely a name, should be helpful. In fact apart from being a favourite of Edwig's, he was a thegn - a landowning nobleman – who also had land in Hampshire (and especially at the Royal Wessex capital of Winchester, where he was buried) and Berkshire, and was living as an adult within the years 932 to 958, dying two years after his grant of land at Newton. In a later charter he is also called *Preng* which translates from the Anglo-Saxon as 'prince', which may imply kinship with the royal house, perhaps by marriage; Aethelgeard was obviously a man of some consequence.[8].

Although Newton-on-Trent, as it came to be called in its earlier stages, was clearly a settlement of Saxon origin, the fifty years of Norse domination of the area would have had its effect, as it did on Derby itself, which was a bi-lingual town by the early medieval period, with an *elite* running it, members of which bore both Saxon and Norse names. Likewise, in Newton, there were clearly people of Norse extraction living and working there, for three of the ancient toponyms which crop up in the very full collection of charters lodged in the County record office by the Every family, are *Swathlinghay, Colingherdwyke* and *Alketwode* which occur in c. 1225, 1330 and 1381 respectively and reveal the Norse personal names Swartling, Colling and Anketil, probably all free peasants who had worked the land in the village after c. 874.[9] The community, like Derby, was probably a mixed one.

The local place names also include one most suggestive example, that of Spellow Cross, mentioned in the 1846 Tithe Award, a locale situated two fields north of Dale Farm, Bretby Lane and to which may be allied Spellow Flat – probably the same location - in a 14th century Every charter. The name is from Anglian *spell* ('speech') + *hlaw* ('low hill') and as 'speech hill', is usually taken to mean a place of communal gathering, upon which subject William Fraser noted that in his day, exactly a century later, the field was often called Sparrow Cross, and was thus

> "...an instructive instance of how a name of great significance and definite meaning can, through distortion by those unaware of its origin, become meaningless."[10]

Two assumptions might be made from this. The first is that the site must have once marked a gathering point for the community, or for elements of the community. In a town, such a place was called a moot, hence in 12th century Derby the *portmannemot*, but such for a small settlement like Newton these are not well attested. It is possible that, as it lay very close to the border with Repton parish, it was a place of mutual discourse for the two settlements, or was memorable for having been used once or twice at a time of crisis as, for instance, when the Viking Great Army was approaching in autumn 873. Yet as Dr. Turner has suggested, these more local assembly places (the Anglo-Saxon ones tended to be restricted to town moots and Hundred – in Norse, *Wapentake* - assembly places) may well be a feature of the Danelaw, the portion of England settled by the Norse invaders after this date, in which Newton lay.[11] The other point is that in the nineteenth century source, Spellow. is suffixed by the word 'cross'. There being no obvious modern explanation for this, it may well be that the *spel-hlaw* gathering place was not merely of a lay communal nature at all but was in fact was adapted after the restoration of the control of the Saxon church in the Danelaw, as a place with a preaching cross, around which the worship of the community was conducted. This indeed was commonly the case before the widespread erection of proprietary churches in rural areas. To risk piling speculation on hypothesis for a moment, it is worth noting that such places were very often hallowed with antiquity even when marked out for Christian use, which might presuppose that the *hlaw*, or low hill, could have once been the site a pre-historic tumulus or burial mound of some important person and hence have survived in communal memory at a place of significance even before the Norse perhaps fixed upon it as an assembly place. If such a mound then existed, it should occasion no surprise today that it is no longer discernable; such features can be all too easily ploughed out.

Wulfric Spot

To return to the thegn Aethelgeard's estate at Newton, there appears to be no known continuity between him and the next person whom we know owned it, another thegn, albeit rather better known, called Wulfric Spot, although there may well have been such a link. Wulfric is better known because he left extensive landed estates to the Abbey of Burton upon Trent in his will. Having the will itself is a bonus, because it gives a picture of the sort of land-holdings a great magnate of the time would have held. In Wulfric's case these consisted of no less than 80 estates, mostly in

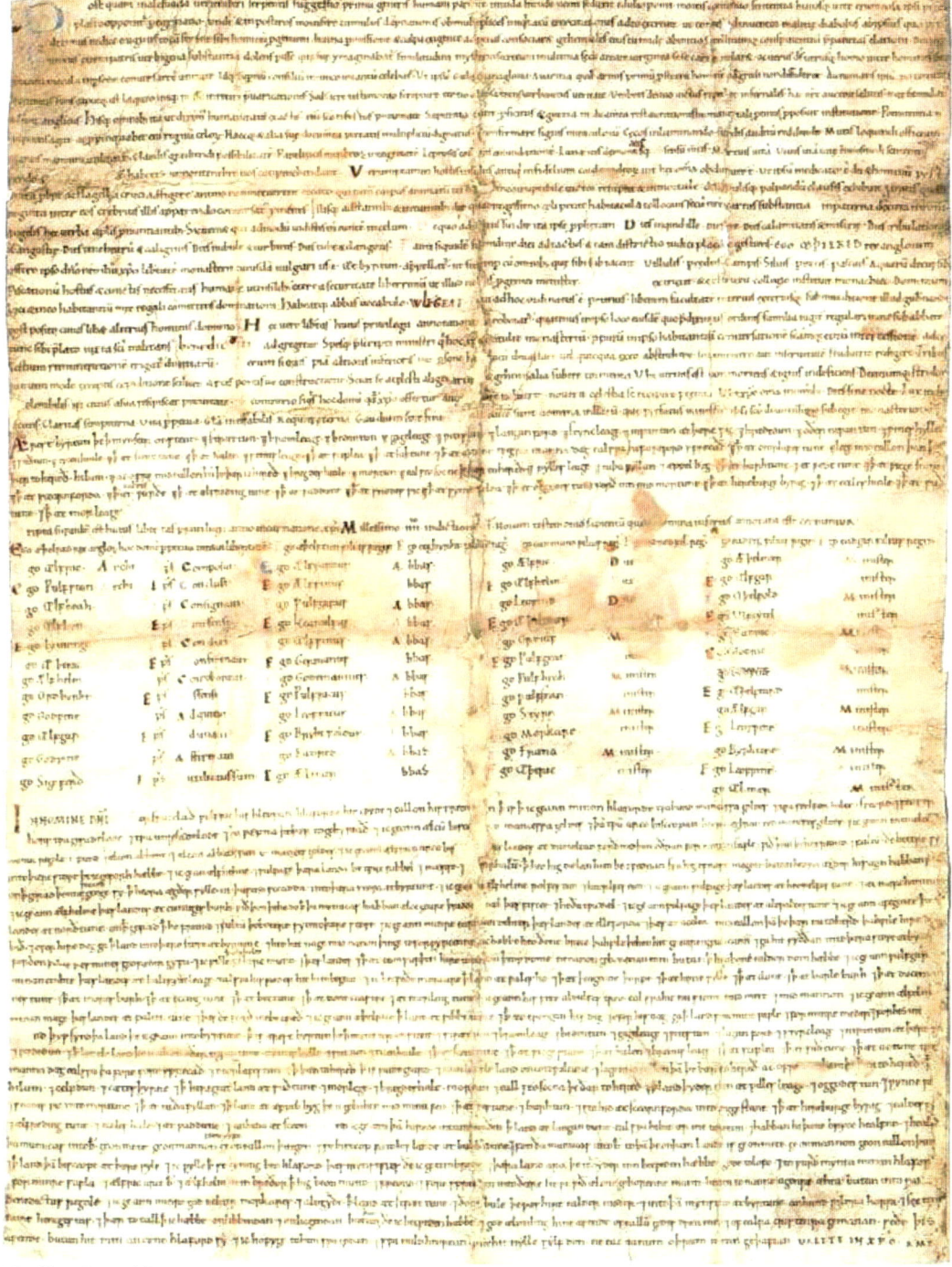

Will of Wulfric Spot [*British Library*]

Staffordshire, Derbyshire and the western portion of Leicestershire. In 1004 he established, through his gifts and endowments, also itemised in his will of the same year, the Abbey of Burton, and King Aethelred II (Ethelred the Unready, where 'unready' actually meant 'ill-advised') duly confirmed it.[12] In the will Newton is called "a little estate at Newton", which is less than specific, especially when one realises that there are several Newtons in the areas where Wulfric held land. Fortunately, as this entry comes right after that of Winshill, a settlement immediately adjacent to Newton-on-Trent to the SW, there can be little doubt but that he was referring to the same estate as that granted to Aethelgeard five decades before, rather than say, King's Newton, further east, which has on occasion caused confusion in later charters.

Unfortunately, not enough is known of Wulfric's family to identify a connection whereby Wulfric could have inherited the estate from Aethelgeard. It could just have easily been recovered by the crown if Aethelgeard had died without issue or in disgrace, and been granted to Wulfric's family. We know from the descent of the bulk of his estate that a thegn called Wulfsige *Maur*, or 'the Black', was his maternal grandfather, and that his mother was Wulfrun, whose eldest son inherited his *Wulf-*prefixed name from her, Anglo Saxon notables being long in the habit of repeatedly using the same first syllable in given names through many generations. It has been suggested that a thegn called Wulfric of Austrey (Warwickshire) was our Wulfric's father, but he might just as easily have been his uncle or great uncle; the only point in common is that both Wulfrics and Wulsige held Austrey. Any of these could have inherited or been granted Newton and passed it on to Wulfric Spot.

There is another explanation, on offer, too. Wulfric *Maur* had, in 942, been granted a huge block of territory on either side of the upper Trent valley, probably as a reward for vital aid to King Aethelstan and his successor Edmund in the great defeat of the combined Danish and British armies under Olaf II King of Dublin at the unlocated *Brunanburh* and the subsequent second re-conquest of Mercia completed that year. Although the three extant charters setting these grants out list a good number of places, including Rolleston-on-Dove, partially opposite Newton, the wording suggests that there may have been at least one other related grant which could have included Newton, If so, it could have been surrendered to the Crown – or taken back as the result of some slight - and re-granted to Aethelgeard. Hence its re-appearance in Wulfric Spot's portfolio before 1004 might represent a restitution.

After Wulfric died – he and his wife Ealhswith appear to have had no surviving children – his family went on to make powerful and royal connections. Although his brother Aelfhelm, Ealdorman of Northumbria was killed and his two sons blinded in 1006, the former's daughter Aelfgifu went on to marry King Cnut (1016-1035) and become the mother of Harald I Harefoot (1035-1040). Another niece, Ealdgyth, married King Edmund Ironside ironically, killed by Cnut in the struggle for the control of England in 1016. Her daughter by her first marriage, however, married Aelfgar, or Algar, Earl of Mercia and East Anglia, who went on to be the most powerful man in the region in which Newton Solney lay in the reign of Edward the Confessor. Again, although his sons failed to survive the Conquest in 1066, his daughter married Welsh King Gruffydd ap Llewellyn (through whose numerous descendants the blood of Wulfric's family has survived to the present) and then the ill-fated King Harald II Godwinson. Of one thing we can be sure: Newton, although in Wulfric's will, was not one of those places granted to the Abbey of Burton.

Whilst the family of Wulfric Spot maintained their position as a recurring thread through the dynastic and racial conflicts of the following six decades, we hear no more of Newton, and can only derive inferences from the next piece of written evidence: *Domesday Book*. Here, we are told that in the time of King Edward (the Confessor) Newton Solney, by now definitely linked to Bretby, was held by Algar, Earl of Mercia who had actually died in 1062, leaving his possessions to his elder son, Edwin. This suggests that the estate had been claimed back from the Abbey of Burton by Wulfric Spot's heirs in some way. Given the upheavals of 1015-1016 and those subsequently, it is no surprise that Wulfric's carefully laid bequests began to unravel. There was strategic value of some of them, especially places commanding stretches of the navigable Trent, like Newton; nor can it be a matter for surprise if the family should succeed in recovering at least some of them. After all, the sheer magnitude of the original grant to the Abbey must have represented a severe diminution of Wulfric's patrimony, to a reasonable share of which his brothers and sister must have felt fully entitled. Hence, Newton might have been recovered by the niece Ealdgyth, later wife of Edmund II Ironside and transmitted to her daughter Aelfgifu whose husband Algar Earl of Mercia would have held it in her right. Hence Newton-on-Trent was still effectively in Wulfric's family when the Conquest supervened, and changed everything for good.[13]

Domesday Book

The Domesday Book entry for Newton Solney reads:

The land of the King
NEWETUN
In the time of King Edward, Earl Algar had 7 carucates
[Now there is] land for 5 ploughs; the king has 11/2 ploughs. [There are] 19
villagers, 1 smallholder (together having 5 ploughs). Land: 12 acres of meadow, 2
leagues by 3 furlongs of woodland pasture, [all] worth 20/- in both 1066 and 1086.[14]

Facsimile of the Newton-on-Trent entry in the Derbyshire section of Domesday Book

It will be noticed that the King had deprived the heirs of the Earls of Mercia of the manor (either in 1066 or 1071) and that the size of the estate had increased from 5 to 7 hides (*Domesday Book* uses the analogous Norse-derived term, carucates) since the grant to Aethelgeard 110 years earlier, thus representing an increase in arable land from 600/750 acres to 840/1050. This almost certainly suggests that further clearance of woodland had occurred. Bearing in mind the combined acreage given in 1846 of

2,906, this means that there was still a minimum of 1,856 acres left not brought into cultivation. And although Bretby is a slightly larger settlement in terms of today's parish boundaries – which, as we have seen, are likely to be quite early – it was only a berewick or outlier of, and subordinate to, the manor of Newton, suggesting an inferior status, perhaps deriving from the fact that Bretby was or had been a British settlement, whether from time immemorial or from the time of the Viking invasion.

Reverting to the Domesday Book, an interesting aspect of Newton is that with the taxable value having remained constant between 1066 and 1086, despite various upheavals like the Stafford Rebellion and the 'harrying of the north', the settlement must have escaped the worst of these deleterious events.[15] The 19 villagers mentioned are not, however, that useful a guide to the total population of the two settlements, but they do represent the free peasants living there; under them there would have been unfree families living in serfdom, called villeins, as well.

There is no mention of an under-tenant, specifically holding the estate at Newton either, although there would have been one. Unfortunately, *Domesday Book* only lists things that yielded tax to the Crown – contrary to the popular belief that everything in England was listed – and frequently omits tenants of the chief lord, especially those holding their manors under the King[16].

For that was the new order. In Saxon times land was granted to a man for life, and then the grant had to be renewed. Later, especially after the Viking invasion, land was granted to be held hereditarily, called *Bocland* (Bookland) because it had been "booked out" of the King's hands. Thus, the manor of Newton had been able to descend through the family of Wulfric. After the Conquest, however, only the King could actually own land, and everyone else held their land from him, either as tenants-in-chief, who held considerable properties, or as sub-tenants, holding under a tenant-in-chief. This also included the monasteries, too. Unfortunately, we get no clear idea who the King's sub-tenant at Newton was, for the paperwork which might have shed light on it has not survived and it is almost a century before we know the identity of a Newton sub-tenant. Evidence elsewhere, however, tends to suggest that the main sub-tenant would almost certainly have taken the place name in addition to his given name in order to distinguish him. Hence the Domesday tenant at Brailsford, Elfin (corrupted in the Book from Aelfwine, and therefore a man of Anglo-Saxon descent) was father of Nicholas and by 1100 both were being called 'de Brailsford' and there are numerous other examples of this in Derbyshire alone. Hence, there must have been an elite family holding the manor of Newton under the King from the post-conquest era, and the likelihood is that they were called Newton from the place. They might well have been of non-Norman stock, too, if similarities with other places are taken into account, perhaps the same family as held the estate under Algar of Mercia.[17]

Indeed, a family of this name emerges early on in the immediate vicinity, the earliest reference being to one Roger de Newton who witnessed a charter of Repton Priory concerning land at Heather, Leics., in 1170 and in the next generation we find Hamo son of John de Newton witnessing a charter of Burton Abbey.[18] There were other Newtons witnessing deeds at Repton Priory in this era, but the charters refer to land at Ticknall where one of them, another John de Newton, was holding land in 1260. With Ticknall being somewhat closer to Newton by Melbourne (King's Newton), a note of caution needs to be signalled: the Ticknall Newtons might be members of a separate family taking their name from there, not from Newton-on-Trent.[19] It is not, indeed, until July 1317, long after any notional early subtenants of this name must have lost their pre-eminent position at Newton, that one can tie a Newton to actual property in the village. This is Richard son of Margery de Newton who was drawing two shillings per annum rent from a house and land there, this being the same era in which two further members of the family were again witnessing Burton Abbey charters.[20] Thereafter one can trace a steady succession of Newtons in the village from William and Thomas de Newton 'chaplains' (probably canons of Repton Priory) having dealings in the village in the 1370s to John Newton of Corbin's Hall, Kingswinford, Staffordshire, who was listed as a Newton Solney freeholder in the Every family's terrier of 1758 and who, two years later, sold some of his property on Landlands Lane (now Bretby/Newton Lane) to Sir John Every, then the lord of the manor. This indeed, was probably the end of the Newtons' association with the village after what might well have been 700 years, and certainly 400, for William Newton, possibly John's father, described as 'Gent., of Burton upon Trent' also sold some land to the Every's thirteen years before.[21]

A new Chief Lord

We know much more about the chief Lordship at this period however which, as it happens, did not for long remain in the King's hands. William had followers to reward, and he came back from Normandy in 1067 and 'gave away every man's land'. Most of the holdings of the King still in his hands in 1086 were lands forfeited by supporters of Harald II or men who had subsequently rebelled. One of the great Norman magnates to be rewarded was Hugh d'Avranches, given the Earldom of Chester, which came with a portfolio of lands designed to support the dignity, and called the Honour of Chester, just as the Honour of Tutbury comprised the lands and manors which supported the de Ferrers family's Earldom of Derby. Hugh was later to stand loyally by William II during the serious rebellion of 1096, and this may well have been the occasion his honour was augmented by further grants, including Newton. The other opportunity for Newton-on-Trent to have been added to the Honour of Chester was as a result of the death, in the *White Ship* disaster on 23rd November 1120, of Hugh's son and successor, Richard, his wife and child, thus rendering his male line suddenly and unexpectedly extinct. Henry I, in the following year, re-conferred the Earldom on Hugh's nephew Ranulf de Meschines. In the grant of the Earldom, Ranulf surrendered to the King some lands in Cumberland he had previously been granted in exchange for an increase in those of the Earldom. On balance, the latter occasion seems the most likely for Newton to have been given to the Earl.[22]

The new earl – he was son of the Viscomte de Bayeux, a Norman who was also lord of Avranches and who had not previously been involved in English affairs - brought in from France a number of his own followers. One change was that a new family was installed, again at an unknown date in the mid-12th century, as the Earl's sub-tenants in Newton: the de Solignys, usually Anglicised to (de) Solney, and with their arrival there opens a new, much better documented era in the history of Newton.

It is worth noting, too, that this era signalled a parting of the ways between Newton and its Domesday berewick of Bretby; they were henceforth no longer part of the same polity, although Bretby had come to the Earls of Chester by the same grant. At some date in the middle 12th century, possibly when the original sub-tenants died out, or were simply supplanted, it was granted as a separate manor to a new sub-tenant, Philip de Kyme, of Kyme, in Kesteven, Lincolnshire. His grandson of the same name, however, sold it back to Ranulf de Blundeville, 6th Earl of Chester in the 1220s, after which it continued on a separate course, being granted by the Earl to the Segraves, from whom it descended to the Berkeleys and eventually the Stanhope Earls of Chesterfield.[23]

Enter the Solneys

There are two important questions concerning Newton's new local lordly family: when precisely did they acquire the lordship of the Manor of Newton, and from whence did they come?

The first mention of the Solney family occurs in a charter of Earl Ranulf granting land to the Norman monastery of St. Evroul., c. 1121-1125 (these early monastic charters are frequently undated but their period can often be fixed by reference to the known period in office of the superior of the religious house in question, which is usually well attested). The man is named as Alured de Soligny, whose Christian name we may henceforth Anglicise as Alfred. There is nothing about this charter to connect him with Newton-on-Trent, except that it is one issued by the 3rd Earl of Chester who by this date had almost certainly been granted Newton by the King.[24] The next time we hear of a member of the family, however, is 1162 when another Alfred (II) de Solney witnessed a confirmation by Hugh, 4th Earl of Chester to the canons of Calke of all their lands and liberties, before going on to witness several later charters up to the first years of the 13th century. He was also forced to pay 40 shillings in Derbyshire for a default.[25] As Calke is so close to Newton, we may be very confident that by the time Alfred witnessed there in 1162, he had been safely installed by the Earl of Chester as lord of Newton, leaving the displaced sub-tenants, whom we have contended were the Newtons, in a subsidiary sole as free landholders under the very people who had supplanted them, hence their prolonged presence in and around Newton.

As to the origins of the de Solneys, this presents some problems, if only because there are no less than five places in Northern France of this name or one close to it. One, in the heartland of William the Conqueror's duchy of Normandy, is Soulangy, Calvados, *arrondisement* of Falaise.; another is Soligne, Curey, near Avranches, there is Subligny, La Haye-Pesnel, Manche, Soligny-la-Trappe, Orne, and another Soligne near Pontorson, Tanis, Brittany. The latter produced a Suligny family whose descendants settled in the West Country and which also produced the later Counts of Dol-Combour, Brittany, whose pedigree got hitched – rightly or wrongly - onto Alfred's by earlier antiquaries, notably by the Revd. S. P. H. Statham, who was the first to try and chronicle the family of the new lords of Newton, in 1927. Another (or, conceivably the same) Alured de Solegni had been attested in 1093 (thus of age and born before 1072) as the brother of one Turstin de Solegni, although they both seem to be from an unrelated family from the Falaise Soligne; yet it is tempting to see in him the same man as he who attested the St. Evroul Charter, but Dr. Katherine Keats-

Rohan cautions against it.[26] In favour of the link, however, is the predilection for Saxon names like 'Alfred' and 'Thurstan'

Our Alfred, whose ancestry is thus unknown to us, was most likely one who took his name from Soligne near Avranches. As Avranches was a premier lordship of Ranulf, Earl of Chester, it is highly likely that he drew his followers of knightly rank from the immediate area, of whom Alfred was clearly one. The only factor to give us pause here is the evidence of early heraldry. The de Solney arms were *quarterly argent and gules* (left) which fits reasonably well with the arms borne by Ralph de Argouges' descendants: *Quarterly or and azure, three cinquefoils gules.* Normally, that would be congruence enough to establish a link, bearing in mind that heraldry developed divergently on either side of the channel, despite having begun in the early 12th century as a unified system, the general motif of the arms of both families being a quartered shield. However, the arms of de Soligne de Dol were: *quarterly argent and gules, a bordure of the second semee of martlets of the first* which is so close to the arms as used in England that it might seem conclusive that Alfred came from the Breton Solignis. Bearing in mind that the de Solney arms are not recorded prior to 1304 (although they could certainly have been older), it may be that the King's heralds merely made that assumption in allowing them to the family.[27]

Arms of de Solney

Having served Ranulf in some notable way, then, Alfred - whatever his ultimate background - was duly rewarded with a lordship in the Earl's newly inherited English lands: Newton-on-Trent. Yet, despite all the charters Alfred attested, not one mentions him as 'of Newton', although the default ties him firmly into the land-holders of Derbyshire.

The first positive mention of Newton in conjunction with a de Solney actually only occurs on the death in around 1204 of Alfred II de Solney. What we find is the elder son of Alfred (II), Ralph de Argosis (occasionally attested, at least in English charters, as Ralph de Solney), granting to his younger brother Alfred (III) de Solney a portion of his inheritance which he had from Alfred his father and his mother Joanna, this portion being all his English possessions, namely the manor *Neutona in Anglia* and somewhere that reads as 'Bawe', possibly intended for Broughton, Nottinghamshire. Thus we can be absolutely certain that Alfred (II) was actually lord of Newton, and pretty certain that his tenure dated back at least to the date of the Calke confirmation. Subsequent deeds confirm that Alfred held Newton from his brother and establish that he also held the manor of Upper Broughton, Nottinghamshire, possibly the 'Bawe' of the 1204 settlement. Upper Broughton lies right on the southern border of Nottinghamshire with Leicestershire, in which latter county lies the adjacent settlement, Nether Broughton. What it has in common with Newton Solney is that both were the property of Earl Algar of Mercia in the 1050s and that both were in the hands of the King at the time of *Domesday Book*; Broughton was not one of Wulfric Spot's possessions, though. Nevertheless, it is interesting that they were in the same hands from the mid-eleventh century and both came to the de Solneys through the benevolence of the 3rd Earl of Chester. The brother's surname of de Argosis or Argouges probably derives from Alfred II's wife Joanna, who was probably the heiress of the Lords of Argouges, to which lordship Ralph seems to have succeeded as Raoul VI, and where his posterity remained for at least five further generations.[28]

Thus we have the de Solney family established holding a knight's fee from the Earls of Chester at Newton and another knight's fee at Upper Broughton. We do not know the name of Alfred's wife, unfortunately, but he had died in or around 1230 to be succeeded in Newton by his elder son Sir Norman de Solney and at Upper Broughton by his younger son, Alfred, who held it from his brother.[29]

It was at this juncture that the chief lordship of Newton changed. In 1232, Earl Ranulf (de Blundeville) died leaving a childless widow, along with two living sisters and co-heiresses, and his lands were divided up. Whilst his widow Clemence was alive, Newton Solney was to be part of her dower. On her death it was to pass to the Earl's sister Alice (also known as Agnes), who was married to William de Ferrers, 5th Earl of Derby. In the event, she lived on until 1252, when the Earl of Derby's son, William, 7th Earl, became Newton's chief lord, but in the end it was not to have long as part of his Honour of Tutbury, for he rebelled in 1265 and suffered attainder the following year for treason. The consequence was that the chief Lordship passed back to the King, eventually becoming part of the lands of a royal kinsman, the Earl of Lancaster, whose descendants later became Dukes of Lancaster (Henry IV being Duke prior to his usurpation of the throne in 1399); thus the manor was henceforth part of what later became the Duchy of Lancaster. Thereafter it plays no noticeable part in the history of the settlement, except that all rather than two thirds of the taxes paid by the villagers now went directly to the Crown. Interestingly, in the Index of Dower of Clemence, Countess of Chester (the list of lands held in dower to provide income for her widowhood), there are included those at 'Newton Solney', which is the first known use of the name as we have it today.[30]

Newton Park, mill and fishery

It is with the succession to the Lordship of Newton of Sir Norman de Solney – he was knighted by 1244 – that we first hear about a park at Newton and about the holdings of the Priory of Repton in the village, too. In 1230, probably on his succession to the lordship, the Prior of Repton relaeased to him the park, mill and fishery at Newton. The fact that this was a release, suggests that they were originally granted as a lease to his father, or even his grandfather; certainly, it establishes the existence of all three to the very early years of the 13th century, and we assume that no mill existed in 1086, although its omission from *Domesday Book,* if such a mill had then existed, is perfectly plausible, as we have seen; it may, for instance, have rendered tax elsewhere than to the Crown. These properties must have been at some time previously a gift to the priory, and were probably given by Countess Maud, widow of Ranulf (3rd) Earl of Chester to endow the foundation of the Priory in 1172.

The park must have been a creation of one of the sub-tenants of the manor undertaken before that date, although whether by a de Newton or by Alfred (II) de Solney is well beyond knowing. Either way, it constitutes an early example of a Derbyshire hunting reserve. Indeed, it may have been an ancient piece of ground devoted to the chase, perhaps once belonging to Earl Algar or to even to Wulfric Spot; which would account for the discrepancy between the acreage mentioned in the latter's will compared with the known extent of the settlement and, being a private hunting ground, would not necessarily be mentioned in *Domesday* in which only royal (hunting) forests were generally itemised. There is no way of establishing whether or not this park was in any way co-terminous with the later parkland of Newton Park House as mapped in the early nineteenth century, although it is topographically likely, but for the appearance of ridge and furrow on part of one of the settlement's common fields being visible within the area, which introduces an element of doubt. Recent research has concluded that the boundary is largely lost, although an ancient embankment which curves round to join Newton Lane on the north edge of The End (the name itself, if ancient, perhaps significant in this respect) may be a last vestige of its pale or boundary. Either way, it constitutes the first mention of Newton Park.[31]

Modern photograph of the so-called mill stream in Newton Park.   *[Michael Day]*

The mill may have stood on the brook running through the park at this early stage, although the presence of small close called Mill Dam slightly to the east of Newton Lane Farm might suggest that it was on the brook the lower part of which forms the parish boundary with Repton, although this could have been a later mill. However, the fact that the same Mill Dam and a *mulneway* ('mill path') are both mentioned in fourteenth century Every charters would seem to confirm that the Newton Lane site the more likely, although in more recent times, the stream in the Park has been thought of as the site of the village water mill.[32]

The fishery was on the Trent, however, at the confluence with the Dove. Later, certainly from the early 14th century, it was usually included with the grant of the parsonage house along with a bovate of land as the endowment of the curate of the church. It was certainly a valuable thing over which to have control. Later, in Tudor times, it appears to have been worth £4 per annum, for a later manorial lord, John Lathbury, borrowed £4 from Sir Ralph Longford on the security of property in Hargate (Heathhouses), Egginton, but, failing to repay it, granted Sir Ralph 'all the weir and waters of the Trent belonging to the lordship of Newton at no cost for one year' A weir on the river here was also attested in a charter of 1566. Nor was this the last grant to a member of the family by a Prior of Repton, another was in 1291 to Alfred de Solney of land at both Newton Solney and Bladon[33].

One interesting adjunct to the foundation of the Priory at Repton and its landholdings in Newton was that the third Prior (and the second at Repton, rather than at Calke) was one Alured, in office at some imprecise date between 1181 and 1200. The name is reasonably scarce, certainly in Derbyshire, at that time and the thought obtrudes that this Prior might easily have been a close kinsman of Alfred II de Solney, especially as the family were favoured retainers of the foundress's husband[34].

The later de Solneys

Sir Norman de Solney paid *scutage* or shield money in order to avoid military service on his knight's fee by which he held the manor of Newton, the sum being assessed at forty shillings (£2) which emerges as the taxable value of the manor for at least the two centuries following. He married Juliana de Ulecotes, by whom he appears to have had at least two sons, neither of whom, in the end, succeeded him and who thus presumably died in his lifetime, although one, Alfred, was still his 'son and heir' in 1280, but thereafter we hear nothing of them, and he was succeeded as lord of Newton by the eldest son of his brother Alfred.[35]

Meanwhile, Sir Norman's younger brother Alfred (IV) de Solney also held a knight's fee – that is, like his elder brother in return for holding Newton, he notionally had to find the service of a mounted and fully equipped knight plus attendants for forty days per annum if the King required it - at Upper Broughton in Nottinghamshire in Sir Norman's lifetime, holding it first of the Earl of Chester but then by 1242/43 of the 6th Earl of Arundel as a co-heir of the Earl of Chester, when it was referred to as 'Broughton Sulleney' (Broughton Solney). He, unlike Sir Norman, did not get out of his 40 day obligation of Knight's service by paying *scutage*, for in 1253 we find him serving the King in Gascony as Constable of the Gironde with a grant of £20 per annum, by which time, of course, he was also a knight. It has been suggested that this was an aged Alfred (III) but this is highly unlikely and, if one accepts Alfred IV as Sir Norman's younger brother – and the genealogical evidence is very persuasive – then we have to be dealing with a younger man. Sir Alfred married, before 1244, Sybil, daughter of John de Braytoft, a Lincolnshire landowner who settled the manor of Surfleet on the happy couple, from which they were excused scutage. He was, though, dead by 1262, when his widow re-married Adam de St. Lo who was able to enjoy the manor of Broughton Solney, in the right of his wife, who had it as her widow's portion.[36]

Thereafter, the lordship of Newton Solney - as it had now become – managed to pass through a succession of de Solneys down to the reign of Richard II (1377-1399). Most were called Alfred – there seem to have been eight in all, starting with the one who witnessed the St. Evroul charter – but their family history is too complex to be recounted here and readers with a taste for the minutiae of genealogy are recommended to refer to the Appendix. Nevertheless, some of them left a mark worth recording, quite apart from the three reclining knightly effigies in the church.

John, younger son of Alfred IV de Solney had Broughton Solney in Nottinghamshire settled on him, which had previously been his mother's dower – the land granted to her to keep her in her widowhood. On later inheriting Newton Solney he sold Broughton Solney – which henceforth tended to lose its suffix in favour of 'Upper' –

to Sir Gervase Clifton of Clifton by Nottingham, with eight virgates of land (around 200/250 acres on land scattered amongst the open fields of the village). John also held a knight's fee at Raydon, Suffolk, possibly inherited from his mother. John de Solney is probably to be identified with one Miles de Solney whose name occurs in one of the Every charters, in which case the reference confirms that he was knighted, for the Latin word for 'soldier', *miles*, was synonymous with 'knight' in charters of this date. His wife was Margaret, daughter of Elias de Egginton which is the first reference to a link with the parish which lies opposite Newton Solney across the Trent and which was later to be united under the same ownership. Elias was fourth son of William son of Henry de Egginton, otherwise FitzWalkelin, a minor landowner in the manor opposite, which had been twice fragmented between the descendants of heiresses. Margaret had good social standing but very little land to bring to the union. In either case, it was a doomed alliance, because they died without producing any surviving children; by 1311 Margaret was widowed.[37]

The next Alfred de Solney – the fifth - seems to have had a fairly wild youth, for he was brought to book in 1282 for illegally taking a buck in the bailiwick of Alrewas, in Needwood Forest, a royal hunting park where the game was strictly off limits without a licence being obtained. The offence was committed ten years or so before, so royal justice had a long memory! He was nevertheless later knighted and also held land as a tenant of the Abbey of Burton at Mickleover and Findern. He married Margery, daughter and ultimately the heiress of Odo de Hodnet. Her mother had been an heiress, too, in her case of Ralph le Poer of Pinxton and South Normanton. Alfred thereby eventually became lord of half of the manor of Pinxton and South Normanton. This enabled him to appoint to the living of the latter his youngest son, John who, with his brother William (priest at Newton Solney itself), were both ordained and possibly canons of Repton Priory.

William, who was curate of Newton Solney in 1304 and in 1327, held land there, along with a house, ten acres and the fishery and these seem to have continued for a couple of centuries as the usual perquisites of office for a curate of Newton. An earlier William, 'chaplain' – not the uncle of this name, who married a Bagot of Bagot's Bromley and who thereafter fades from view, but a first cousin - also held the fishing and was thus also probably also the local priest. He was probably an otherwise unrecorded son of Sir Norman, for sons who had entered Holy Orders were disbarred from inheriting. In which case he was again probably seconded to the chapel at Newton from the Priory at Repton of which he would have been a canon.[38]

There were younger sons of the family living on small patrimonies in Newton Solney in the fourteenth century, too. Geoffrey de Solney paid a considerable £4 poll tax there in 1327 and Robert third son of a later Sir Alfred de Solney de Solney was granted a ten shilling rent in Newton 16/6/1347. It may be that either or both of these men may have succumbed to the plague in 1348-49. However, one or other of them must have been the father of the Richard de Solney who witnessed a charter at Newton Solney in 1354. The year before (1353), he was described as 'of Newton Solney' and had a wife, Alice. Another Richard, referred to as 'chaplain' in 1375-1379 was probably his son. If Richard could afford to allow a son to take the cloth, he presumably had another to inherit his property who, however, must have died prematurely, as the elder Richard eventually left only a daughter and heiress who married, and by 1375 had a son, Richard le Warde of Winshill who was his grandfather's heir.[39]

The eighth Alfred de Solney was born in 1286 or 1287. Like several of his forebears, for instance, his father in 1302, he paid forty shillings feudal dues for Newton Solney to the chief lord (by this time the County Palatine, later Duchy, of Lancaster) in 1346, presumably on his succession. He held various other lands, too, including Pixton, Bilby & Ranby, Nottinghamshire, and must have held a manorial estate of some kind at Coggeshall, Essex, for he was granted a licence for an oratory there. This may have been related to his father's holding of a knight's fee at Raydon, Suffolk which had come to him from a maternal uncle, but which had been settled on Alfred's elder brother. It had, however, been sold by him prior to his death without issue. Despite these considerable landholdings, like several of his much later successors, he was still in debt - to the tune of £1,000 in 1320. His creditor was Robert, Lord Holand, but they came to an arrangement that Sir Alfred should surrender the inheritance of the manor of Orby in Lindsey, Lincolnshire, to Lord Holand of Melbourne Castle to cancel the debt, the record of which was lodged with the Prior of Repton, which gives an interesting insight as to how such matters were dealt with amongst the elite in that period. Orby had been the inheritance of Alfred's mother, Sybil, daughter and heiress of John de Orby a third moiety of which he had inherited in 1317 on the death of his uncle John de Orby of Orby, Lincs. In 1326 he had also done homage for Basford in

The alabaster effigy of a de Solney knight in the church is dateable to c. 1375 and thus must be of Sir Alfred VIII de Solney. It is the work of the notable Burton-upon -Trent school of carvers.

Nottinghamshire following the death of another uncle, Simon de Orby of that place. He had been knighted by 1356 and died at a very good age for the period in 1379. His is almost certainly the alabaster reclining image in the church, usually stated to be that of his son, Sir John, for whom it is stylistically a fraction too late. He married Margaret, daughter of Sir John Trussell of Cubblesdon, Staffs., who eventually

18

became the heiress of a knight called Baldwin Frynell of Tamworth, who had married one of her Trussell cousins.[40]

Sir Alfred VIII de Solney, too, had a younger brother, William de Solney, who paid poll tax of £2 in 1327, quitclaimed some land to his father in 1337 and was still living in 1359. He was perhaps the father of two otherwise unplaced de Solneys, William and Nicholas, who both witnessed family land grants to tenants at Newton Solney in 1379. They must both have died without leaving issue, however, for Alfred VIII de Solney's elder son, Sir John, despite a glittering marriage to Margaret, daughter of Sir Robert Hastings, died without issue – or surviving issue - a decade later, sometime between 1390 and 1392, when the estates were divided between the heirs of his sisters, Ermentrude and Agnes[41].

This brought to an end the de Solney family at Newton – and, as far as is known, anywhere else, at least of the descendants of Alfred II de Solney – after an unbroken succession of two centuries or more. A new era was about to dawn, in which the family's patrimony and thus the lordship of Newton Solney would be divided and remain so for around 240 years.

The de Solney Village

Newton Solney's prosperity came largely from agriculture, although the importance of the fishery in the surviving charters suggests that the fruits of the Trent were an element of that prosperity. There must also have been some trade generated by the village's controlling position on the river just opposite the mouth of the Dove, too. Added to which the ford across the Trent from Newton Solney to Egginton was part of a thriving trade route, as is emphasised by Coalpit Way Field, which appears on the 1797 Every estate terrier for Egginton. An earlier account of the estate of 1605 calls it

The Trent-Dove confluence from near the ford, with the fields on the north side.
[Maxwell Craven]

Coale Pitt Way Close and it actually lies on Hargate Lane which leads from the village of Egginton to the ford over the Trent to Newton Solney. It was via this route that coal from the south Derbyshire pits, the lime from Ticknall and bricks from the Newton Solney brickyard (the two latter not provably as early as the de Solney period of course) could reach the settlements on the north bank of the river and which probably attracted a toll, not to mention a fee for specialist help in actually crossing the river on what, as early as 1346 was referred to as *Neutonford*.[42]

The detached portion of the parish on the north side of the river included Hargate Pasture, Bretby Meadow, The Callinge – anciently Callingeherdwick and probably Scarsey, mentioned earlier. Both Hargate (earlier called Heathhouses) and Hardwick were subsidiary manors in Egginton, which was fragmented, as we have seen, by frequent failures in the lordly male line, into four separate manorial estates, the others being Egginton itself and Seymour's Place[43].

Added to these, the village of Newton Solney itself would have operated the typical medieval three field system, and identifying which the three common fields were is something of a challenge. An attempt was made by William Fraser to reconstruct them from name evidence. Two appear to have been Bladon Field & Hough Field, otherwise The Howgh. The other was probably Newton, or Dale, Field, first mentioned in a deed of about 1580[44]. Certainly, some ridge and furrow can still be seen, although confusingly some of it lies within the area now called The Park, which clearly implies that the enclosed park itself, referred to as early as 1230 as we have seen, may not have been co-terminous with the parkland created in the early nineteenth century.

Mention of Bladon Field is a reminder that the westerly portion of the parish is called Bladon along with the eminence nearest the river which stretches into the adjoining parish of Winshill. The name probably means 'bleak hill' from Old English *blaw* = 'cold, cheerless', and *dun* = 'hill', although Fraser favoured 'black hill', which might be right, for even Kenneth Cameron admits that there are not enough early versions of the name for its development, and thus its precise etymology, to be clear[45]. It is possible that Bladon originally included a subsidiary settlement which subsequently vanished. Bladonfields Farm may mark its approximate site, but it barely shows up on the extant charters and therefore as an entity has to be treated with caution. Nevertheless, this supposition gains strength when it is realised that there was a family, long resident in the parish, who took their name from the place. Now, although the place name is not uncommon in England, the early appearance of this family on the spot, as it were, would appear to be convincing proof of the derivation of the name.

Thomas de Bladenlone – that is, Bladon Lane – appears in a deed of 1385 and as Thomas de Blawedon in another concerning Newton church of 1397. A generation later Adam de Bladon of Newton Solney appears as a person of elevated status, for in his will, John de Lathbury of Newton Solney stated,

> "Know ye that I have appointed, constituted and put in my place my beloved
> in Christ Adam de Blawden of Newton Sulny to be my true and lawful
> attorney to deliver for me and in my name …full and peaceful seisin of and
> in all my manors, lands and tenements with appurtenances…"

As "beloved in Christ" it is likely that Adam was the curate of Newton Solney, too. Just over sixty years on, and we find Matthew de Bladen as a freeholder at Newton Solney although by 1584 another member of the family was described as tenant and a husbandman, or small holder. Nevertheless, there was still a family freeholding in Newton in the 1758 terrier, owned then by John Bladon, a man born in 1701, but whose father and grandfather, John and Francis, were not listed for hearth tax in 1662. Yet, after this John, the family fades from sight after at least four hundred years in the parish. Nevertheless, their very presence makes something of a case for Bladon to have once been a place of more consequence that a common field, a hill and a modern farmstead[46].

It is during the de Solney period, indeed, that we get a clear picture of the free men of the parish, for the 1327 poll tax list has survived.

1327-28 POLL TAX RETURN[47]

Galfridus de Solney	£4 – 0s – 4d	Adam [de] Saveney	£2 – 0s – 8d
Adam Pychard	£2 – 0s – 2d	Adam le Revesme	£2 – 0s – 8d
Rob le Wodeward	£2 – 0s – 8d	Wills. Adcok	£2 – 0s – 2d
Johes [ ]	£2 – 0s – 2d	Adam Thomassone	£2 – 0s – 2d
Rog de Saveney	£2 – 0s – 2d	Ric. Williame	£2 – 0s – 8d
Wills. de Soln[e]y	£2 – 0s – 2d	Thom. Heyne	£2 - 0s – 8d
Walt le W[a]yte	£1 – 10s – 0d		

There are thirteen names on this list: thirteen free men, but the village population was probably something in the order of 100, if we assume that there were probably an average of four persons per family of those itemised above – thus some fifty two – plus something like twenty un-free families with a similar average number, thus another sixty persons, plus Alfred de Solney (not on the poll tax list at all) and his immediate family who probably accounted for another six, which gives a very approximate figure of 118 all told. 'Galfridus and Wills. de Solney' are the Geoffrey and William de Solney mentioned above. Some of these names reassuringly recur in other documents, like the Walter Adcock who is a witness to a deed signed at Newton in 1311. On 10th March 1346, William Woodward of Newton Solney, perhaps the son of the man listed above rather the same, was pardoned for all possible crimes on the recommendation of the Earl of Lancaster, with whom he had served in Gascony. It will be recalled that Sir Alfred IV de Solney had served in Gascony in 1253, and it may be that Woodward was actually serving under Sir Alfred VIII in France, bearing in mind that the paramount commander under whom he had served, Henry de Grosmont, 3rd Earl of Lancaster, was the chief lord of Newton at that time[48]. If Alfred VIII de Solney had fought in the early part of the Hundred Years' war, it would account for his martial effigy in the church.

Continuity: some Newton families

Another man, Roger de Saveney also occurs later on, as Roger Savery (*sic*) of Newton, who with Agnes his wife, granted a messuage, 4 virgates and 6 acres of wood in Newton to John son of William Burwes. He is also mentioned as having been granted land at Newton for life in 1316. Later, in January 1335, we find him taking a lease of lands at Newton from Sir Alfred de Solney at 5/6d per annum rent. Roger's is one name that is of interest out of several on this list. His family were of considerable status, too. An earlier Roger de Saveney was of Newton in the mid 13th century and was probably father of Adam le Saveney of Newton living 20/9/1303 and 1316; thus the Adam in the Roll Tax return was a grandson of the first Roger. Roger the younger, more likely another son of the original Roger, was granted five and a half acres at Newton by Sir Alfred de Solney at a rent of five shillings and sixpence, a transaction which Adam witnessed. A slightly later contemporary was Thomas de Saveney who witnessed a Burton Charter on 1342. John son of Roger de Saveney granted Robert son of Alfred de Solney 10/- annual rent for life from land at Newton in 1347 and made grants in 1353 & 1354, in one of which Roger and Thomas de Saveney witnessed. John's wife was Matilda, and they granted land to a third Adam de Saveney. It may have been this same John Saveney of Newton Solney (widowed and re-married or a son, bearing in mind the different name of his wife) who granted all his property in Newton Solney to Sir Alfred de Solney in 1375. In 1370 he was recorded with Alice his wife, and a last mention occurs in 1379 where the surname is given one of its more modern forms, of Sawney. Strangely, the name, having vanished from the record in the immediate local area for more than two centuries, recurs at Repton in the person of Norton Chaveney (*sic*), born at Quarndon in 1636, and married to a sister of the first of the Borough family of Castlefield, Derby. They even sent their two sons to the school from 1679[49].

The Saveney/Chaveney family suggest a sort of continuity, although it is not possible to connect Francis Chaveney of Quarndon, Norton's grandfather, which one of the Saveneys in fourteenth century Newton. Yet two other names on this 1327 list survived in the village: the descendants of Adam Pychard (modern Pickard) and those of Walter le Wayte.

The Pychards can be traced to the time of the earliest de Solneys, in the person of another Adam, living in the last two decades of the 12th century, and his son John *filius* Adam Pychard can actually be pinned down to Newton in 1257, where he quitclaimed a garden there which stretched from the path leading to the church, to the river Trent, along with half an acre on *Derlestow* – thought to be the field called Dastow of the 1846 tithe map - to Sir Norman de Solney[50].

A measure of the status of this family comes in a Repton Priory charter of about 1275 where William Pychard of Newton was a witness, attesting the charter after Sir Englehard de Curzon (of Kedleston) and Robert de Shobnall, and again witnessed another, his name this time appearing after William de Hartshorne. All these families were at the time of knightly rank, and witnesses were invariably made to attest in an agreed order of social standing, which accords the Pychards almost knightly status. Later, this William witnessed a grant by Sir Alfred (V) de Solney to the Abbey of Burton that the monks might enclose forty acres of his woodland at Winshill – probably in part of Bladon, which then straddled the parish boundary with Winshill – presumably so they could profitably run their pigs there. He also witnessed after the magnate Sir Peter de Gresley and the landowner William de Ingwardby. The Adam Pychard of the Poll Tax list was witnessing documents at or concerning Newton Solney up to 1342 and another William witnessed a charter at Egginton, his name appearing between those of Nicholas de Fynderne of Findern and William de Appleby of Appleby Parva, both of knightly rank.

Indeed, from one of the seals, it can be seen that his bore arms: *quarterly,* which Sir Bernard Burke, from a medieval roll of arms supplied tinctures: *quarterly or and azure.* This is essentially the same as the arms of Ralph de Argouges' descendants, without the superimposed *cinqefoils,* which were clearly added as a difference mark; in other words it is a de Solney based coat. As Cecil Humphery-Smith has established, families frequently in this period took arms based on those of their feudal overlords, and this can be seen in Derbyshire where a whole ground of families have arms incorporating the *vaire or and gules* or the horseshoes of the powerful de Ferrers Earls of Derby. With the Pychards, we appear to be seeing the same sort of thing happening, *vis-à-vis* the de Solneys, whose chief retainers they clearly were. They may even have been a cadet branch of the de Solney family in some way. The Pychards can be traced at Newton down to the mid-fifteenth century, but thereafter they moved away and declined; by the time of the Hearth Tax assessments in 1664 their representatives were at Barton Blount, apparently in very reduced circumstances[51].

It is only with William le Wayte that we are presented with a truly remarkable element of continuity at Newton. Le Wayte (sometimes written *le Wyte* and thus a derivative of the name 'White' but modified by a regional inflection) was probably of much lower status that the Pychards or de Saveneys, but still, of course, a free man, for villeinage was still a significant factor in rural life in this era. Richard son of Robert le Wayte of Burton occurs in one of that Abbey's charters for the reign of Edward I – the last quarter of the 13th century – and an exactly contemporary William son of William le Wayte held a bovate in villeinage from Isabella, widow of John de Stapenhill of Stapenhill. If Isabella had dower land in Newton, it is likely that she or perhaps her mother-in-law was from there originally, perhaps even a de Solney daughter who has escaped record, for the de Stapenhills were themselves a high status family[52]. This William, as a villein was clearly close kin to a Matilda le Wayte, 'born a bondwoman' and mother of another William who was presumably free, if we are correct in interpreting the expression 'born a bondwoman' to imply that she was no longer so at the time of her appearance in the Egginton Manor court roll (1307/1311). Her son, we learn, married an Amicia and was presumably the father of the Walter in the Poll Tax assessment or an elder brother, by which time Walter was a free man for sure, or he wouldn't have been assessed for the tax. It may even be that the Walter Plantation recorded in the tithe award bore his name.

Thereafter, we find a Henry Wayte in 1436, a Richard of Newton Solney aged (about) sixty at an inquest there in 1476 and another Richard (son of Richard) leasing part of one of Repton's open fields, called the Westfield, which abutted Newton Solney's boundary (where it was called *Neutonfield*) along with two kinsmen, John and Henry Wayte, from Gilbert Thacker (the man who tore down the Priory) for fifty two years at a rental of 2/5d in September 1550[53].

From Richard Wayte junior of Repton (elements of the family migrated over the boundary to Repton from time to time, no doubt in search of the most favourable tenancies) one can trace a family tree through baptismal records down to William Wayte, by whose time the family had gone up in the world from their 13th century villeinage, for he was a Newton Solney freeholder and farmer in 1827 and 1841. In 1846 he had married at Newton Solney parish church, Sarah, daughter of William

Morley of Trent Farm, Newton and had a daughter Ellen, the last of the family by 1895, and still a freeholder, and William, whose ultimate fate has defied elucidation.[54]

There are many more families whose presence in Newton Solney stretched over many centuries, but nearly all date from after the Black Death, which hit England in 1348-49 and killed almost a third of everyone then alive. It is clear that this calamity seriously affected Newton, for this is the one element that explains why only the de Saveneys, Pychards and le Waytes managed to survive the holocaust out of the thirteen families listed on the Poll Tax assessment, as well as the de Solneys of course, who also survived, although it is likely their younger sons William and Geoffrey de Solney, whose names appeared on the list, did not, for their names fail to recur.

The Black Death reached Derbyshire by May 1349 and is well attested as having been particularly virulent in central Derbyshire; the chartulary of the chantries of the Wakebridge family of Wakebridge in Crich church chronicles the almost complete demise of a family of similar standing to the de Solneys and the Pychards in the period of the plague, leaving alive, by the early 1350s, only the *paterfamilias* and an heiress. An inquisition involving the surviving Wakebridges refers to the crippling effect the Black Death had on property values, messuages and cottages referred to being untenanted and the surrounding land uncultivated. Recent estimates have calculated that the population of England rose from a *Domesday Book* level of 1.5-2 million to about 4 to 4.5 million before the onset of the Black Death, following which it seems to have dropped to between 2.5 and 3 million, a very drastic fall by any account. It was not until the beginning of the 15th century that the level of population began to rise again. Some villages never recovered, like Canons Ashby, Northamptonshire, where a Domesday Book estimated population of 50-65 rose to 75-90 by 1302 and then spectacularly to just under 200 in 1343, six years before the onset of the plague. Twenty five years later there were less than 100 again, and the village was finally abandoned in the 15th century[55].

The pestilence, by its devastating effect, changed the composition of the landed elite to an enormous extent, and in so doing provided opportunities for those in a lesser station who had survived and had the leverage, either fiscal or personal, to acquire derelict land, make something of it and found new dynasties. That, combined with the failure, forty five years later, of the de Solneys in the male line, changed things at Newton Solney for ever and ushered in a new era.

*

[1] Finberg (1957) *passim.* ; Todd (1973) 54; Whitwell (1982) 51f.; Roffe (1986) 22-25.

[2] Information in Gogh's Cave Guide Book, 2007.

[3] DAJ XCIX (1979) 78; Aston: DAJ LXXXI (1981) 149; LXXXVI (1966) 103, XC (1970) 10-21; Findern: *ibid.* 4-7; Twyford: DAJ LXXXI (1961) 149; Swarkestone: DAJ LXXV (1955) 125149; LXXVI (1956) 10-27; LXXX (1960) 1-48 & LXXXI (1961) 149; Stenson: DAJ LXXIII (1953) 121-126; Shardlow: DAJ LXXXVIII (1968) 68-81.

[4] Cameron (1959) III. 623; Ine's laws, Kirby (1991) 124-126; Waltons, Ekwall (1951) 471-472; on David, note that his first biographer, Rhygfarch ap Sulien, was late, c. 1090, but incorporates genuine records interspersed with legendary material; elements not elsewhere attested – the Repton story being one – could be authentic, but have to be treated with caution and assessed ion degrees of likelihood, cf. James (1967) 33 – if true, though an important confirmation of a substantial surviving British population in the area.

[5] On the name of Repton: Gelling (1984) 145, 155; Cameron (1959) III. 653; on the tribal area: Turbutt (1999) I. 295,343; Cox III (1877) 441-464; DB 1. 20-26, 3.3, 14.6; DB *Leics.*.E 3 & 11; *Luitcoit*, BL Harleian MS 3859; Aethelflaeda was more commonly referred to as 'Lady of the Mercians', but several charters refer to her as *regina* (= queen) and she should really be so styled.

[6] Hart (1975) No. 16

[7] Bagshaw (1846) 256; Bretby contained a little more, 1505 acres (*ibid.* 224)

[8] Hart, *op. cit.*, 285.

[9] On Anglo-Norse Derby, see Craven (1988) 36-37; toponyms, Cameron (1959) 648.

[10] Cameron, *loc.cit.*; Fraser (1947) 102.

[11] *Portmannemot*: Darlington (1945) DC B6; Danelaw assemblies: Turner (2000) 7-10.

[12] Sawyer (1979) 25-26: Will and charter; Jeayes & Deanesley (1937) 5: royal confirmation.

[13] Wulfsige *Maur's* acquisitions: Sawyer (1979) xxix, 14, 23, 55; Turbutt (1999) 346; possible acquisitions, cf. Jeayes & Deanesley (1937) 6-7; On Wulfric's family, Higham (1997) 46 & Hart (1975) 373-376.

[14] *Domesday Book*: Morris (1978) I. 18.

[15] Stenton (1971) 602-605

[16] Roffe, *loc.cit.*

[17] DB 6. 40, 52, 58, 60; Tutbury Charter 52

[18] RC 27; BC 49 of 1197/1213

[19] Edwin & Geoffrey de Newton witnesses at Ticknall c. 1200/1218 [RC 62]; John de Newton, holding at Ticknall 1260 [RC 72]

[20] Richard f. Margery de Newton: DRO D5236/9/5 of 23/7/1317; Alan de Newton: BC 293 of 1280/1305 & Adam de Newton: BC 420, 1/1/1317/18

[21] William de Newton, chaplain, 1375 [PEC CXXI]; Thomas de Newton chaplain confirmed a grant of land at Egginton 1359, 1370 & 1379 [D 5236/3/40; PEC II, CXXXV & LXXXVI]; John Newton of Newton Solney granted land there 1500 [D5236/4/45]; Nicholas Newton husbandman of Newton granted 21 yr. lease of cottage etc. in 'Hardwick in the town and fields of Newton Solney' 9/5/1572 [D5236/4/57]; Tho. Newton, taxed on 1 hearth 1662 (Edw. Newton taxed on 1 hearth at Bretby, probably forebear of Joseph Newton of Bretby who suffered a forced sale of livestock, crops & property to enable Henry Every to recover unpaid rent on property at Newton Solney 29th March 1743 [D5236/27/8]; 1726: Henry Newton of Smithy House, Egginton [PEC];1743: William Newton of Burton D5236/18/12/8]; John Newton of Kingswinford 1760: D5236/18/12/111

[22] CP III. 164-179; the disaster was alleged to have been caused by a drunken crew.

[23] There appears to have been a family holding Bretby as sub-tenants of the Earl previously called de Bretby, latter corrupted to Bratby. RC 2; sale of manor: J. 486; regrant to Segrave : J. 487; on the Kymes, CP VII. 354-359

[24] Barraclough (1988) No. 10

[25] Baraclough, *op. cit.* Nos. 147 (Calke), 206, 322, 337 & 338; default: *Pipe Rolls* 31 Henry II 15.

[26] Keats-Rohan (1999, 2002) II. 715, 725-726, cf. Statham, in DAJ XLIX (1927) 317-328

[27] de Solney arms' first appearance on a seal attached to a document of 1307, PEC LIX; Argouges: Rietstap (1861) 55; Soligni de Dol: *op. cit.* 985.

[28] J. 1753; see also VCH *Derbyshire*, forthcoming; on Upper Broughton, see DB Notts. 1.59.

[29] Barraclough (1988) 413, 273.

[30] FF 196; On the Earl of Chester, CP IV 170-179.; on Ferrers, *op. cit.* III. 194-204; Newton Solney: *Book of Fees* 1001

[31] The Hundred of Repton to be held by Matilda Countess of Chester (wife of 4th Earl) with all

liberties & customs 1159, confirmed by Queen Eleanor to Sheriff of Notts. & Derbys. (Duchy of Lancaster 1174-1189, DLSL refs. missing); Barracough (1988) 273; J. 1755-1756; on Repton Priory, Cox III (1877) 425; on the park, see also now Wiltshire & Woore (2009) 1289-129.

[32] Cameron III 648.

[33] Cameron, *loc. cit.*; Fraser (1947) 104; 1291 grant, PEC XLIX

[34] Cox III (1877) 428; Turbutt (1999) II. 782

[35] scutage: *Book of Fees*, 994; knight: J. 1757 & BC 99 of 10/8/1243; death: PEC LIII; sons: DRO D5236/4/5

[36] Throsby (1796) I. 103; Surfleet *Cal. Close Rolls* 221. 403; William: PEC quoting *Feudary*, 1283-84.

[37] Throsby, *loc. cit.,* recording that Sir Gervase held half a fee at Broughton in 1302, was Lord there in 1316 and his grandson Gervase held it in 1346; marriage: PEC LXXII of 1311

[38] John: D5236/4/4, confirmed to him by Alfred de Solney (VII) 1304, J. 1758; confirmed FF 519 and granted 10 acres at Newton in 1304, PEC LXV and 1316: FF 624; paid poll tax in 1327. On the Pinxton inheritance, J. 1862-1874, 1877. The youngest brother, John de Solney, presented to South Normanton by Sir Alfred: *Plea Rolls* 16 Edw. IV, wherein Nicholas de Longford was claiming the patronage through descent from the other le Poer heiress.

[39] Geoffrey and Robert: DRO D5236/4/22 Richard: PEC LII as 'Rico Sulny'; his wife: PEC XIX; son: PEC, CLXXXVIII, LXXII & XVII and heirs: D5236/4/28

[40] Inheritance: *Feudal Aids*, i 251, 260; landholdings: D5236/9/8 of 1348; Salt Arch. Soc. Vol. VIII (1907), Bishop's Register; Raydon: J. 1470; Orby connections: Cal. IPM VI 71, PEC XXI; knighted: J. 1863 & Burton Charter 524 ;death: Salt. Arch. Soc. Vol. VII (1906) 44; marriage (she was Elizabeth according to D5236/9 of 3/10/1348) and Trussell connections: D5236/9/6].

[41] Sir Alfred VIII and William: D5236/4/19, PEC CLV of 1342 & LXIII of 1359; William and Nicholas, [DRO D5236/4/18

[42] Fraser (1947) 47; Cameron (1959) III. 647.

[43] Cameron, 648, cf. Fraser 101-2, 144.

[44] Fraser (1947) 101-102, cf. Cameron 648.

[45] Cameron (1959) III. 647; Fraser (1947) 101

[46] Thomas: Staffs RO Bagot MSS, D(W) 1721/3/30/13; Adam: DRO D5236/6/17, D5236/9/21; will: PEC LXVIII; Matthew: PEC XLVII of 1500; husbandman: D5236/4/66 of 14/10/1584; 1587: note the Robert Bladen of Newton on the 1588 Muster Roll, DAJ XVII (1895) 18

[47] DAJ XXX (1908) 52-53

[48] Deed of 1311, PEC XX; Cal. Pat. Rolls 1345-8, 82

[49] Roger, FF679 of 13-20/1/1323/4, D5236/4/14 of 9/1/1316 & D5236/4/17; earlier Roger D5236/4/2; Adam 1303, D5236/4/7 & 1316, PEC VIII; Roger the younger, PEC VIII of 1316; Thomas BC506 of 15/8/1342; Repton School Register; Fletcher (1887) 108-109; John son of Roger PEC LII of 16/6/1347; D5236/4/22, 24; John son of Adam, D5236/4/20 of 6/5/1341 & D5236/4/31 of 3/6/1375; John & Alice, PEC LXII; Sawney, 1379, D5236/4/18, cf. PEC XVII; the heiress married into the Farnhams of Quorn (Leics.) Upper Hall.

[50] BC 43; D5236/4/1; PEC LIII].

[51] William Pychard, RC 24 of c. 1275; RC 25 of 1291, cf. PEC XLIX; BC 394 of c. 1277/1307; Pychard arms, Burke (1884) 381, but unsourced; feudal arms, Humphery-Smith (1973) 11, H. Lawrance, in DAJ XLVI & XLVII; hearth tax, Edwards (1982) 6.

[52] Richard, Burton Charter (BC) 372; William, PEC XLVI.

[53] Henry, RC 37; Richard, D5236/4/42 of 1476; Richard, John and William, RC 53, 55 & 57 all of 12/9/1550

[54] Glover's *Directory*, 1827; Census 1841; Bulmer's *Directory*, 1895

[55] Black death, Joyce (1991) 9; Wakebridge: Saltman (1976) 2, 4, 110-111; effects, Taylor (1983) 151- 152.

II

A DIVIDED PATRIMONY

The death of Sir John de Solney somewhere in between 1390 and 1392 not only meant the extinction of the senior male line of the de Solneys, but worse from the point of view of the village, caused the de Solney inheritance to be divided between the offspring of his sisters.

This was the result of medieval rules on inheritance, and had a good deal to do with the fact that women had no status in law. If a man died without a son but left a daughter - the heiress - then his property would pass to her husband, who held it *jure uxoris* – in the right of his wife – and then to his heir male. And if he, too, were to have only a daughter, it would in turn pass to her husband *jure uxoris* and so on, until a male heir of the original person's blood line actually appeared. If a man left more than one daughter (co-heiresses) and no sons, then the property was divided as near as possible into equal portions, or moieties, and thereafter each portion descended in exactly the same was as described above. Thus each lineal male descendant, or the husband of each heiress or co-heiress, was entitled to a share of the original piece of property. If a man died leaving a brother, on the other hand, the property went to the brother entire, but if the nearest male was a cousin and there were heiresses in a closer degree of kinship, the property would divide amongst the daughters. It was worse with parliamentary baronies created by writ of summons, for the right to be summoned to the House of Lords cannot be divided in practice. If a peer left two daughters, the right to received a summons in the father's peerage rested equally with their heirs male and the King had to decide which one was the senior (or more suitable) and summon him, thus terminating the state of suspended animation (abeyance) into which the honour had fallen.

The de Solney inheritance was not, at least, complicated by a peerage falling into abeyance. Yet, on the death of Sir John in 1390/92 without any surviving issue, he did leave a married sister, Ermentrude, and the issue of a younger sibling, Agnes, who had pre-deceased him. Ermentrude had married in 1330, which suggests she must have been born around 1312/1315 (upper class girls married young in those days) and her husband was Robert Lathbury of Egginton (1310-1360), by whom she had four sons and three daughters. After her husband's death, however, she re-married John Folcher, whose family had inherited Osmaston-by-Derby from the de Osmaston family. He did not long outlive Sir John Solney, but laid a claim to half the manor in the right of Ermentrude as soon as he could.[1]

Agnes must have been a lot younger than her sister, for she did not marry until 1348, suggesting that she must have been born at about the time her older sister was getting married. Her husband was Sir Edmund de Appleby of Appleby, a village long split between Appleby Magna, in Leicestershire, and Appleby Parva, then in Derbyshire, the division dating from the ending of the Appleby dynasty with two heiresses in the earlier 16th century, although the settlement had always straddled the county boundary – at least until the anomaly was rectified in the late nineteenth century. Sir Edmund only managed to father two children with Agnes, for she died fairly young and he re-married, although the name of his new wife is lost to us. The two daughters, however, who were called Margaret and Alice, each inherited a half share in their mother's half of the manor of Newton Solney, although when Sir John de Solney died, Margaret, the elder, was already married to Sir Nicholas de Longford of Longford, who claimed his resulting quarter share of Newton. Alice, on the other hand was a serial widow, having married three times and outlived each husband, all Staffordshire gentry: Robert Pype of Pype, Sir Thomas Stafford and William Spernore of Spernore. However, by Sir Thomas, she did mange to have two sons, Thomas and John, of whom Thomas inherited his quarter share of Newton Solney.[2]

TABLE I
THE SUCCESSION TO NEWTON SOLNEY
1390/92

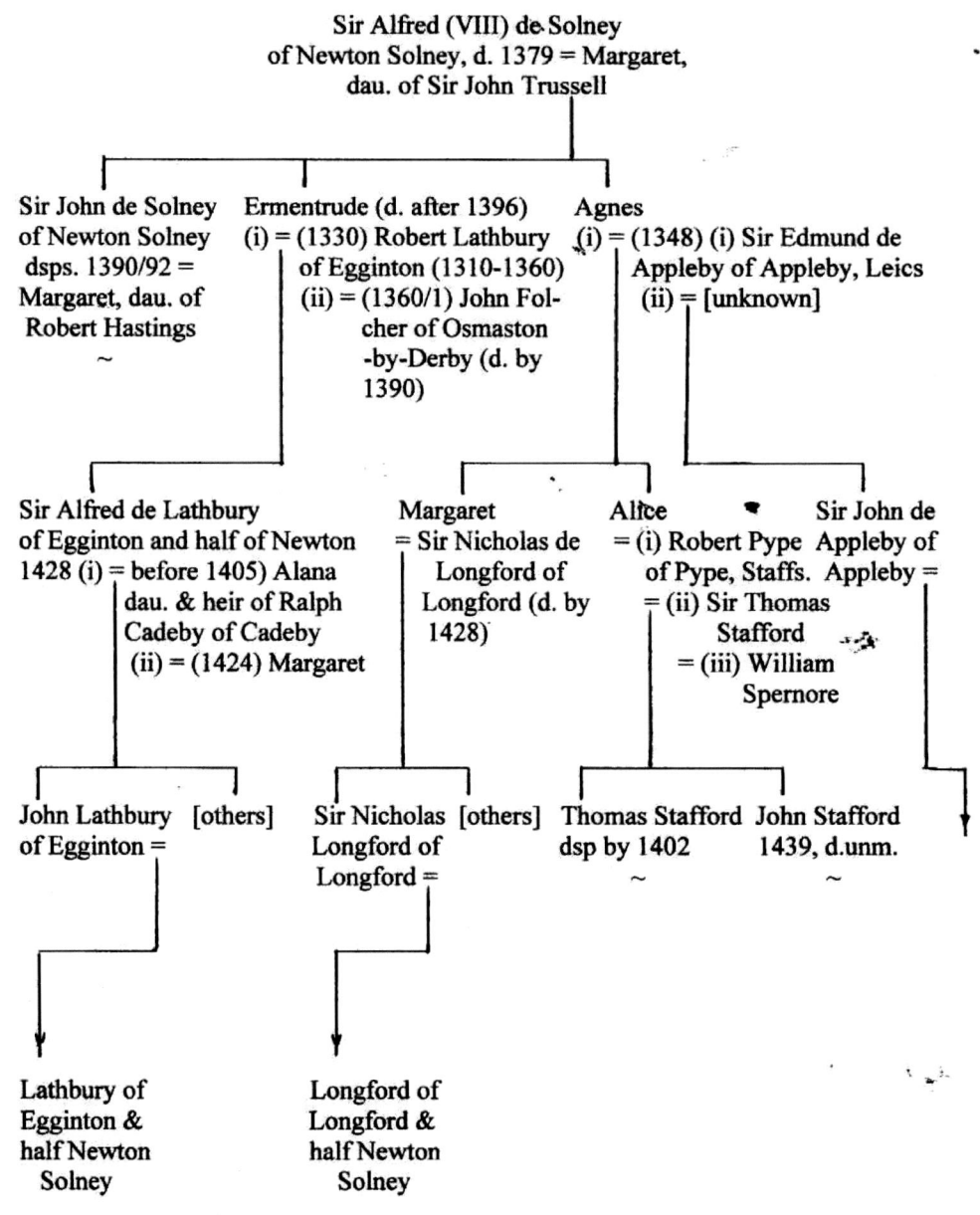

Sir Alfred (VIII) de Solney
of Newton Solney, d. 1379 = Margaret,
dau. of Sir John Trussell

Sir John de Solney of Newton Solney dsps. 1390/92 = Margaret, dau. of Robert Hastings ~

Ermentrude (d. after 1396) (i) = (1330) Robert Lathbury of Egginton (1310-1360) (ii) = (1360/1) John Folcher of Osmaston -by-Derby (d. by 1390)

Agnes (i) = (1348) (i) Sir Edmund de Appleby of Appleby, Leics (ii) = [unknown]

Sir Alfred de Lathbury of Egginton and half of Newton 1428 (i) = before 1405) Alana dau. & heir of Ralph Cadeby of Cadeby (ii) = (1424) Margaret

Margaret = Sir Nicholas de Longford of Longford (d. by 1428)

Alice = (i) Robert Pype of Pype, Staffs. = (ii) Sir Thomas Stafford = (iii) William Spernore

Sir John de Appleby of Appleby =

John Lathbury of Egginton = [others]

Sir Nicholas Longford of Longford = [others]

Thomas Stafford dsp by 1402 ~

John Stafford 1439, d.unm. ~

Lathbury of Egginton & half Newton Solney

Longford of Longford & half Newton Solney

However, there had been a settlement, when Agnes had originally married Sir Edmund de Appleby in 1348 (unless the marriage was earlier and the settlement an afterthought, which is possible but less probable) that should the male line of the de Solneys fail, the Applebys would waive all claim to Newton Solney in return for the manors of Bilby and Ranby in Nottinghamshire, This was clearly long forgotten by the time Sir John de Solney died, for we find John de Appleby, the son of Sir Edmund's second marriage, busy trying to claim a share in Newton against his half-sister Alice's son Thomas Stafford and then, after the latter's death without issue in 1402, against his brother John who, as a leading cleric, could not actually inherit, but who was nevertheless, entitled to the right to his portion of the manor. In the end, the entire process ground on for decades – as Medieval lawsuits tended to do – before, in the end, John Stafford died and the entire moiety passed to the surviving senior heir male of Agnes and Sir Edmund, Sir Nicholas Longford, the grandson of the man who had married the Appleby's elder daughter.[3]

Thus by the middle of the fifteenth century, the manor of Newton was in two halves, (having previously been in three fractions or moieties) held by the neighbouring knightly families of Longford and Lathbury.

The manor house

One thing about this settlement, was that neither family had any particular need to settle in Newton, which was very similar either to Longford or the Lathbury's estate at Egginton, both of which had substantial manor houses in which Newton's new joint lords continued to live. Yet the de Solneys would have had a manor house at Newton, as it was their chief manor and, according to the evidence of their charters, their residence too. Henceforth, however, it was to become largely redundant.

One of the great mysteries of Newton Solney – or so previous writers have averred – is the location of the original manor house. Most suggestions have centered on the vicinity of the church, the position now occupied by Rock House or by Newton Park house. Yet in all conscience, the precedents would suggest that the former is correct, especially when one realises that the 1758 Every estate terrier mentions a Hall Field which was clearly adjacent to the church, or almost so. As Rock House is itself adjacent to the church and is built on the one part of the river bank in Newton from which one can obtain a commanding view of the river in either direction, so strategic a position would seem an extremely likely one on which the first de Solneys – or even an earlier Newton – would probably wish to construct his main residence. Thus two of the three classic suggestions are essentially one and the same. The site of Newton Park is less likely at this stage, simply because the present house and its demesne sit on what was then still part of the open fields of Newton; as we have seen, the original park was not necessarily on the same footprint. In fact, the stream which bisects the present parkland, was probably the dividing line between Bladon (open) Field and The Howghe (pronounced 'Huff').

Thus we can be sure that there was a manor house, and that it was situated between the church and the river and was referred to as the hall, if only from the later field name. What we do not know was what it was like, for very few unfortified manor houses survive from the Medieval period to give up any clues. It was probably timber framed, there being no immediate source of building stone, although its position on the river bank would have meant that Keuper Sandstone from Weston Cliff, further east along the river, could have been used to build it, as it was with the contemporary church. The house itself would have consisted of a great hall and probably a cross-wing; and we do know it had a separate gatehouse. The only examples nearby are those at Norbury - a high quality house of the right date (c. 1305), but of stone – and Appleby Parva, where the house is timber framed and moated, but has experienced too many later alterations for us to be sure of its original form. It does, however, boast a stone gatehouse, and we know that the hall at Newton had a gatehouse, too. Moated houses were a feature of the later 12th and early 13th century, too, but the topography rules out any possibility of a viable moat at Newton, a there is certainly no vestige of one in the parish today.[4]

Norbury Hall, medieval wing, from west, 1980   [*Maxwell Craven*]

Appleby Hall, Appleby Parva, from Nichols' Leicestershire, *Vol. IV (1811)*

Surprisingly, and perhaps supporting the supposition of a family absence fighting in France or merely residing in Nottinghamshire on the other family estate at Broughton Solney, we find the house occupied by someone who was not a member of the de

Solney family as early as 1370 when Thomas de Chandos was described as "of Newton". This presents us with a problem in identifying him. Sir John Chandos KG of Radburne was one of the great heroes of the Hundred Years' War and was of a cadet branch of the Herefordshire Chandos family of Snodhill, whose forebear had married one of the FitzWalkelin heiresses and inherited the Radbourne estate. Yet there is no Thomas on Sir John's pedigree, which can be fairly completely recovered from the Chandos-Pole and Every charters. The only man who fits in date and name is a third cousin, Thomas Chandos, son and heir of 1st Lord Chandos of Snodhill who did not bear his father's title, as he was never summoned to Parliament, but why he should be living at Newton Solney is hard to imagine. One explanation might be that he was a boon companion from the French wars of Sir Alfred, but the evidence for this is flimsy in the extreme. More likely that he was an unrecorded younger brother of Sir John Chandos lodging there. If so, he must have died by the time Sir John Chandos was killed in action in the autumn of 1370, for by then, only a sister remained, who brought the estate to the Poles of Newborough.[5]

When Sir John Solney died, it was John Folcher and his wife, Sir John's sister Ermentrude, who received the portion of the manor containing 'le Aula' (the hall), with the maltchamber, presshouse, gatehouse and great grange, all itemised. After Folcher's death, however, it was included in the moiety that Sir Alfred Lathbury inherited from his mother, and it continued with the Lathbury family thereafter. It was used, often as not, to house a deserving younger son, for instance, in 1423 when William Lathbury, a lawyer, described as "of Newton Solney". Similarly with John Lathbury, Sir Alfred's grandson and heir in 1431. Thereafter, John succeeded to both estates in around 1428 and presumably went to reside at Egginton for, a decade later, we find another William Lathbury – also an attorney and possibly the earlier William's son - in residence at 'his capital messuage at Newton Solney', his sojourn lasting until at least 1469. Thereafter is appears to have been let to one John Babington to whom we will return shortly. It will be necessary to resume the story of the hall later, however, for the saga grew more complex as time went on.[6]

The village

One asset we do have is a list of the tenants of one half of the manor, from 1381 giving us another snapshot of the ordinary folk of the village to compare with the pre-Black Death Poll tax return of 1327 reproduced in Chapter I:

Peter Thorold ('serf')	Thomas de Bressington	Robert Magge
Adam Thorold	Ann Webster	William Magge
John Paphowe	Thomas le Shepherd	Thomas Sterre
John Gamel	Richard Smyth	Henry de Melton
William Carter	Matilda Miller	William fisher
John Mondore	John Pr[i]estman	Anota de Bromley
John de Chesterfield	Matilda Draper	Richard Swan
Ralph Parr	John le Roo	Matilda Hobbeswyfe
John Adam	William de Chopenhall	John Hancockson
William Adam	Adam Wilson	Adam Vessy
Robert Adam	William Annoys	

Only heads of households were listed, hence the paucity of women, the only ones in evidence – Ann Webster, Matilda Miller and Anota de Bromley – almost certainly being widows. Adam Thorold was at the time the priest of the Newton Solney church and, although unfree, Peter Thorold must have been a near relative. The names Smith and Shepherd as family names continue thorough the ages in Newton, right up until the present, although there is no guarantee that they all belong to the same stock for, even in 1391, surnames were still fluid, as witness Matilda Hobbeswyfe who was probably a widow bearing her late husband's name, along with his status as a newly coined surname! The three Adams and John Hancockson all bear patronymics, quite probably of recent coinage. 'Hancock' for instance is formed from the middle English name 'Hann' with a common familiarity added as a suffix. Likewise 'Swan' derives from the occupational name 'Swain' and John Gamel was probably so named because he or a forebear was a twin (from the Latin *gemellus* = twin).[7]

We get another snapshot of a clutch of villagers nearly a century later, when Sir Nicholas de Longford was engaged in consolidating his claim to his portion of Newton Solney, in 1476. All the elderly residents of the Longford moiety of the village were summoned to help attest the claim, although their ages (in brackets in the list) are clearly extremely approximate, mainly rounded up in the original document to the nearest ten!

William Boyleston (60)	John Laurence (60)
Thomas Carrott of Bretby (72)	William Michell (66)
Robert Cawke [Calke] (60)	Richard Nyke (60)
John Clandon (60)	John Pole (60)
John Gifford (60)	Richard Pratt (60)
Robert Gilbert of Winshill (90)	Richard Wayte (60)
Thomas Hendley (60)	Thomas Webster (50)
Richard Hunt of Repton (80)	William Winshill of Winshill (80)

Two of these were residents of Winshill, one of Bretby and another of Repton but this did not disqualify them from giving evidence; all probably had close links with the village or had perhaps lived there at one time. The Longfords were, however, not unwilling to grant land in their portion of Newton to their own established tenants at Longford, as with a 30 year lease of a farm there granted by the last Nicholas Longford to Thomas Hankey of Longford yeoman, in 1557. Some of the men in this list may have owed their presence to a similar arrangement. Yet there are some familiar names here, too, like the Waytes, which family we have already encountered. William Winshill was minor gentry, and the Abbey of Burton's tenant at Winshill, descendant of a long line of his family going back to the 12th century.[8]

Another very long-lasting dynasty were the Boyl(e)stons (*sic*), represented by William on this list. The first of the family pops up in 1401 on the Egginton manor court roll. It would be entirely reasonable to presume that they were a junior branch of the Medieval landholding dynasty which took its name from Boylestone, in western Derbyshire, perhaps in Egginton through a younger son having married one of the seemingly numerous heiresses of the de Egginton/FitzWalkelin clan. The William on the list was born in 1416 (or thereabouts) and may have been granted a tenancy by the Lathburys, who would have been the feudal lords in Egginton of the John Boyleston there of 1401, quite plausibly William's father or grandfather. This supposition is strengthened when we find that only a decade earlier than the list, a Thomas Boyleston and Margery his wife were granted land in Newton Solney by John Lathbury, senior and junior. This may indeed be the same Thomas still holding land in the village in 1500, along with Thomas Boylston junior, presumably his son. They certainly enjoyed a measure of status, too, for the widow of this Thomas Boyleston, herself born a Shepherd of Newton Solney, re-married James Burton of Lyndley, Leicestershire, a gentleman, who died in 1544. Furthermore, in Queen Elizabeth's time a Richard Boyleston of Newton married a Joan Pype of Pype, in Staffordshire, making him a relative by marriage of much-married Alice Appleby, the grand-daughter of Sir Alfred (VIII) de Solney (see chart above). At the same time Richard's brother Henry had married a Bladon of Newton, thus demonstrating the continuing interlinking of these ancient village families. They seem to have farmed Town Lands at Newton Solney, for in 1614 William Boyleston of Newton Solney, yeoman was granted a lease of three lives on a cottage, farm buildings and land there bearing this name and the likelihood is that this was a fresh grant of a long-tenanted property. Two of the family later made careers outside the village, for in 1603 we encounter John Boylston, of London as a haberdasher but holding land in the village, for he effectively acknowledged that a moiety of the manor was the right of a man called Hugh Beeston, whom we shall encounter below. Another scion of the family was Dr. John Boyleston, who trained as a physician and by 1649 was living and working in Weston-on-Trent. He must have been a very successful doctor, too, for he occupied an eight hearth house there in 1670 – larger than some manor houses! After the time of Richard Boyleston of Newton, who married a member of the Newton family at Burton in 1685, however, the name ceases to crop up in the village records.[9]

The community was not entirely cut off from the tide of national events, either, for duties were from time to time imposed on the villagers quite apart from the obligations of tax. In 1539 for instance, eighteen men were summoned from the village to undertaker military service and fifty years later, with a threat from Spain looming, there was another muster, the roll containing the names of:
Thomas Eaton (pikeman)
Robert Bladon (armoured spearman.)
Richard Sharpe, (archer)
And there was a further muster the following year when the beacon that endowed Beacon Hill, west of Newton Lane, with its name may have been erected. This is locally reputed to have been Napoleonic, but the Armada is a much more likely period for it, especially as the toponym had to have time to mutate subsequently into Bacon Hill. Further military demands were no doubt also made during the Civil War, in the following era, although fewer details of these *vis-a-vis* Newton Solney survive.[10]

From these occasional surviving lists of inhabitants, then, it is possible to see in action the continuity that underlies so much of English rural life, and are afforded at least glimpses of their doings over and above the constant round of husbandry and the imperatives of the changing seasons.

The Longfords

The Longfords were a family of similar standing to the Solneys: old established, knightly in almost every generation and very definitely Norman in origin. Indeed, they were descended from Ralph de Toeni, *gonfalonier* (standard bearer) of the Conqueror – a genuine example of a family with an ancestor who actually fought at Hastings. Indeed, Ralph himself was the great-great-grandson of Hugh de Calvacamp, one of the Norse followers of Rollo 1st Duke of Normandy, and he was the common ancestor of four Derbyshire families, the Gresleys, the Staffords, the FitzNicholases and the Longfords. Nigel de Stafford was one of Derbyshire's tenants-in-chief in 1086, and Nicholas *fitz* Nigel, one of his sons married Margaret, a daughter and co-heiress of Ralph *fitz* Ercald who held Longford at the time of *Domesday Book*. Their eldest son was ancestor of Sir Nicholas de Longford of Longford who inherited a quarter of Newton Solney in 1392 or thereabouts, and their second son, Ralph was ancestor of Ralph FitzNicholas, created 1st Lord Pipard by Edward I, who brought the de Lathbury's into Derbyshire from their native Buckinghamshire[11]..

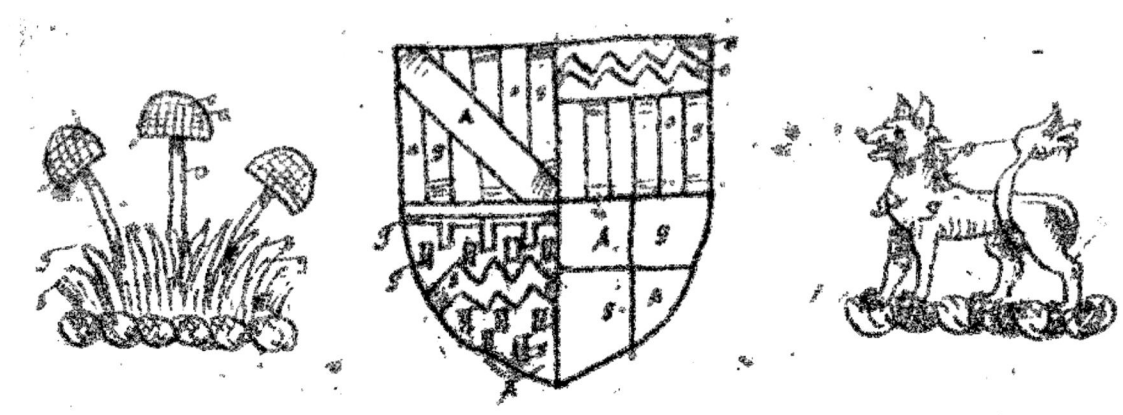

The arms of the Longfords and their two crests, 1569; the quarterings of the shield are, 2: Hathersage, 3: d'Eyncourt and 4: Solney. [*Derby Local Studies Library*]

Although Sir Nicholas Longford succeeded to a quarter of Newton, in 1392, in 1405 he inherited the other quarter of Sir John's younger sister Agnes's half of the manor on the death of Thomas Stafford, but when his son and heir, another Nicholas, died in his own lifetime in 1416, he was still in dispute with John Stafford, Thomas's clerical brother, and as late as 1447 with John Appleby of Appleby, still vainly trying to claim his step-mother's share of the inheritance. The identity of Thomas Stafford's clerical brother presents an interesting conundrum, for it clearly emerges from the charters at at the time of the disputes, notably in 1431and 1439, that he was Bishop of Bath and Wells. Now all the published biographies of this Bishop, appointed in 1425 and in 1443 translated to Canterbury as Archbishop, make him the son (illegitimate in some versions) of Humphrey de Stafford of Southwick, Wiltshire, a grandson of one of the Earls of Stafford. In fact the evidence of the charters concerning Newton Solney clearly suggest that he was son and brother of Thomas Staffords and perfectly legitimate to boot![12]

Nevertheless, back in the 1390s, things had been less confrontational, for he and his wife had joined with Thomas Stafford and his mother to establish a chantry in the church at Newton wherein masses might be said for the souls of Sir John, his father, and Sir William le Wyne of Pinxton, a kinsman. A chantry was a sort of independent chapel within an existing church, ministered to by a separate priest paid for wholly by the donor; needless to say they were all abolished at the Reformation for many had accumulated handsome endowments on which Henry VIII was keen to lay hands. In 1408, after having been widowed, Margery Longford, who later had to go and live in Chesterfield, agreed to pay her share on the cost of this from her portion of the manor of Pinxton[13].

Sir Nicholas Longford was succeeded in turn by his three grandsons: Sir Nicholas, who had died before 1476, then Sir Roger, who died after 1484 and before 1498, and thereafter by Sir Ralph, who died in 1513 but who had also had the misfortune to have lost his eldest son, Nicholas in 1510.

Under Sir Nicholas an extraordinary incident is recorded relating to Newton Solney. In 1474, John Babington, described as 'armiger' – that is, a gentleman entitled to a coat-of-arms - sued Sir Nicholas Longford for breaking into his close and house at Newton Solney and for expelling him by force. John's presence in the village is explained by the fact that his father, William Babington of Chilwell held 'a free tenement' in demesne by socage for which he paid £3 per annum in 1431. Now Babington, although a younger son, was a grandee of the County, and his mother was Isabella, daughter and heiress of Robert Dethick of Dethick; his father Thomas (who had died in 1464) was thus of Dethick in the right of his wife. The house broken into, judging from his status, must have been the hall, and he must have been the tenant following the death of William Lathbury. This whole incident appears to have arisen out of the discord in the County during the Civil Wars in which Sir Nicholas Longford had led the Lancastrian faction.

Longford Hall, built between 1513 and 15476, pictured in the 1890s.   [*M. Craven*]

In 1454, one confrere, Walter Blount, had defected to the Yorkists, and over the following two years, Longford had launched a violent campaign against him, sacking his Derby town house and his seat at Elvaston in the process, riding at the head of what amounted to a private army. Clearly Sir Nicholas was now harassing Babington, despite the passage of almost two decades and the accession of Edward IV, which should have put the lid on such activities. It may be that he perceived that Babington too had supported the Blounts, or even taken against him for some other reason. In any case, the attempt to turf him out of his home failed and sanity prevailed[14].

Another Sir Ralph, succeeded to the estate and the portion of Newton Solney that pertained to it in 1513. Sir Ralph the elder had held considerable property, quite apart from Longford and half of Newton Solney, numbering manors, or portions of manors at Barlborough, Blackwell, Boythorpe, Duckmanton, Hathersage, Killamarsh, Morton, North Wingfield, Pilsley, South Normanton, Pinxton, Whitwell, and in Staffordshire, Ellastone amongst his possessions. As a result, there was little presence of the family on their part of Newton Solney, although there is a record that Sir Ralph's fourth son, Henry Longford was 'of Newton Park' in 1494/95 and again in 1521 whilst acting as his father's and then his nephew's collector of rents at Longford and Ellastone - in other words he was agent for the estate in that part of Derbyshire. This is a helpful piece of information, as it establishes the original Newton Park as being part of the Longford moiety of the estate, and further, that there must have been a capital messuage, an important residence, within it, although there is no hint as to where this might have been situated. That is not to say that the Longfords failed to manage their moiety of Newton, and we have a court roll for 1437 and Nicholas Longford (1530-1610), the last of the family to hold the estates of Longford, held a great court at Newton Solney in May1564. One legacy of their long tenure, however, is the cover known as Longford Wood, south of Newton Park, which also lend weight to the suggestion that their portion of the manor lay to the south of the parish.[15]

Yet by the Elizabethan period the writing seems to have been on the wall for the Longfords, for all their massive landholdings, and they appear to have been short of capital. Perhaps it was the expense of building their huge new brick mansion at Longford, the work after 1513 of Sir Ralph Longford who died in 1544. Either way, they were beginning to dispose of assets at this period. Sir Ralph's son Nicholas, for instance, sold the fishing rights in the river to the future Lord Mayor of London, Nicholas Mosley and his first wife Margaret for £143 – 6s – 8d in 1579 This sale underscores the importance of the fishing in the Trent, which at Newton Solney appears, as we have seen, to have been worth £4 per annum in early Tudor times. The Longfords had acquired 'all the weir and waters of the Trent belonging to the lordship of Newton...' from John Lathbury (in whose portion of the manor it had originally

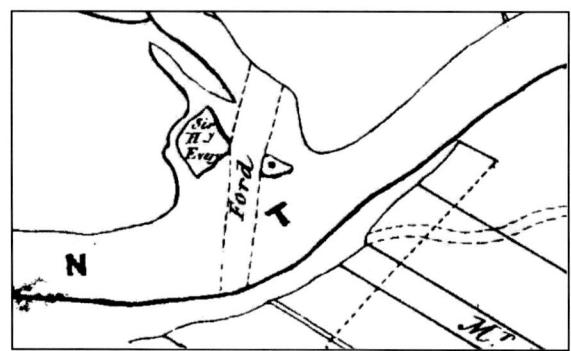

been) in 1502 when Lathbury had used the fishery as collateral for a debt which he had failed to redeem. This was initially for a year, but seems to have become permanent thereafter and the weir and fishery were mentioned again in 1566. A century later Blome remarked that there were plenty of salmon in the Trent and that 'The salmon here taken are sent to London.'[16]

Site of the fishery and the ford over the Trent at the Dove confluence (1836 sale catalogue map). [*Derby Local Studies Library*]

Mosley was thus presumably expecting to make a handsome profit by sub-letting the fishery to a London fishmonger. Interestingly, his posterity not so long afterwards bought the Rolleston Hall estate in Staffordshire, adjacent to Stretton the parish opposite Newton on the NW side of the Trent, parts of which were barely half a mile from this fishery.

One of the Longford family tenants at Newton had been one Nicholas Forde and his wife Agnes, who, however were both dead by 1578, when Nicholas Longford granted a 21 year lease of their farm to George Dicken. The importance of this is that this is the debut on the Newton stage of the Dicken family, prominent fixtures in village life well into the twentieth century. Their legacy in topographical terms included the survival of their name in Dicken's Hill and Dicken's Meadow, both field names recorded in the 1846 Tithe Award. Not that George of 1578 was the first, for his probable father was certainly in the parish in 1564, when a John Dykyns occurs, again on the Longford moiety. George, meanwhile, had married at Egginton on 11th February 1566/7 Joyce Forth (Forde) who was without doubt the daughter and heiress of the Nicholas and Agnes Forde whom in 1578 George had succeeded, emphasising the essentially hereditary nature of agricultural tenancies through the ages. George Dicken's son was probably the William Dicken of Newton Solney, yeoman (also married to an Agnes, clearly a popular name on the estate) who was granted a fresh lease of 21 years there in 1608. This was almost certainly the same farm as George's, whose 1578 lease would have expired in 1599, whereupon he would have obtained another for a similar period. The survivor of the couple had probably died in 1608, requiring William as the son and heir to apply for a renewal in his own name. This William's younger brother John (of Egginton) seems to have been the progenitor of all the members of the Dicken family who came after, whose family history is traceable through the pages of the Newton church registers. In 1758 two Dicken brothers farmed 141 acres between them in the village, and members of the family served as parish clerks throughout most of the 19th century up until the Great War.[17]

Later, in 1592, Nicholas Longford sold a moiety of the Newton estate to a speculator, Hugh Beeston of the Strand, London, the man to whom one of the Boylestons quitclaimed in 1603. Not that this was the first such sale, for we find a Longford cousin, John, a son of a Nicholas Longford who had settled at St. Germans in Cornwall, acquiring another moiety of Newton in 1584 for £150. He, too, was acting as a speculator, for eight years later he sold it to Richard Taylor, a London physician for £300, although to be fair, he did give his cousin Nicholas the profit! Needless to say, Dr. Taylor sold this portion on a year later to the same Hugh Beeston who had bought the other portion direct from Nicholas the year before. Nevertheless, by 1599, Beeston and Sir Nicholas seem to have been holding this combined moiety of Newton – presumably the full half share of the estate – jointly, presumably on the understanding that it would revert to Beeston on Nicholas's expected demise without issue. This duly occurred in 1610, although there were several Longford families (the name latterly mutated to Langford) still settled on parts of the estate, as well as a long-lived branch at Mansfield. The remaining Longford estates passed to the families of Nicholas Longford's sisters, the Vernons of Haddon, the Hastings of Cadbury, Somerset and the Dethicks of Newhall. The half of Newton Solney, however, reverted to Hugh Beeston who thereupon sold it, finding a willing buyer in Sir Henry Leigh of Egginton, long the owner of the other portion. This sale thus at last re-united Newton Solney under one ownership for the first time since the death of Sir John de Solney in the late 14th century[18].

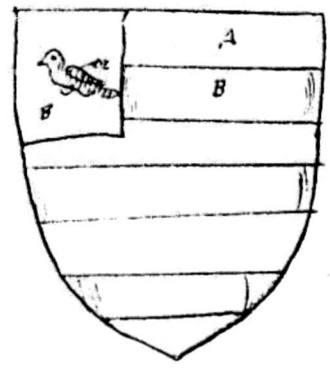

Lathbury arms, 1611

ROBERT DE LATHBURY, the husband from 1330 of the senior de Solney heiress, Ermentrude, was born in 1309 or 1310 but, dying in 1360, was comfortably outlived by his nephew, Sir John de Solney. Consequently the half portion or moiety of Newton Solney, including, as we have seen, the manor house, was in fact inherited by his eldest son – named after his de Solney grandfather - Sir Alfred de Lathbury, once it had been released from the hands of his mother. This must have been irksome for Sir Alfred, for his mother must have been around 45 when she made her late re-marriage to John Folcher of Osmaston, especially as he enjoyed the benefits of it in the right of his wife. It was irksome because Sir Alfred was nothing like as wealthy in either land or capital as Sir Nicholas Longford, being the lord only of a major part of Egginton.[19]

The Lathburys were, in essence, a new family, who had made it to landownership as officials (and possibly kinsfolk) of a much grander family, the Lords Pipard. Henry de Lathbury was of (and took his name from) Lathbury, near Newport Pagnell, in Buckinghamshire, and was a lawyer. In the Barons' Wars at the end of Henry III's reign he was granted a Royal exemption for life from serving on juries, assizes and similar obligations in recognition of having been made coroner against his will, probably as a result of the upheavals the wars had caused. This convenient happenstance had been arranged courtesy of an uncle, who happened to be the King's Clerk.

Henry left two sons and, the elder dying early, the family's meagre Buckinghamshire lands went to John, the younger son. In 1312, this John de Lathbury's son, Ralph, was Chamberlain (steward) to Ralph, 1st Lord Pipard of Linford. Although the Pipards were a great Baronial family with estates on the Oxford-Buckinghamshire border, Lord Pipard also had considerable Derbyshire estates, for he was a FitzNicholas by birth, of a younger branch of the de Longford family, whose mother had married the daughter and heiress of the last Pipard. Their son was summoned to Parliament in 1298 by Edward I in his grandfather's name – hence the title. In 1300 and 1301, Lord Pipard granted lands in Derbyshire, including the manor of Hargate, in Egginton, to his loyal steward, thus setting the family on their road to success. Interestingly, the Lathburys bore arms, *Argent two bars azure and on a canton of the second a martlet or* (see illustration above), which very closely resembles those of their feudal masters, which Lord Pipard assumed on inheriting: *Argent two bars azure and on a canton of the second a cinquefoil or.* Either the Pipards allowed their chamberlain astonishingly similar arms because of their position as senior feudal functionaries, as with the Mackworths and the Touchets, or they were actually of a junior line of the family, which took their name from having been settled on land at Lathbury.[20]

Of Ralph de Lathbury's two sons, Ralph, the elder, who was of Hargate Manor, Egginton, succeeded his father as Chamberlain to the Lords Pipard, but whose only son an heir pre-deceased him. Thus it was his second son, Robert, who eventually inherited Hargate-in-Egginton, which he consolidated with half of Newton Solney by his marriage to Ermentrude. Naturally, their eldest son was called Alfred after his grandfather. He also managed to acquire the Egginton manorial estate of Hardwick, too, thus increasing his holdings there, too, and he settled his third brother Ralph on it at some date prior to 1361 when this Ralph's son inherited it. It was probably this son of Ralph Lathbury who was the father of the William Lathbury whom we saw living in the manor house at Newton Solney in the early 15th century. This branch of the family were also probably the ancestors of the Lathburys of Hoon, recorded in the 1611 heralds' visitation of Derbyshire, and whose posterity were of Wetmore Hall, Burton, in the following century and tenants of the Everys, the eventual successors of the Lathburys at Eggington and Newton Solney - how fortunes change! Amazingly, the name still is current in Newton Solney.[21]

Sir Alfred de Lathbury eventually held land in various pockets of the Trent valley, quite a few inherited from his mother: Egginton, Heathhouses (the older name for Hargate-in-Egginton), Newton, Ambaston, Thulston, Chaddesden, Radbourne, Bearwardcote and Trusley. These lands are known about in some detail, as he settled them on his son John in 1424, but his young heir died shortly afterwards and they all had to be settled again on his grandson, yet another John, in 1428, his fourth son Reginald Lathbury being the chief trustee for the lad. In fact the elder John had been unfortunate in his marriage, as his wife, Joan, daughter of Henry Parr of West Broughton, in Sudbury, having borne him the younger John, then began an *affaire* with a member of Sir Alfred's retinue, Robert de Kythen, a distant cousin of the Lathburys - which probably explains his position on the family following. Although something like this was often papered over or settled with a civil case and a fine, the fact that de Kythen was only a member of staff, as it were, made the adultery the more heinous in those days when social position was paramount, and this therefore led to an annulment in 1399, and it was on the death of his second wife, a Bradbourne, in 1422 that caused Sir Alfred to make a new settlement.[22]

Sir Alfred's grandson, John was described as of 'of Newton Solney' before he succeeded in 1431 (so was presumably living in the hall there), but he died also quite young in 1438 although not without, again, marrying twice. He was the first of three John Lathburys, the last of whom left a son, Alfred, who once again pre-deceased his father, leaving an only daughter who, despite having three living male uncles, inherited everything, as medieval succession law dictated. In 1500, John Lathbury II confirmed a grant of his "capital messuage at Newton Solney with all its appurtenances all its demesnes, lands and tenements, feedings and pastures now in the tenure of Thomas Boylston and Matthew Bladon, together with a parcel of land there covered over by the water of the Trent, which is in English called 'a greyfe place' to accomplish his will" to Sir Ralph Longford. The impression one gets from this document, is that the Hall was divided as two farmhouses and let to Boylston and Bladon, members of two of the parish's oldest yeoman families who, as we have seen, were later inter-related by marriage (and for all we know, probably already were by some alliance now lost to record). The parcel of land 'covered over by the water of the Trent' must relate to part of that valuable commodity, the fishery. The transaction - presumably a temporary arrangement - was perhaps to do with Longford needing the rents from the two farms, for with the house divided, it is unlikely that he wanted it for a member of his family to inhabit. Nor is it known how long this lease was to last, but in the year of his death, William Leigh (1512-1546), the eldest son and heir of Anne, the Lathbury heiress, was described in a deed to have been 'of Newton Solney, armiger'. This clearly implies that he too then occupied the hall at Newton Solney, probably because his mother was still alive and was living in her ancestral home at Egginton. This also means that the lease to Boyleston, originally granted in 1466 for three lives, had fallen in along with that of Matthew Bladon, leaving the house available to be adapted back into a single residence. It is even possible that opportunity was taken to rebuild it. The situation was swiftly reversed, however, for with William Leigh dead, his widow Dorothy, a daughter of Thomas Eyre of Highlow Hall, Hathersage, moved into the hall at Newton Solney and she appears to have died there in 1563, although long re-married to Richard Needham of Snitterton Hall who was, like her father, a rich lead-mining entrepreneur, both also being members of ancient local families.[23]

The Leighs

The last John Lathbury of Egginton died in 1508, leaving his grand-daughter and heiress Anne as his heiress; she was by that time already married to Robert, a younger son of Reginald Leigh of Annesley, in Nottinghamshire. As part of the settlement, the half knight's fee for the tenure of the manor of Newton was released to the Duchy of Lancaster – still the notional chief lord of Newton in succession to the Ferrers - to be duly granted back to Robert to formalise the settlement.[24]

Arms of Leigh, quartering Lathbury (3) & Solney (4)

The Leigh family were a notable one, originally from High Leigh in Cheshire, and roughly equivalent in antiquity and distinction to the de Solneys and, like them, once vassals of the Earls of Chester. Robert Leigh of Adlington, Cheshire, also held a moiety of South Normanton, Derbyshire, and was fifth in descent from Sir John Leigh of Booths, in the same county, second son of William Venables and Agnes, daughter and heiress of Richard de Leigh of High Leigh, a son of William *fitz* Hamo de Leigh, first of Leigh. Robert Leigh of Adlington died 1415 having had numerous sons, but was in fact succeeded by his grandson, another Robert, whose sixth son was Reginald, of Annesley, Nottinghamshire. Another brother (or uncle) was given an estate in NW Derbyshire which, due to his son having produced no issue, devolved back on to Robert, Reginald's son, who was already, in the right of his wife, lord of Egginton and the former Lathbury half of Newton Solney. This estate included lands at Bowdon, Wormhill and Whitfield, confirmed to his father in 1476, along with Blackbrook and land at Glossop, Chapel-en-le-Frith, Hope and Whitehall. He also inherited land at the Booths, Cheadle, and Kingsley, Staffs., confirmed to his father by Richard Leigh of Adlington, Chapel-en-le-Frith, Hope, Wormhill, Whitehall and Bowdon. Before inheriting Egginton, he was styled as 'of Blackbrook, Esq.' All this land thus became, from 1508, part of the holdings of this formerly obscure branch of the Leighs[25].

40

In 1525 the new squire of Newton Solney was party to a bond for £300 for wool from the Staple at Calais from his cousin, Roger Leigh of Clapham, Surrey, which suggests that he was supporting Roger's lucrative wool stapling business, the export of this commodity being then in the ascendant. Indeed, wool must have been a staple product of his NW Derbyshire estates, all on windswept upland pasture. After all, the neighbouring Thackers bought the dissolved Repton Priory with the profits of a similar undertaking a generation later. Not all family relationships were so fruitful, however. A year after depositing his bond, he found himself in dispute with one John Lathbury over custody of "evidence concerning his inheritance". John was probably a son of one of Robert's mother's uncles, Henry Ralph and Thomas, and appears to have been trying to prove that the estate was actually entailed upon the senior heir male rather than upon Anne, elder daughter of the senior brother, Alfred. Very sensibly, in view of the expense of a lawsuit, the matter was instead referred to Henry, the Prior of Repton, for arbitration, who found for Robert Leigh over his importunate cousin, although John Lathbury appears later as a witness to one of the Leigh family's legal transactions, which suggests any rift was patched up in the wake of the Prior's wise counsel[26].

Robert Leigh's eldest son, William married twice, first to a Kniveton, and secondly to Dorothy Eyre, whom we have already encountered. Both were lead-mining families, as was that of Robert Leigh's mother, Anne, sister of Sir Richard Vernon of Haddon. This must have been a period of considerable prosperity for this emergent branch of the Leighs, therefore, which reached its fulfilment in the grandson of Robert and Anne Leigh, Thomas, being knighted shortly after 1572. At that time, Sir Thomas was still holding the supposed manor of Blackbrook (Bowdon Edge, Chapel-en-le-Frith) which, with its appurtenances, he was renting out, the manor house itself being let to the Carringtons, who lived there for a very long time. In 1570 he managed to recover the manor of Newton from his mother's widower, Richard Needham, along with the hall, where Dorothy had been living until her death. This enabled him to get some income on stream from the village, as for instance the income from the Newton Solney tithe barn – which without doubt lay near the church and hall – which had long before been let to his father-in-law, William Dethick of Newhall.[27]

Sir Thomas Leigh thus married Anne Dethick in 1552, whose sister Elizabeth had also married a Leigh, in this case Sir Thomas's younger brother Ralph, who appears to have been living at Newton Hall after 1570, along with their two sons, Humphrey and William. Sir Thomas and Anne had three sons and four daughters. Then, Anne died in childbirth and her husband re-married in 1587, his bride being Elizabeth, daughter of Thomas Curzon of Croxall by whom he had three, possibly four, more sons. Several of the Leigh offspring married and had issue, and when the estates passed to the Every family in the 17th century, most still lived round and about on very modest patrimonies. A descendant of Joseph, the youngest son - appointed rector of Egginton 1631-1640 by his brother - was Revd. John Leigh of Belmont, Lancashire, who was also ironically made rector of Egginton two centuries later, in 1824, appointed by Sir Oswald Mosley Bt., perhaps to discomfort his fellow patron, Sir Henry Every, by re-introducing a scion of his predecessors into the parish! However, Sir Thomas did not long outlive his second wife, and died in 1591 after four years of marriage, to be succeeded by his eldest son Henry. His widow re-married Sir Francis Coke of nearby Trusley, so presumably did not require a capital mansion like Newton Hall to live in.[28]

It was under the last of the Leigh family that the Newton Solney estate was largely re-united. Sir Henry Leigh was born in 1573 or '74, and was thus only seventeen when his father died. Coming of age in 1595, he at once seems to have been perceived to have been in the market for the Longford portion of the Newton Solney estate and after acquiring ever smaller moieties which had been granted to various Longfords, eventually acquired the bulk of it in February 1602/3 from Hugh Beeston for £4,582. It was shortly after this and before 1608 that he was knighted by James I. The re-unification of Newton Solney may have cost Sir Henry more than he had bargained for, because in 1605 we find him selling part of his north Derbyshire estates to Thomas Bagshawe of Ridge Hall, Chapel-en-le-Frith for £300. Indeed, as time went on he must have been getting into considerable debt, for in 1627 he sold a substantial chunk of land at Egginton to his future son-in-law, Simon Every. Again, this may all go back to the Newton Solney purchase of 1603, for it is quite possible that he had been obliged to borrow most of the principal at an unfavourable rate of interest.[29]

Sir Henry married on 6th July 1591, when still well under age, and just after his father's death. His bride was Catherine, daughter of John Horton of Catton Hall right in the far south western corner of the County. They had only three daughters, Mary, Anne and Catherine, of whom only Catherine married and had children It was to her husband that the entire Leigh estates eventually passed on Sir Henry's death in 1635, shortly after he had vested some of his lands in a trustee, including a moiety of Newton Solney. The trustee was his cousin once removed James Milward of Egginton, whose father Arthur - a member of an old and distinguished Derbyshire family seated at Eaton Dovedale - had married the sole heiress of John Leigh, a great uncle of Sir Henry's and had settled on land granted to him in Egginton. This included no less than 30 messuages (houses with attached land), 20 tofts, 40 gardens, 1120 acres of various land with rents in Newton Solney & Repton. This is the first indication that some of the Leigh family's lands lay in Repton; how this came to be will become clear in the next chapter.[30]

From 1633, then, the story of Newton Solney continues for some 160 years once again under one undivided ownership. The village enters its next major phase.

*

[1] Ermentrude, DRO D5236.6.9; Folcher settlement, PEC XL]

[2] Appleby family, Glover (1831/33) II. 24-29; Longford marriage, settlement and moiety of Newton, J 1761, 1763, D5236/9/13.

[3] Agnes's marriage settlement, PEC XXXV of 1348 which reads as if John, Alfred's son, had not yet been born; Appleby vs. Stafford, D5236/9/15, D5236/9/17 & J. 1763

[4] Norbury, Emery II (2000) 425-427; Appleby, Nichols IV (1811) 429; moated sites, Craven & Stanley (2001) I. 22-23

[5] Thomas de Chandos, D5236/3/41 of 1/1/1369/70; Chandos, CP III. 126; Sir John, DNB

[6] Hall, PEC XXVII; William Lathbury, D5236/3/62; John Lathbury, *Fuedal Aids*, I 308; the younger William, D5236/3/62; PEC LXVIII; J. 1185

[7] Tax return, DAJ XXX (1908) 52-53; PEC XXVII; surnames, Hanks & Hodges (1996) 238, 519

[8] List, D5236/4/42; Hankey: D5236/4/49 of 13th May; Winshill family, see BC *passim*.

[9] 1401, Manor Court roll, Egginton, 1399-1417; Thomas and Margery, D5236/4/41 of 30/10/1466; Thomas sr. & jr., D5236/4/47 of 30th Aug. & D5236/4/47 of 21/6/1505; Burton & Pype marriages, V. Staffs., 1614; Boyleston/Bladon marriage: Egginton PR 4/2/1566/67; Town Lands, D5236/4/95 of 1/6/1614; John Boyleston, D5236/4/81 of 1/2/1602/3

[10] 1539, L P Hen. VIII xiv (1) 267; 1587 muster DAJ XVII (1895) 18; Beacon/Bacon, Cameron, *loc.cit.*

[11] de Toeni, CP XII. i. 753; Pipard, *ibid.*, X 531-532].

[12] Disputes, John Stafford, *Feudal Aids,* I 264, 308; with John Appleby, J. 1763; John Stafford the Archbishop, DNB II. 1977

[13] Chantry, *Calendar of Close Rolls,* (1389-1392) 342-343; endowment: J. 1769.

[14] *Plea Rolls* 15 Edward IV; on the Longford-Blount feud, Turbutt (1999) II. 468-469.

[15] Sir Nicholas, DRO D5236/4/38 & /42; J. 1763; wife, Margaret Shaw, DRO D185B/Culland; DC, B6, I8, K2, O8; Sir Roger, DLSL deed 597; DRO D185B; Sir Ralph, IPM 7/6/1513; (RLC) 242; DRO D5236/4/43; Henry at Newton Park, RLC 238, 551-552; 1437 court roll, J. 1762; 1564 manor court, DRO D5236/12/19; Longford Wood, Pounds (2000) 17.

[16] Sale of fishing, D5236/4/63-64; on Mosley, the founder of the family of that name now represented by Lord Ravensdale, BP (2003) III. 3283; 1502 agreement, D5236/4/46 of 25th March; weir 1566, D5236/4/53 of 2nd Jan.; salmon, Blome (1673) 128

[17] Lease PEC CI of 20/7/1578; topography, Cameron III 648; 1608 lease, D5236/4/90

[18] Sale to Beeston, D5236/4/73 of 29th April; sale by John Longford, DLSL deed 3434, D5236/4/65 of 4th Feb. 1584, D5236/4/72 of 25th March 1592, D5236/4/71 of 14th June 1592, D5236/4/76 of 27th July 1593; joint ownership, D5236/4/78, /80 of 4th June 1599 and 25th Feb. 1599/1600, contradicting the assertion of the Lysons – *op.cit.*(1817) 245 - that the unification took place in Henry VIII's reign; Longford cadets, DLSL MS 6341 & *Reliquary* VII (1866-67) 74-75 cf. V. Notts. 1569

[19] On Ermentrude's settlement and Folcher, PEC XL, D5236/6/9; the arms of Longford (with crests), Lathbury and Leigh are the herald's tricks (sketches) from the Visitation of Derbyshire of 1569.

[20] Henry's career, *Cal. Close Rolls* 1266-72; the sons' inheritance, *Cal. Pat. Rolls* 17 Edward II, ii. 103; grant of lands, D5236/6/1-2 of 13/5/1300, PEC XXXV, LXII, the latter dated Rotherfield Pipard 5/1301; Pipard, CP X. 531-534; arms: Lathbury, Visit. 1569, 1611; Pipard, Falkirk Roll, 1298 & seal on PEC XXXV, dated 1300; Touchet grant to Mackworth 1404, Craven (1991) 105

[21] Ralph II, J. 919; Salt Arch. Soc. Vol. V (1904) 99; PEC LXXIV, LXXXIII of 1326; D5236/6/5 of 13/10/1340; Hardwick manor, J. 1202; Lathbury of Hoon, V. 1611

[22] Holdings of Sir Alfred, PEC XXIV; settlement, PEC XXIV, XLII, LI; marriage & annulment, PEC LXXXII; D5236/10/7; DLSL deed 3258

[23] John Lathbury I, *Feudal Aids,* i 308; death, IPM; will dat. 20/8/1438, PEC LXVIII; John II, J.1185, 1764, D5236/10/10, RLC 545; John III, PEC XLVII of 1500, D5236/4/47 of 1505, J. 1764; uncles of heiress, DLSL deed 3169; grant of mansion, PEC XLVII of 1/4/1500 & of the original lease to Boyleston D52376/4/42; William Leigh, IPM 18/10/1549, Notts. RO Mi6/175/52; Dorothy 'of Newton Solney', D5236/4/51

[24] DRO5236/9/21

[25] On this family, see V. Chesh. 1580; Robert of Adlington, IPM 9/12/1415; NW Derbys land 1476, D5236/5/20; IPM 6/11/1525, D5236/10/18; Staffs. lands, where he is described as 'of Blackbrook Esq.' PEC LXXXVII of 1492

[26] £300 bond, PEC XXXV; Anne Leigh's uncles, D5236/15/19-20, *ibid.*, /4/476; DLSL Deed 3169 of 1506 & PEC; dispute with John, D5236/15/19-20 of 30/1/1526/7

[27] Visit. 1569, 1611, V. Chesh., 1580; knighthood, D52376/4/5 of 1572; Blackbrook, *ibid.* /10/19, 5/276, 5/44; recovers Newton Solney, *ibid.*/4/56; tithe barn, J. 1765

[28] Marriage bond 27/10/1552, D52376/5/26; Ralph Leigh of Newton Solney, V. 17611; Chaloner's MS DLSL MS 6341; Rev'd John Leigh, MI in Egginton church, Cox IV (1879) 187-188

[29] Newton purchase, DRO D5236/4/83-85; Bagshaw purchase, D5236/5/60-61; sale to Every, DRO D5236/4/97

[30] Settlement of the estate, D5236/4/102 of 10/11/1632.

*

III

THE EVERY ERA

The Every family

On the death of Sir Henry Leigh, inheritance law dictated that the estates he held should pass to his three daughters and co-heiresses but, thanks to the settlement he had made with James Milward, the whole estate, including almost all of Newton Solney, passed to Simon Every, the husband of the middle daughter, Anne, who held it in the right of his wife, a situation that would be repeated all over the country until the passage of the Married Women's Property Act in 1882, after which an heiress could at last own property in her own right.

The Everys claimed descent from a family of that name long settled in the area where Devon, Dorset and Somerset meet; they were, it was said, scions of the Norman house of d'Ivry. John Every was of Weycroft Castle at Axminster, in Devonshire in the age of Queen Elizabeth, and his son William married Margaret, daughter of Robert Haydon of Cadhay, a well known medieval house nearby. This must have encouraged him to live in an equally ancient house, and in 1605 he bought Cothay Manor, Somerset, although in the family it was always said to have been granted to the Everys by Queen Elizabeth, who had seized it from the Catholic Bluetts of Holcombe Regis. Here his posterity remained for nearly a century, and which the Every's heirs owned until the turn of the 19th century. A year earlier he had applied for a grant of arms and William Camden had allowed him *or four chevronels gules* (four red chevrons on a gold shield) which establishes that Camden, a careful scholar, considered the claim of descent from d'Ivry to hold some water at least, for their arms were similar but with one less *chevronel*. For crest he granted them *a demi unicorn*

Original Every arms, as used by Sir Edward Every 8th Bt., quartering (inter alia) Leigh, Lathbury and Solney

Every arms as granted in 1804

45

couped gules armed un-guled and maned or. The Simon Every who married Anne Leigh, however, was the son of John Every of Chardstock – only five miles from Weycroft Castle - and of Oxford, grandson of another John, originally from Chaffcombe, Somerset, who had been a royal servant to every monarch from Henry VIII to Elizabeth I, being appointed Sergeant at Arms by the latter. This John, according to the copious notes towards a family history compiled by the late Miss E. M. Every, was the uncle of the John Every granted arms in 1604 and, although his descendants used those arms for two hundred years, they were not strictly speaking entitled to them, not being descended from the grantee. This situation was not rectified until 1804.[1]

John Every of Chardstock had bought a 63-year lease of the manor and advowson of the village in 1581 and died three years later leaving it to his eldest son, John (1570-1628, a Fellow of Magdalen College, Oxford. Simon was his eldest son, born in 1602, matriculated at Wadham College, Oxford 27th November 1618 and proceeded to the Middle Temple in 1620; education for the elite went at a much faster pace than today! He married Anne Leigh probably in 1628, although the family aver that he came to Egginton to wed her in 1623, they clearly did not marry in the parish, for the records are complete for this period. !628 was the year that Sir Henry Leigh settled land at Egginton on him, followed a month later by the entire manor of Newton Solney, the yearly value of which was set at £350. The manor house "and certain lands, parcel of the demesnes" were assessed at £100 per annum. Miss Every asserts that the Everys "lived at Egginton with his father-in-law", but this seems unlikely in view of the fact that Sir Henry and his wife and their two unmarried daughters already inhabited the house; it is much more likely that they lived at Newton Solney until Sir Henry's death in 1635, when, as had happened before, they probably swapped houses with his widow. This would have been all the more appreciated by the Leighs at Egginton, as Simon and Anne started a family without delay. Whilst there, too, Simon spent £500

Repton Priory's former Grange Farm: The 19th century farm buildings on Main Street
[Maxwell Craven]

46

buying the rectory and tithes of Newton Solney from Godfrey Thacker, whose ancestor had acquired them with the rectory of Repton from the dissolved Priory there. From then until the 19th century, the Everys were patrons of the living at Newton Solney. He also purchased some land in Repton from Henry Beresford of Newton Grange, north of Ashbourne.[2]

Although he had the manor of Newton Solney settled on him, he did not own all the land within the manor, for ownership of a manor by this date did not imply ownership of all or even necessarily any of the land within it. There were a number of freeholds in Newton, most of which were parcels of land granted to religious houses by the de Solneys and their successors, and 'privatised' at the Dissolution of the Monasteries, mainly through sales organised by the Crown's commissioners. For instance in 1553, some former Gresley Priory lands at Newton were sold to Leonard Brown of Skymande, Lincs., and Anthony Trappes of London, Gent., who were essentially speculators, who took over the land and its two tenants, Richard Platon and John Hanby, the latter being a name found in the Longford family charters suggesting that this holding, wherever precisely it lay, was in the former Longford moiety of the manor, and thus most likely south of the Repton to Stapenhill Road. Repton Priory also held land in Newton for, in 1564, some of its former holdings there was granted to Robert and William Caldwell and, a decade later, a grange in Newton Solney, again formerly belonging to the Priory of Repton and owned by the Thackers, was let for 21 years at 40/- per annum to Alan Matthew, Gent. & William Cox, yeoman, both minor court officials, who no doubt also put in tenants. This, of course, was the farm on Main Street subsequently called Grange Farm, on the lands of which the late 19th century residence called the Grange was also erected. Later still, in 1580, a lease of a house and land formerly property of Repton Priory was granted for 89 years to John Boylston, whom we have already met, this to begin as soon as a previous lease, granted by the Priory itself in 1508 to his grandfather Thomas Boylston, his wife Alice and son Richard, had expired.[3]

Nor was there land up for grabs just from the religious houses at this period, for the chantries – like that set up in 1390 in memory of Sir Alfred VIII de Solney at Newton - were also dissolved. This chantry land was part of a large agglomeration of property seized from "chantries, religious houses and attainted persons" – members of the political *elite* convicted of treason and who had their property forfeited as a result – and granted by Henry VIII to the Perpetual Hospital of The Savoy in London, and which was given a fresh investment under Mary I who confirmed the gift in 1556. Six years later, under Elizabeth I the same Newton chantry lands had been detached from the endowment of the Savoy and granted to Cecily, widow of John Pickerell, himself no doubt another favoured land speculator.[4]

The Civil War and After

More land was lost to the manorial estate at Newton as a result of the Civil War, too, and in the context of that conflict, Simon Every held a prominent position. Having inherited his father-in-law's estate in 1635, he was appointed Receiver General of Rents for the Duchy of Lancaster on 3rd May 1636 along with his neighbour, John Curzon of Kedleston who, a fortnight later and for reasons that remain obscure, was created a baronet of Nova Scotia. Simon was the same year appointed to the Derby-

TABLE II: THE EVERY SUCCESSION

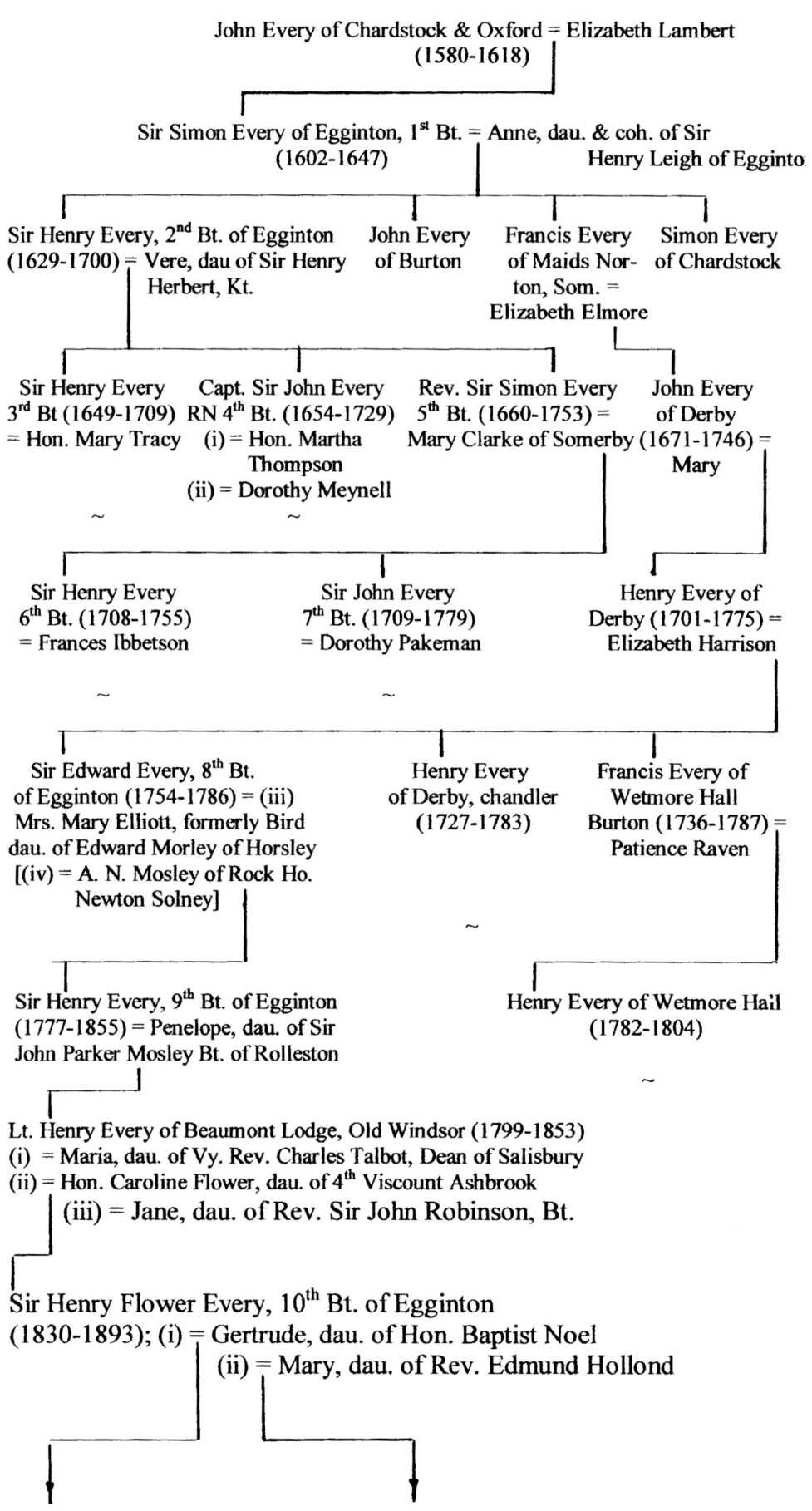

John Every of Chardstock & Oxford = Elizabeth Lambert
(1580-1618)

Sir Simon Every of Egginton, 1st Bt. = Anne, dau. & coh. of Sir
(1602-1647)   Henry Leigh of Egginto

Sir Henry Every, 2nd Bt. of Egginton   John Every   Francis Every   Simon Every
(1629-1700) = Vere, dau of Sir Henry   of Burton   of Maids Nor-   of Chardstock
     Herbert, Kt.   ton, Som. =
                                Elizabeth Elmore

Sir Henry Every   Capt. Sir John Every   Rev. Sir Simon Every   John Every
3rd Bt (1649-1709)   RN 4th Bt. (1654-1729)   5th Bt. (1660-1753) =   of Derby
= Hon. Mary Tracy   (i) = Hon. Martha   Mary Clarke of Somerby   (1671-1746) =
                Thompson   Mary
               (ii) = Dorothy Meynell

     ~   ~

Sir Henry Every   Sir John Every   Henry Every of
6th Bt. (1708-1755)   7th Bt. (1709-1779)   Derby (1701-1775) =
= Frances Ibbetson   = Dorothy Pakeman   Elizabeth Harrison

     ~   ~

Sir Edward Every, 8th Bt.   Henry Every   Francis Every of
of Egginton (1754-1786) = (iii)   of Derby, chandler   Wetmore Hall
Mrs. Mary Elliott, formerly Bird   (1727-1783)   Burton (1736-1787) =
dau. of Edward Morley of Horsley   Patience Raven
[(iv) = A. N. Mosley of Rock Ho.
Newton Solney]

                                ~

Sir Henry Every, 9th Bt. of Egginton   Henry Every of Wetmore Hall
(1777-1855) = Penelope, dau. of Sir   (1782-1804)
John Parker Mosley Bt. of Rolleston

                                ~

Lt. Henry Every of Beaumont Lodge, Old Windsor (1799-1853)
(i) = Maria, dau. of Vy. Rev. Charles Talbot, Dean of Salisbury
(ii) = Hon. Caroline Flower, dau. of 4th Viscount Ashbrook
    (iii) = Jane, dau. of Rev. Sir John Robinson, Bt.

Sir Henry Flower Every, 10th Bt. of Egginton
(1830-1893); (i) = Gertrude, dau. of Hon. Baptist Noel
        (ii) = Mary, dau. of Rev. Edmund Hollond

48

shire bench and in March 1640 was elected to Parliament for Leicester, although in the event he did not serve long, for this was the famous Short Parliament, dissolved by the King in the May following. A year later, however, no doubt in an attempt to ensure his loyalty, Simon Every was raised to a baronetage – effectively an hereditary knighthood, but carrying no ex officio legislative function – 26th May 1641, just as the clouds of civil conflict were gathering ominously. Baronetcies, of course, had been instigated by James I in 1611 in order to raise money for the plantation of Ulster. From the Conquest, the second tier of the *elite* had mainly been knights, charged with keeping order and administrating justice within their manors. Subsequently, as we have seen with the de Solneys – almost all knighted – the Lathburys, Longfords and Leighs, the head of the family could usually expect that a knighthood would be conferred upon him. For those fighting in France in the Hundred Years' War, the superior knighthood of banneret was created, and baronetcies were an attempt to replace the expected knighthood for the more important members of the gentry with a hereditary equivalent, modelled on the old rank of Knight Banneret, hence, indeed, the style, baronet. The catch was, that in order to receive one, a fine had to be paid to the Crown. For those who demurred, a similar financial penalty was exacted as a penalty for refusing, resulting in a fairly healthy take-up on the honour, the Gresleys of Drakelow, and the Knivetons of Mercaston for instance, being amongst the very first families in Derbyshire to receive the honour in 1611. Sir Simon paid a fine of £1,095 for his baronetcy, which was supposed to keep 30 infantry for three years at 3d per day for the colonisation of Ulster. A similar scheme was also instigated in Scotland, but here the fine was spent on the colonisation of Nova Scotia – it was one of these that Sir John Curzon received – and later Irish baronetcies were conferred[5]

Sir Simon Every, 1st Bt., circle of Sir Anthony van Dyck [*Sir Henry Every, Bt.*]

During the Civil War, Sir Simon Every, although known as a Royalist, did waver and his position at times was equivocal, mainly out of self-interest. When the war broke out in 1642, Sir John Gell of Hopton, Bt. raised a regiment of tenants and lead miners, seized control of Derby and thereafter slowly brought the entire county under his sway. Hearing what had happened in Derby, Sir Simon was one of a group of local notables opposed to Parliament – the others included the Earls of Devonshire and Chesterfield, two Sir John Harpurs (of Calke and of Swarkestone), Sir John FitzHerbert of Norbury and Sir Edward Vernon of Sudbury - who signed a strongly worded remonstrance, in order to make their objections to his actions plain, at Tutbury Castle, which Gell, needless to say, ignored. These grandees then raised a regiment for the King from their tenantry, into which Sir Simon was commissioned, thereafter moving to take command of the garrison at Lichfield, being promoted to Lieutenant-Colonel by December 1643. The Every family aver that that Sir Simon was in charge of munitions and supplies at Tutbury and several other castles like Loughborough and Kenilworth.

Unfortunately, he fell out rather drastically with the Royalist C-in-C in the Midlands, Lord Loughborough, which had serious consequences. Loughborough eventually accused Every of disloyalty, though the disloyalty was principally against Loughborough, not the King. The accusation had arisen because Sir Simon had failed to collect the outstanding Duchy of Lancaster rents before Sir John Gell had closed parts of Derbyshire off to such exactions. Sir Simon therefore found his estates seized, Lord Loughborough's aim being to sell part of them in order to make up the perceived fiscal shortfall caused by their owner's failure – hardly his fault in the circumstances – to collect the rents, which were desperately needed to fund the Royalist war machine. Worse, hard on the heels of this indignity, Sir Simon found that, in his absence, Sir John Gell had plundered Egginton Hall and his properties at Newton Solney, presumably the hall there, too. Having protested but obtained no satisfaction, Sir Simon "Having neither Men nor Armes and wanting Meanes to trouble this County, he went to Oxford to expect the success of the ante-Parliament there", an action which laid him open to Royalist accusations of treachery. As it turned out, a party of marauding Cavaliers captured him at Stony Stratford, and they took him forthwith to the King's headquarters at Oxford where he was charged with 'being a friend to Parliament'.[6]

This contretemps was resolved eventually and he was re-instated with honour and sent to north east Derbyshire at the head of an armed troop to try and collect the Duchy's rents due at Bolsover and thereafter at Ashbourne, Tutbury and Lichfield, in which tricky mission he had rather mixed fortunes, bringing back little cash. In 1643 he was relieved by Parliament of his Duchy receivership and was succeeded by Sir John Curzon, who was a leading supporter of Gell. Thereafter, Sir Simon took a commission in the army raised by the Queen in the July of that year at Burton, where he helped to capture the town in a desperate cavalry charge under Col. Thomas Tyldesley across the medieval bridge there on 2nd July, watched by Henrietta Maria herself and establishing his credentials at last as a dashing cavalier. Thereafter he was in arms in the West Midlands, Derbyshire and Staffordshire through 1644 and to May 1645, also playing a leading role in the capture of Leicester. He fought with honour at the Battle of Naseby, in which the Royalist army was thoroughly defeated, and fled to Wales where he remained for some time.

Before the war had really got under way, Sir Simon had attempted to protect some of his property for the benefit of his children. In 1641, he had obtained a confirmation from the Crown through the Duchy of Lancaster (remembering that Newton Solney lay within the Honour of Tutbury, part of the Duchy) of the rights and customs of the residents, which was a considerable benefit which, resuscitated at the Restoration, continued for some time. This was followed by a grant from Charles I of toll-free status to the tenants and inhabitants. In the year following, however, Sir Simon granted the tithes of Newton for 99 years in trust by a deed of entail to finance the education of his younger children. Because of his actions in the Civil War, though, he was subsequently thought to have done this solely to keep his land out of the Parliamentary Commissioners' hands and he was adjudged a 'delinquent' by the *junta* which ran the County for Sir John Gell, called the County Committee, and an Act of Parliament of 1643 disqualified him from disposing of his estate except by sale. His delinquency was assessed at a mere £100 by the Parliamentary Committee for the Advance of Money, but by November 1645 this sum had been increased to £2000, although he was granted a respite to pay in May 1646.[7]

Because of the Civil War, there were a remarkable number of people around who were on the take, always prepared to lay accusations with the County Committee against almost anyone they didn't like or on whose property they thought they might get their hands under the pretext of delinquency. Sir Simon suffered in this way early on. A keen radical, Richard Ford of Repton, mercer, 'shopped' him to the county Sequestration Committee – set up to oversee the engrossing and disposal of Royalist sympathisers' estates - on his return from Wales, on the grounds that he was in breach of the 1643 Act and had concealed assets especially estates in Worcestershire and Gloucestershire. Sir Simon countered that he had made the provision for his children by granting them the Newton tithes *before* his delinquency had been declared under the 1643 Act. At this point, Sir Simon died, leaving his eldest son Sir Henry, thenceforward 2nd Baronet (Bt.) to argue the case, which he did, adding the argument that, as he had not been involved with his father's Royalist actions, he should not be discriminated against. Against this, it was argued that his father had already been declared a delinquent when making his settlement for his children – a debateable point, to say the least.[8]

Royalists who had had their estates seized but who had returned after the war had ended were made to compound for their estates – that is, to pay a substantial fine of up to two thirds their value - to get them back. The case already outlined against Sir Henry (standing in for his deceased father) was thus eventually adjourned pending the outcome of the compounding process. Sir Henry therefore petitioned the Compounding Committee (which by 1650 had been amalgamated with the Committee for the Advancement of Money) that his father in trying to protect his offspring was merely settling the estate and was not intending to defraud the state, his case bolstered by the provisions of Sir Simon's will, proved 1st December 1649. Furthermore, he alleged that Mr. Ford and his two supporters had fabricated the entire accusation levied earlier in order to enrich themselves, for informers whose allegations led to successful prosecutions being entitled to 20% of the sum exacted. What with the compounding of the estate, which required a substantial sum to be raised, and the exactions of Lord Loughborough in trying to claw back money Sir Simon had failed to collect from the Duchy of Lancaster's tenants, a great deal of land in the village seems to have been lost to the estate by the end of the Civil War. Thus, over the following century, the family were constantly, when in funds, buying land back when and where they could. In the long term, Parliament's impositions were settled by a single fine of £2,000 paid by Sir Simon's son, Henry, who had contrived to stretch proceedings out until September 1652 alleging that his father was merely a life tenant of his estates which, by the outbreak of hostilities, were all held in various trusts for the benefit of the family. The dispute over the money owed to the Duchy of Lancaster ground on until the Restoration.[9]

Sir Henry, understandably disenchanted with the Commonwealth, was quick to join Sir George Booth's Royalist rising of summer 1659, being described by the turbulent Republican Col. Thomas Sanders of Little Ireton as "the principal Actor and Promoter of the Rebellion in Derby". The rising collapsed, and Sir Henry was arrested and once again his remaining estates were sequestrated. He was only saved by the collapse of the port-Cromwellian regime and the Restoration in May 1660, as a result of which he was absolved of all his and his father's alleged 'delinquencies' and appointed a deputy lieutenant of the County.

After the Restoration

One innovation which followed the Restoration was the imposition of a hearth tax, from which only the poorest in each community were exempt. An assessment was undertaken for the Hundred of Repton and Gresley in 1662, and from it we get a cross-section of all the households in Newton Solney, from which we are able to make some estimate of the status of people from the size of their houses and also, to some extent of the population.[10]

The list reveals that there were 41 householders, giving an estimated population of something like 165. It also tells us that there were only two houses of any size, both apparently of four hearths, which is about the size of a large farm house or small manor house, although some names may indicate a house divided between more than one family, examples being the Widow and William Dickyn (i.e. Dicken) in a three hearth house, along with John and Thomas Dicken and the two John Shepherds both sharing two hearth houses. These were about par for the course in size for tenanted farmhouses in the 17th century, and it is a shame no house of this size in the village has survived, although there is a photograph of one, taken by Derby photographer Richard Keene of Derby in 1877, thought perhaps to have been the fore-runner of Museum cottage. John Smedley had the only other three hearth house, marking him out as a substantial farmer, probably with a freehold, for this family were still freeholders, albeit of a small acreage, in 1758 and 1827 (see Chapter V). One very

---

1662: HEARTH TAX ASSESSMENT FOR NEWTON SOLNEY

Name	Hearths	Name	Hearths	Name	Hearths
Henry Byard*	4	John Spratley	1	John Smedley*	3
Widd. Fisher	2	Humfr[e]y Alsop	1	Widd. Wayne	4
Tho. Smyth[*]	1	Geo. Shenton	1	Tho. Newton*	1
Will. Hakesley	1	Will. Hatchett	1	Will. Bateman*	1
Tho. Dakyn*	1	Will. Dickyn*	1	Tho. Holmes*	1
Tho. Bird	1	Widd. Dickyn*	2	Henry Willson*	1
John Smedley*	3	Will. Garner	1	Richard Reynoldson*	1
Will. Reynoldson*	2	Will. Reynoldson*	2	Geo. Rivett	1
Humfr[e]y Alsop	1	John Shepard sen*	1	Tho. Hide	1
Tho. Newton*	1	John Shepard jun*	1	Mr. Wiseman	2
Will. Hatchett	1	Will. Bateman*	1	Mi[le]s Bryan	2
Tho. Dakyn*	1	Tho. Bird	1	Robert Wright	2
John Dickyn*	1	John Symson	1	Francis Atkyn*	1
Tho. Dickyn*	1	John Wright*	1		

From this Thomas Dicken, the parish constable was able to raise £1 – 1s - 8d (£1.08p). Names with asterisks appear in the 1758 terrier as well.

---

interesting entry is that of Henry Byard. Although four hearths seems very little he was probably occupying part at least of the hall. However, later evidence, indicates that the property had been split and that Byard had a tenant. This was almost certainly (on the precedent of properties known to have been divided at the time of the assessment elsewhere) the person next named in the list, therefore widow Fisher, whose family, as we shall see, had obtained a freehold of the hall at Newton. Thus the hall was in all probability a six-hearth house, equivalent in size therefore to the decayed manor house at Findern, Little Hallam Hall or Hartshorne Upper Hall. Other parts of the old house may have also been adapted for agricultural use.[11]

The hearth tax lists 33 households, probably in thirty or thirty one buildings. If one may postulate an average family size of four, then one has a figure of 132 people, but with servants and living-in farm labourers, this figure is probably nearer 200. 11 of these families were still in the village in 1758 – the Byards, Smedleys, Newtons, Wilsons, Holmes, Dickens, Reynoldsons (later spelt Rennison), Wrights, Atkins, Shepherd and Wayte, the latter being recorded also in the 1321 poll tax list along with (possibly) the Shepherds: continuity if you like! Wayte, incidentally, was in 1662 occupying the other 4 hearth house, and this may be the capital messuage that we know was situated on the former Longford portion of the manorial estate. Again, the family were freeholders latterly, although whether it was a small residual freehold of land or a substantial property is difficult to discern. In 1758, there were eight substantial farms, tenanted by two Dickens, a Wilson, an Atkins and a Holmes. We also know from the 1758 terrier that the Thomas Newton of 1662 was a freeholder and ancestor of John Newton, whose holding was just over 24 acres at the latter date.

Richard Keene's 1877 view of a typical 17th century brick-built small farmhouse, this one situated on the edge of Newton Park.   *[Brian Appleby]*

None of the people on the hearth tax list except Mr. Wiseman appear to have enjoyed any real status, although had widow Fisher's husband John Fisher of Foremark still been alive, he would have been accorded the style of Gentleman. Mr. Wiseman was almost certainly the incumbent of Newton church, probably put in to replace a non-conformist predecessor installed during Sir Simon Every's sequestration by the

County Committee to replace the "disaffected" Mr. Bryan, who was there at the time of the Committee's visitation in 1650. Clearly, the house of the perpetual curate of Newton was far from palatial at this date.

Egginton Hall from near Rock House, 1821, after a painting by Henry Moore of Derby. [*M. Craven*]

A missing name is that of Eaton, for we have encountered a member of this family on the 1587 muster roll, and they re-appear again in 1758 and flourished as farmers and cattle dealers through the 19th century until we find the widow of the last of the line living in Rose Cottage in the 1880s and 1890s (see Chapter V). Perhaps there was no member of the family of age, only children or teenagers living with differently named maternal grandparents at the time of the survey. Alternatively, they might just have temporarily moved away. A number of farming families moved to tenancies in Egginton over the years, just as some Newton families, like the Byards and Dickens, seem to have originated the other village. Some came from further afield. For instance, Joan Dicken married Thomas Shenton in March 1683, as his second wife, and thereby imported another name to the village, for they proceeded to farm in Newton Solney (where a cousin, George Shenton also farmed) and were succeeded by their son Thomas, whose sister Mary married Newton husbandman (small farmer) Richard Atkins in 1723. The Shentons had originally farmed for some generations at Alkmonton Hospital, which ancient building appears to have been demolished by the landowner after Thomas moved to Newton and replaced by Top Farm.

There is one particularly new name on the list, apart from the parson, that of William and Richard Reynoldson. The family first appear in Newton Solney in 1563, when John Raynoldson (*sic*) leased a share in a 'tenement (in the village) with all houses, barns and 2 oxgangs of land pertaining' for 21 years at 24/- (£1 – 20p) per annum from Sir Thomas Leigh of Egginton. Again, he was probably an Egginton man, perhaps the father or brother of the William Reynoldson of Egginton who married an Alice Bennett there in 1576. A descendant of John was probably William, of Newton Solney, yeoman, who acquired a 1,000 year lease on a house and 5.5 acres of land in Walton on Trent from Christopher Nevall (Neville) of Barton-under-Needwood, Gentleman, for £148 in 1656, Neville having been a Royalist victim of sequestration. This is the same William whose two hearths were taxed six years later. Richard was probably a younger brother. A grandson, John Rennison (1650-1728) – note the change in the spelling of the name, a mutation from local phonetic usage - seems to have been a freeholder in Newton and Egginton, for his farm in the latter village was mortgaged in 1720-1728, although he also held a tenancy from the Gresleys in Overseal which he seems to have acquired through his marriage to Mrs. Collins, a widow there in 1696. We know he also held a freehold in Newton, for his two sons, William and John, held it jointly with John's son, Thomas Rennison. Unfortunately, the family got into financial difficulties and William was summoned for debt in 1742, by which time they had already had to sell some land to the Everys, and in 1744 were obliged to sell what remained to them, too. Thomas's was the last generation of the family to live in the village, however.[12]

Rebuilding the Estate

From the Restoration, then, the Everys began a campaign to re-acquire lost territory in Newton. Fifteen years after Charles II managed to regain his throne, Sir Henry Every, 2nd Bt., "obtained a piece of ground in Newton Solney from Philip (Stanhope, 2nd) Earl of Chesterfield in exchange for the right to erect and maintain a fishpond with free fishing in the same in a close there" This underlines the importance, in the kitchens of elite families, of plentiful supplies of fresh fish. It also reminds us that Lord Chesterfield and Sir Henry Every were neighbours on the southern boundary of Newton Solney who enjoyed cordial relations. Not only that, but the Everys had enjoyed the patronage of the Stanhope family, for Sir Henry's brother John – later of The Great House, High Street, Burton-upon-Trent - had been a Captain in Lord Chesterfield's Regiment of Foot eight years earlier, in 1667. A point which arises from mention of Sir Henry's brother John, is that he was a very talented man, a keen entrepreneur and made a fortune in his own right. For many years he managed and improved the Every family estate for his brother, spending a total of £5,375 on various improvement projects. This must have been especially welcome, for the estate at first was encumbered with the debt arising from the Civil War sequestration, the compounding and other depredations. A testament to his success, is that in 1702, Sir Henry Every had 20 houses with land, 1000 acres of land, 300 acres of meadow, 100 acres of pasture, 100 acres of woods, 40 acres of heath & gorse (total acreage, 1540) worth £1360, and by 1713, the income from the Newton Solney estate was estimated by William Woolley at £1,500.[13]

One reason why little improvement at Newton Solney was undertaken especially in the years immediately following the death of Sir Henry, 2nd Bt, in 1700, was that his successor let Egginton Hall and resided in his uncle John's residence, The Great House, High Street, Burton, and on his death in September 1709, his widow was granted the manor of Newton Solney for life "excluding Newton (later called Bladon) Wood", site of a favourite family shoot, which rather precluded any of his immediate successors taking any part in its improvement. Yet even then, some was retained by the Everys and not assigned in dower to the widow of the 3rd Bt., for a farm at Newton Solney had to be mortgaged to Thomas Wright of Bretby, yeoman, by Sir Henry for a short time in order to raise some ready money.[14]

It really took until the third decade of the 18th century before more serious re-acquisition of land in Newton Solney could take place, although strengthening of hol-

Thomas Carter's effigy of Sir Henry Every, 3rd Bt., in Newton church, 2008.

[*M. Craven*]

dings in Egginton had been embarked upon some time before this. Furthermore, there had been a fairly rapid succession of baronets following the death of Sir Henry in 1700, for he had been succeeded in turn by three of his sons, the last of whom. Revd Sir Simon Every, 5th Bt., formerly a long-serving Lincolnshire parson, succeeded at the age of 69 and died aged 92 in 1753. He, in turn, was succeeded by his two sons, Sir Henry (6th Bt.) and Sir John (7th Bt.). In the event, it was the 6th Bt. who began to re-acquire land, doing so long before he ever succeeded to the title, starting with "a small estate" there in 1731 (paying £1000), a house and land attached in 1735, a farmhouse the following year with land there and in Repton (for £311), a further house and 34 acres in the village in 1737 and some land from the Rennisons in 1739. In 1744 he bought the remainder of the Rennison land along with a cottage for £14, and two years before had splashed £800 on a farmhouse and 27 acres at Newton, which also came with 8 acres in the Egginton manor of Hargate and 2 roods in the open fields of Repton (the Westfield, immediately abutting Newton). The year following the Rennison purchase, Henry Every bought what is described as a 'capital messuage', which probably refers to the hall or to the house that various members of the Longford family had retired to in the sixteenth century. All this activity at Newton by an heir apparent strongly suggests that Henry Every was actually living in the village. Yet, if he was, the question arises as to which house he occupied. As a gentlemen, it would have to be the Hall or a dwelling of similar status. It may be that he resided nearby in the Great House in Burton, or perhaps at Wetmore Hall, the latter certainly in the family's ownership in the later part of the 18th century, but Newton Hall, is another possibility. This might well be identifiable with the "capital messuage" he had bought in 1747. Wherever he was living, he inherited the estate on his father Sir Simon's death in 1753 and died eighteen months later, to be succeeded by his younger brother Sir John as 7th Bt. Sir John inherited 1,200 acres "including Bladon Wood" in Newton Solney, but which had been put into trust in July 1741 for his brother's widow, which rather prevented further activity until she died in 1770. Thereafter, Sir John made several acquisitions in Newton, including the reversion of a cottage for eight guineas (£8.40p), a house, 17 acres and a "little decayed cottage" for £1100 from William King of Caldwell, Gentleman, and five closes totalling 21 acres for £570, which his brother had previously exchanged with Newton freeholder, William Newton. As we have seen it is possible that he was perhaps a descendant of the medieval pre-de Solney under-tenants of the manor, and at this date once again acknowledged in the relevant deeds as a gentleman. This earlier exchange of land, which Sir Henry had undertaken with various local freeholders in 1760, had been to try to consolidate the family's holdings into one bloc and in 1770 Sir John was also able to re-purchase 13 acres affected by that arrangement from Alexander Byard, and also bought from him "a mansion house and premises" although it is not entirely clear where this 'mansion house' was; the Grange has been suggested, but there is little evidence to show that the Grange was high status building. On his death, Sir John gave to 38 poor families in Egginton and Newton Solney 2/6d each.[15]

1758 Wyatt Survey
(Every family terrier)

Farmers	Small tenements	Freeholders
Thomas Atkins*	Daniel Bateman*	Alexander Byard*
William Belcher	William Deakin*	John Bladon
Samuel Bull	James Gibson	Mr. John Newton*
Joseph Dicken*	Thomas Holmes, senior	Mrs. Smedley*
John Dicken*	Thomas Holmes, junior	Thomas Smedley*
William Dicken*	Ann Mansfield	Francis Tivey
Thomas Eaton	Elizabeth Richardson	Ralph Wright*
John Gibson	George Smith*	
John Holmes*	John Ticklebank	**Cottagers**
Joseph Payne		John Mawley
Peter Payne & 1748		William Richardson
Thomas Powis		Ellen Midlam
John Rennison*		Mary Collier
Thomas Smedley* (blacksmith)		Thomas Moor
Thomas Shepherd*		[ ] Ashmore
Aaron Thorp	**Farmers** (cont.)	Josiah Mawley
Job Thickbroom	John Dicken Wilson*	Thomas Smedley*

One of the reasons why there was a property exchange in Newton Solney in 1760 was the result of a survey of the manor undertaken for the 7th Bt. shortly after his succession, conducted by William Wyatt of Great Heywood, Staffordshire (1701-1782), an experienced surveyor and an uncle of the architect Samuel Wyatt who, two decades later, was commissioned by Sir John to rebuild Egginton Hall along up-to-the-minute Neo-classical lines. The resulting survey, or terrier, which may have been as Philip Heath has suggested, the central element of what was effectively an 'in-house' enclosure of the estate at Newton, survives although its accompanying map, very regrettably, does not.[16]

With 42 householders, we can see that the population has hardly changed from 1662; it was probably still about 165-170. Regarding our *leitmotif* of continuity, those names marked with an asterisk (*) represent families also recorded in the 1662 hearth tax assessment, amounting to twelve, prominent amongst whom being the Dickens and Smedleys. It will be noted that, following their having had to sell up to the Everys in 1739 and 1744, the Rennisons were reduced by 1758 to tenant farmers, probably on a 49 acre fraction of what had been their own holdings.

The largest tenant farmer was Peter Payne (actually written Pain by Wyatt, but here corrected from other records) with 146 acres, followed by William Belcher and John Holmes with 112 and 121 respectively. Payne was related to the Fisher family of Repton, whose heirs had once rented part of the hall. He occupied its immediate outbuildings and two acres of paddock; the remainder was occupied as a farmhouse by John Holmes. His family were certainly prosperous, for in 1703, his father William had made a bequest to the poor of Newton Solney in his will, confirmed in that of his son, the John Holmes named above, dated 28th October 1773. In the century following they re-appear as freeholders at Grange Farm.[17]

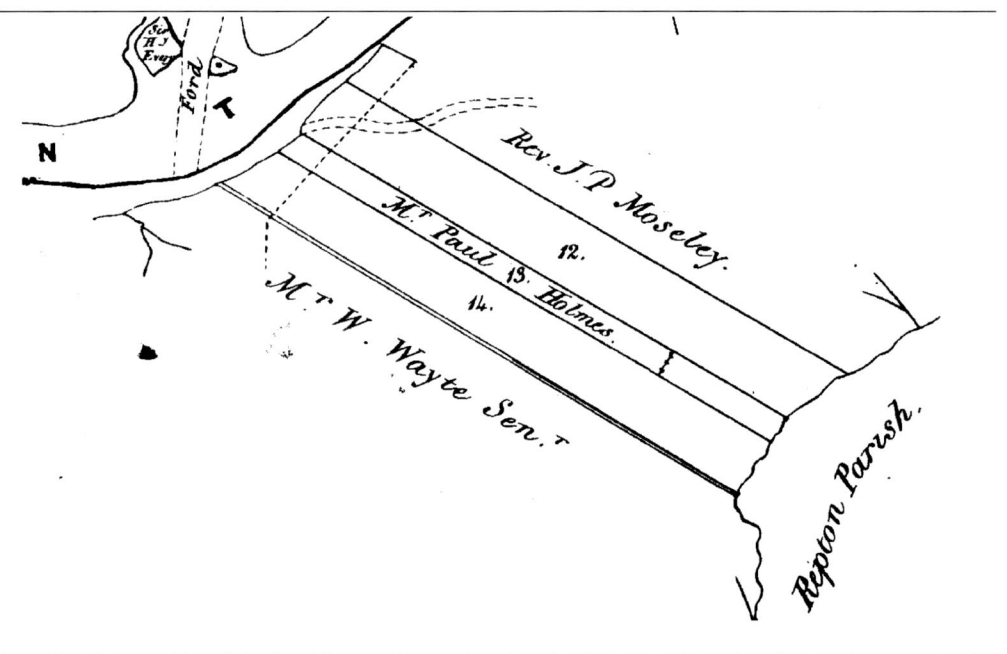

Section of the map from the 1836 sale catalogue showing the surviving strips in Town Field. Nos. 12 & 14 were in the sale   [*Private Collection*]

At this date, most of the farmhouses were arranged along the main street of the village, for it was usually enclosure awards that led to the building of dispersed farmsteads, although well-managed estates also built farmhouses away from their village, something that had never really happened in Newton Solney, which was never subject to formal enclosure. Joseph and John Dicken, along with Thomas Atkin all had farms of over 70 acres, as well as Aaron Thorpe with 63, and Peter Payne's brother Joseph who farmed 87 acres. The remainder were essentially small husbandmen and small-holders and there was something over 4 acres of common land with a further two acres lying within Repton Parish.

These farms were still working parcels of land scattered across the parish, for the three field system of medieval days was still essentially in place, with strips in Town Meadow (lying between the river and the Repton boundary) still being worked there as late as 1836, where they appear on the sale catalogue of that year. Indeed the three common fields were still going strong in 1758, albeit that some had suffered a change of name, but thereafter a more efficient land disposition was the order of the day, however. The easternmost field was by this time split mostly by the road from Repton to Stapenhill, the north part being Town Meadow and the more southerly portion Dale Field. Dale Field extended to just over 104 acres, and Town Meadow was 25 acres, from which we can deduce that the original field extended to about 130 acres. Bladon Field by this date was only 56 acres and The Howgh (revealingly spelt phonetically 'Huff' by Wyatt) extended to a shade over 164 acres. The 25 acres of Town Meadow was divided between John Holmes, Peter Payne, John and Joseph Dicken, John Dicken Wilson and the smallholders, Thomas Eaton, John Powis and Samuel Bull. Hall Meadow lay just west of Town Meadow, and was only 20 acres, but must have represented the former hall's immediate grounds, put out to agricultural use.

The islands in the Trent still existed, and were farmed, Scarsey extending to over 17 acres with three different tenants working various parts of it, and there were two other small islets by the weir each of just over a quarter of an acre in extent. There was also a close called The Butts, which takes us back to the time of the muster rolls encountered in the previous chapter, for the name implies a place where target practice could by done, no doubt by those summoned under the muster as archers both under the threat of the Armada and, without doubt at previous times of trouble, like the Wars of the Roses and the Hundred Years War before them. Not that shooting was a dead art, for we find the Everys were still keeping "the rides in Bladon Wood…clear for shooting and hunting" in 1803 (held back from the 1799 sale of much of the estate), and the closes called Repton Brook Shoot, Dastal Shoot and Crabtree Shoot all suggest that fragments of the early park were still being kept for game shooting, a vital diet supplement for the *elite* table during the winter months. Even after the sale of much of their estate in Newton, there were still efforts to improve what remained. For instance, in the same year the remaining tenants there were paid £2 – 14s – 0d for making 2,700 holes for tree planting at 2d per hole and later another 76,200 were made shortly afterwards![18]

The Hall & The Grange

In the previous chapter we saw how the manor house or hall, as it seems to have been called, was put to use as a secondary residence during the years it fell within the portion of the manor of the Lathburys and then the Leighs. The problem is, that by the end of the eighteenth century, it appears to have vanished leaving few traces behind - or so we are led to believe. Nevertheless, it continued to crop up in the record, and also left a legacy of place names on the 1758 terrier, at which time part of it at least was certainly still extant.

In 1649, John Every, Sir Simon's second son, was described as "of Newton Solney" at this crucial period, just when his elder brother was striving to extricate the estate from the County Committee and the Commission of Sequestration. Clearly, he was then living in Newton, and, given his status, the hall is the only place that obtrudes as at all likely. The next indication we have is the Hearth Tax return of 1662 (by which time John Every was living in the Great House at Burton), in which, as we have seen, it would appear that the hall was split between Henry Byard and the widow Fisher[19]

It would seem that the freehold of the hall was probably that re-acquired by (Sir) Henry Every in 1747 and that of the Grange by his successor in 1770. What appears to have happened is that at the end of the Civil War, the hall and other parts of Newton, were expropriated and sold off to other people, sympathetic to the Parliamentary cause, when the Everys' estate was sequestrated. Fortunately, we can track something of the progress of this, although in the case of the hall, matters remain a trifle obscure. However we learn that in 1712, the Byard family bought a capital mansion and over 25 acres of land from John Fisher of Foremark (1663-1731). Now the Fishers were an ancient and well known Repton family, which, in later years produced Geoffrey Fisher, an illustrious headmaster of Repton School who went on the be Archbishop of Canterbury and Lord Fisher of Lambeth. John Fisher's father, Thomas Fisher of Repton, married there in 1659, Ann Payne, of the same family that we find farming in Newton Solney a few decades later, which goes some way to explain Peter Payne's presence in the village as tenant at Hall Barn Yard, Hall Barns and Rock Tower in 1758. In fact, this capital mansion appears, in 1655, to have been sold by the sequestered Royalist supporter Sir John Harpur to the Parliamentary supporter William Fisher, a London merchant living at Newington Green, London, probably acting as a speculator. How Harpur had come by it, remains obscure; did he buy it from the sequestrators or did Every sell it to him directly? If the house referred to is The Grange, then it may be that his family acquired it from the dissolution of Repton Priory, the Harpurs being subsequently involved with the founding of the School there. Be that as it may, Fisher, having acquired it, died very shortly after buying the property, leaving a daughter and sole heiress, Ann, who brought the property to her husband, Nathaniel Tench. When he in turn died in 1706, he left a son, Fisher Tench (later Sir Fisher Tench, 1st Bt., of Low Leyton, Essex) to whom he left his main estate, but the Newton property went to John Fisher, his cousin. Subsequently, in 1712, Fisher sold it on to Henry Byard, a prosperous Repton farmer, who retained it only until 1719 when it went to the ancestor of the vendor in 1770, William King. The Mrs. Fisher, who was occupying part of the Hall in 1662 (if we have interpreted the Hearth Tax return correctly) was a local girl, widow of William of Newington Green, and keen to see out her declining years closer to her family. One has the impression that the Fisher involvement ran to both Hall and probably the Grange, but that the former was re-acquired by the Everys a generation earlier.[20]

Thus the hall would appear to have been still there in 1758 and appears to have been let to Peter Payne and John Holmes, which arrangement was presumably facilitated by the division that the house had undergone prior to the 1662 Hearth Tax assessment. Thus both Payne and Holmes were substantial farmers, working land owned by the Everys. Holmes for instance, had a house, garden and workshop, outbuildings, yard, garden and a lodge, which sounds as if his portion was the larger one, whereas Payne clearly lived in the smaller portion and enjoyed the use of the barn yard, barns and Rock Tower, the latter being a building to which we will return. Payne was then nearly seventy, had a daughter married to the Every tenant Aaron Thorpe. Their daughter married one John Higgott, a family which cast a fairly long shadow in the village's agricultural community in the mid-19th century, on the basis of inheriting the tenancies of Payne and Thorpe along with the Payne freehold.

Rock House

Rock House is an existing Newton Solney residence, but its origins are complex and would appear to lie in the demise of the hall. As we have seen, local farmer Peter Payne was the tenant of Hall Barn Yard, Hall Barns and a structure called Rock Tower, all in 1758. The next thing which comes to record is a spectacular tower like building called Rock House, first recorded in a competent watercolour (above) still in the possession of the Every family. It is signed by Ashton Nicholas Mosley, the second husband of the widow of Sir Edward Every, 8th baronet, and third son of the Every's neighbour, Sir John Parker Mosley 1st Bt. of Rolleston Hall Staffordshire. One the reverse is written, in a contemporary hand – presumably the artist's

"The Rock House, Newton Solney, Drawn by A. N. Mosley for
Lady Every previous to their marriage, viz. in AD 1789."

Rock House as depicted by Nicholas Mosley in 1789   [*Sir Henry Every, Bt.*]

An entry from A. N. Mosley's diary, quoted in Miss E. M. Every's family history confirms that this house was where they were to live following their marriage on 10th March 1790. Although initially at Egginton Hall, he recorded, that between February and May 1791 the couple gave a "party and a dance at Rock House etc." We have seen how, before the 17th century, the hall at Newton tended to be used as a dower house, and here we seem to have a similar situation. Once Sir Edward had died in 1786, his widow seems to have been assigned a dower house at Newton, as specified in Sir Edward's will. Once affianced to Ashton Mosley, they clearly intended to remain there until something larger could be made available, and in the event they remained until Park Hill, Egginton, was completed in 1798, and into which they moved on 5th June that year. Any suggestion that Rock House was used merely for partying is negated by the fact that it was successfully let as a residence - prior to its subsequently total rebuilding after 1872 – throughout most of the earlier nineteenth century and without any discernable enlargement. A low extension can be seen to the left in the 1789 view and this can be seen to have been fairly substantial on later maps.[21]

The question is, therefore, does Rock House occupy the same site as Rock Tower, if so, what was the origin of the Tower and when did Rock House come into existence?

Mosley's picture, of course, seems to establish the position of the house, and from the position of Hall Barn, Hall Orchard, and adjacent closes on an estate map of 1827, on which Rock House is also marked, it seems likely that Rock House was erected on the footprint, and perhaps even incorporating part of, its predecessor Rock Tower. If one consults the position of Rock House on a map, it will also be seen that it lies on the outer extremity of a southern kink in the Trent and must have commanded a lengthy view both up and down the river. Given the extra height of any structure worthy of being accorded the name 'Tower', the visual command of the river at this point would thus have been impressive. Now the old hall at Newton was not a fortified house as such, for it is absent from the list of Royal Licences to crenellate, issued during the Medieval period. That is not to say that it could not have had a tower or towers. It might, therefore, be safe to assume that the Rock Tower was a remnant of the medieval house, probably by the 18th century, detached from the surviving six hearth portion of the hall (if this was not a replacement building entirely) by the progressive reduction of the old mansion. Why exactly it was suffered to remain as late at 1758 is anyone's guess. The name is explained by its position on a rocky outcrop of Keuper Sandstone, the existence of which probably explains why this bend in the river never moved further southwards.

There is, of course, the possibility that the tower was built in the 1660s by Sir Simon's Every's widow's second husband, Lawrence Squibb, who lived at the hall and is known to have re-landscaped the setting. It is, however, an early date for an eye-catcher of this sort, but not impossibly so. Perhaps more likely it was an ancient remnant and the decision to fashion a house from Rock Tower was probably connected to the extensive landscaping of the park at Egginton Hall which followed on from Samuel Wyatt's completion of the rebuilding of the house in 1780. Miss Every's account notes that the work was done in 1784-85, although she omits to mention by whom. The likelihood is that this was undertaken by William Emes (1729-1802) who had worked at Kedleston realizing Robert Adam's vision of the land

An anonymous view of the re-landscaped park at Egginton from the Dove, c. 1795 by Henry Moore of Derby   *[Private collection]*

scape there, whilst Samuel Wyatt was serving as clerk of works. He later worked in tandem with Joseph Pickford, Wyatt's successor at Kedleston, beginning with Foremark Hall in 1760 (alongside work at Kedleston), and seems to have followed in Pickford's wake until the Derby architect's death in 1782, when he attached his star to the Wyatts, both Samuel and James[22].

One has the strong suspicion that, in landscaping the park, which had the disadvantage of being relentlessly flat, an opportunity was taken to make use the old Rock Tower at Newton Solney as an eye-catcher, set as it was on the high point of the Trent's far bank. One suspects that it was rebuilt as a piece of romantic Gothicism,

Rock House (1789) left, and Richard Keene's 18766 view of King's Mills, right
[Sir Henry Every, Bt.]   *[Derby Museum]*

63

and, the Everys being anything but extravagant, finished as an occasional residence or indeed, as first envisaged, perhaps as a summer banqueting house, just as their neighbours, the Burdetts of Foremark, had adapted Knowle Hill two decades before. The distance from Egginton Hall to Rock House in line of sight was just over a mile and a furlong with nothing, in those days, in between and the planting of the park seems to have been arranged to leave the line of sight clear.[23]

Use as a dower house might well have been an afterthought, following Sir Edward Every's death. If this suggestion is correct, then the architect was likely to have been 'Sam' Wyatt (as the family seem to have referred to him), whose final payment was only made in 1784. As for the form the building took at his hands (if indeed, he was responsible) an obvious comparison has to be drawn with the King's Mills at Castle Donington, where the main building, a narrower version of Rock House, was Gothicised in an extremely similar manner and certainly formed an eye-catcher for Aston Hall, where the Holdens had an interest in the ferry there, if not in the mills, although the same was true for Shardlow Hall, built in 1684 by the proprietors of the ferry, the Fosbrookes. The King's Mills building, a gypsum mill taking much of its raw material from Aston pits, is well-known for its narrow front, but is also long behind, and no doubt Rock House as built presented its shorter side to the river, especially if there was room for the Mosleys to hold a dance there. The possibility that both Rock House and King's Mills were by the same architect and dated from the same period must be strong, although Samuel Wyatt has no known connection with King's Mills. Rock House's verticality, its lancet windows and irregular cresting make for a strikingly original and romantic composition. The oriel window overlooking the river must have made for an agreeable room behind, and below it there appears to have been a sort of water-gate giving access to the river, which was, even in the early twentieth century much resorted to by those with access to it. The cave like opening to the right being probably a boat house, and there was a low crenellated service wing to the left. It is believed that the Gothick façade was of brick, stuccoed over and painted.[24]

After 1798, Rock House's use is unclear, although it remained in Every family ownership until 1871, when it was sold. No occupant is on record from 1798 to about 1830 when Edward Thornewill (d. 1866) was the tenant. He stayed there until around 1837/38 when he retired to Dove Cliff, Stretton, his father Thomas's home. Thomas'

Boating on the Trent between Cliffe House and Rock House, 1920s.   [*Private coll'n*]

own father, incidentally, had in 1767 prevented Sir John Every from building a new water mill on the Old Dove, opposite the Thornewill estate. With Thornewill gone, the house was let to Richard Yates from The Cedars, who left in 1846 when he was succeeded by Francis Sacheverell Wilmot, nephew of the third Chaddesden baronet. Who had married three years previously. In 1854 James Mitchell, a well-known and successful theatrical agent in Bond Street took the tenancy but moved out in 1857. He died in 1870 and left his son George, by then tenant of The Mount, £70,000 but he rapidly managed to lose his inheritance and had been declared bankrupt. R. E. Neave moved in after that, but the house was sold to the Salts in 1871, and the saga will be resumed in the following chapter.[25]

The Brickworks

It is not known when bricks were first made in Newton Solney. It was probably after the period 1591 to 1603 in which we find Roger Hoult, 'freemason of Newton Solney' with Joanna his wife and Edmund their son. This description suggests that he is likely to have worked in stone. Nevertheless, the small-scale clay diggings and brick-making facility were certainly old-established and, judging by the tenacious manner in which the Everys held on to them, they must have brought in a reasonable income, for they appear to have been run in hand at least up to the beginning of the 19th century. In 1758, the brick pit and kiln were on Newton Lane, where now stands (Newton) Hill Farm, previously Brickyard Farm. The first positive reference we have to brick-making in the village is in 1710 when the Egginton vestry minutes record "Fetching 15 Hundred of Brick from Newton for building of Labon's and Bradbury's Houses." These bricks were transported by pack animals through the village, down Trent Lane and across the ford thence to Egginton village via Coale Pitt Way.[26]

The End, looking east, 2008; the brickworks lay to the S, on the right of the picture.
[M. Craven]

In 1824 Sir Henry Every changed policy and let the works in exchange for a rent, to an incomer (but experienced brick maker) William Hopkins, who had been his paid brickmaker (or tenant) on site since 1811. He also farmed some adjoining land rented from the Everys. On his death, he was at first succeeded by his son Samuel (born 1786) who in 1841 lived on site with wife Jane, five years his senior, other sons John and William, junior, and daughter Anne. William continued to farm nearby on Bretby Lane and was still alive in 1881, leaving a daughter, Rosa who went to Australia and died in 1945. Anne married John Marbrow who took the whole operation over about four years later, and local man thirty-five-year old William Shepherd who was living in; probably he dug the clay. In 1841, Marbrow was a farmer only, but by 1846 he had taken over the firm as a maker of "bricks, tiles, drainpipes and kiln-tiles", and his rather well-proportioned new farmhouse in a mildly *cottage ornee* style – which still exists, although with the original windows replaced - seems to date from precisely this period; it may be the work of Joseph Somers, a Repton Builder. Sometime between 1857 and 1870, he too had died and was succeeded by his son William Hopkins Marbrow, who acquired the freehold from the Everys prior to 1873 (it was probably

Newton Hill Farm (formerly Brickyard Farm) in 2008.   [*M. Craven*]

sold at the same time as Rock House), when he was the freeholder there of just over 26 acres. He made bricks on the site until 1891, when he gave up, put out of business by larger, semi-mechanised brickworks with immensely greater output; thereafter he just farmed there until around 1910 when he was succeeded by Joseph Watson Smith.[27]

There can be little doubt that much of the village (not to mention Egginton, including the former hall) is built of locally made bricks, and the Every's estate foremen would have been responsible for much of the construction work over the years. We do not have the names of many of these, and indeed, they may have been based in Egginton. The ground floor of Heage windmill is paved with tiles stamped 'Newton Brick Company' and Philip Heath reports kiln tiles with the legend 'J Marbrow/Newton

Solney', so the products of the works, although a small operation compared to many, especially in the later 19th century, certainly found a market in a wider area than the immediate locality.[28]

A miscellany - crime

Misdemeanours occurred as in all human societies. Not many are recorded for Newton Solney, though. Indeed, the most heinous, murder, only occurred in the fifteent century, as for instance when John Barton of Newton Solney was accused of the murder of William Draper, also of Newton, but was acquitted, on a finding that he was " indicted by malice" – by whom, is lost to us. Nor does it appear that the true culprit was ever brought to book. Earlier we have seen how William Woodward of Newton Solney was pardoned for all possible crimes on recommendation of the Earl of Lancaster with whom he had served in Gascony. What we are not told was whether this pardon was in response to Woodward behaving badly, or whether it was merely a privilege which, whilst making him feel good, was unlikely to need to be invoked. Later, at the tail end of the Civil War, John Gilbert of Newton stole six sheep from Robert Dowman of Smisby, husbandman. He wasn't very subtle, though for they were later identified on grazing on ground in the village belonging to Gilbert, who was duly convicted and punished, late in March 1648. Local punishments were confined to periods in the village stocks; the stocks lasted to about 1850, when they were removed and replaced by a lock-up, which itself has vanished, too. These were both reserved mainly for drunks, perpetrators of loutish behaviour and similar petty offences.[29]

- fishing

Fishing continued in the Trent. The cost of two nets for salmon fishing, which were bought by Sir Simon Every in 1740 from Thos. Wilcox of Sawley Ferry, was £4 – 0s – 6d, so the 5th Bt. was obviously a keen angler himself. In 1764, 58 salmon were taken, Trent salmon being then, as in the previous era, marketed in London. The weight recorded of the biggest fish taken at that time there was 35lbs, but in 1783 a fish of 25lbs was taken simultaneously with another of 26lbs, netted together. The hole at Monk's Bridge, Egginton, on the very northern edge of the parish, was a particularly good draw. Sir John Every 7th Bt. introduced 200 store carp in the 1770s to his lake and other ponds (including the one at Newton the 2nd Baronet had obtained from Lord Chesterfield). Lamprey and grayling fisheries were natural to the Dove but these were destroyed by pollution before the end of the 19th century. In the 1820s there was a surge in popularity of Newton Solney as a fishing destination, but a century later only pike, perch, dace, roach, chub, bull-head gudgeon and loach remained plus 'numerous eels and sticklebacks'.[30]

The fishing on the Trent was sold by the Everys to the Cliffe House Ratcliffs (see next chapter) from whom they became therefore part of the Newton Park estate. Joe Bailey of Newton Hill bought the rights at the break-up of the estate. The Trent is no longer as good as it was before the Environment Agency began a campaign to de-pollute the river, although officially salmon and Trout are returning to it. Nevertheless, if, contrary to received o[pinion the Trent does once again teem with these classic coarse fish, then the fishing will again become as popular as it was in the early 19th century.

Sir Edward Every, 11th Bt., fishing the Trent from the Newton Solney side 1913   *[Private Collection]*

- Pinfold, bull & boat

Stolen sheep were one thing, but strayed ones another. A pinfold had long been provided, but a new one was built in 1779 at a cost to the estate of £5 – 18s - 0d. Nor could most farmers necessarily afford to run a bull, and in 1758 one was provided for parishioners' use. It cost £6 – 4s – 0d and was fetched from Egginton across the ford for 1/-. Having made what use of the happy animal they could, it was sold on, but made only £4 – 19s – 0d: some depreciation! Mention of the ford brings to mind the fact that it was not always possible to use it, if the river was high, to which end a parish boat was kept. By 1771, when a man was paid 6d for "for cutting the boat out of the ice", it had handily been provided with a lock to prevent unauthorised use[31].

- Every benevolence

The Everys were, as the majority of English landowners, kind to their tenants, even thought they were worked hard too. Apart from bequests to the poor of the parish in the wills of various baronets, we find Mary daughter of George Smith apprenticed in 1749 to Thomas Brown of Walsall, of all places, for 5 years to learn 'housewifery', with the fairly hefty premium being paid by Sir Henry Every. Housewifery is not a common apprenticeship, but may indicate that George's wife had died and he was looking for his daughter to be trained up to keep his large and young family. Not enough is known about who was in which trade, however, although we know that the Smedley family provided the village blacksmith from at least the 1740s to around 1830[32].

The topography of the village was rather different in the eighteenth century. Newton Solney escaped enclosure because at the crucial period it was in Chancery, during the minority of Sir Henry Every 9th Bt. Thus it still had some of the strips and headlands surviving from the medieval period, although the Every estate had amalgamated many into closes and small fields over the two centuries they had owned the larger portion of the parish. This, though, meant that all the farmhouses were clustered in the nucleated centre of the village, and it was not until the estate began to be broken up from 1799 that farmhouses began to be built in the midst of the fields which they cultivated. Even today, Grange and Trent Farms are still in Main Street, almost opposite one an other, with Poplars Farm slightly further east but also on the main road, with Waterside Farm only a close's width north of the village street, where it remains to this day, albeit surrounded by modern houses. This is clearly shown on Peter Perez Burdett's map of 1767, with only a single house marked, isolated from the village, well down Newton Lane and on the west side.

Trent Lane, October 2008 [Maxwell Craven]

The street pattern in 1767 shows the Repton-Stapenhill Road passing through the village much as it does today, although it was kinked north, away from his house, by Hoskins in 1809. It would then have been little more than a lane, and was never turnpiked. In the village, Blacksmith's Lane and Trent Lane are shown, virtually parallel and, of course, the latter is as old as the ford to which it leads. Indeed, it has all the characteristics of a classic sunken lane – carved down between earthen banks by centuries of heavy use - and thus may well be a millennium or more old. Parallel to it, then as now, was the road to the church. South West from the end of Blacksmith's Lane is Newton Lane which, then as now, made a junction with Knight's Lane which runs past Broken Flats Farm just across the boundary in Repton Parish. Burdett also shows as a thoroughfare a lane running from Winshill, north of the present Hawfield Lane (which he does not show) and followed today by a footpath. It leaves Winshill at the apex of Hollow Lane and crosses the parish to Beaconhill Plantation, where its course is still a track, to the point where it crossed Newton Lane, and then headed east out of the parish, past Cokhey Barn Farm and thence to Repton village. This road seems to have fallen out of use in the nineteenth century, although it is marked on the 1836 map of the Newton Park estate but only west of Newton Lane.

As with previous eras, the population is difficult to measure with any precision. From the 1758 survey we learn that there were 43 houses, and thus a population of around 172. In 1789 there were 47 houses, suggesting a population of some 188; a partial census in 1801 revealed that there were 181 inhabitants. More reliable figures became available in the nineteenth century however, and the population estimates generally will be found Chapter VI.[33]

The great sale

Sir Edward Every 8th Bt. had succeeded his distant cousin and come into his inheritance from his simpler life in Derby as a chandler, to find it encumbered with debt, mainly from the expense of Wyatt's drastic rebuilding of the Hall and the re-landscaping of the park. His predecessor Sir John had tried to pump some cash back into the estate through the sale in 1772 of an outlying piece of it, Hanson Grange, with 208 acres. This estate, like the Grange at Newton Solney, was once a grange of Burton Abbey, to which it was given by Roger de Hanson. At the Dissolution it had been granted, along with the rest of Burton Abbey's lands, to William, 1st Lord Paget, and this part of it appears to have come to the Leighs through their alliance with a junior member of the house of Milward of Thorpe (in which parish Hanson Grange lies), descending thus to the Everys. The buyer who paid £4,250 – a straw in the wind if ever there was one – was one Abraham Hoskins (1728-1805), a Burton solicitor and no stranger to bankruptcy himself, although it emerges from a letter he wrote that he was at the time a personal friend of Sir John. Hoskins also bought one of the freehold farms in Egginton and then proceeded to stampede the Everys into seeking an Enclosure Award from which he hoped to expand his holdings. Thus even at that stage, it could be discerned that he had laid predatory eyes on the estate which, as the family lawyer, he could see was probably heading for trouble. Worse, Sir John died intestate on 29th June 1779 leaving only a draft will and a male heir who was a distant cousin, albeit one who had been drawn gradually into the family circle over the latter part of Sir John's time. It was at this stage, it is worth adding, that Abraham Hoskins, the friend who purchased the Hanson Grange estate, became the family lawyer.[34]

Sir Edward Every had a struggle to make ends meet. Short-term sums of ready money were raised by mortgages, for example when several closes and other premises on Landlands Lane Newton Solney were mortgaged to Thomas Green; the mortgage was discharged in 1800, probably using money liberated by the 1799 sale. The estate certainly tried to make some improvements: Newton Farms, perhaps identifiable with Middle House, which in 1758 was tenanted by William Dicken, was demolished leaving only a yard with barns and stables left, which was clearly an attempt to amalgamate two farms to make one more efficient one. This house, though, does not appear to have been replaced and, indeed, after Sir Edward's death, it could probably not have been, as the whole was in Chancery and effectively in limbo.[35]

Sir Edward died unexpectedly prematurely in 1786, by which time the already encumbered estate was mortgaged for up to £14,000. The tradesmen's bills alone amounted to £2,3763, so with the heir Sir Henry (9th Bt.) being well under age (he was only 8yrs. and 6 months old), the estate was put by its trustees into Chancery to avoid it having to be split up and sold off in parcels. This, however, prevented any further sales or mortgages, so the whole estate was effectively in limbo for thirteen years. In this state, the rents still had to be collected and, after due allowance for maintaining the family and the hall at Egginton, the residue applied to the reduction of debt. Ominously, by 1793, the duly appointed 'receiver of rents and profits' for the estate was none other than the wily old family lawyer who had been investing in the Every's estate two decades before, Abraham Hoskins. Indeed, he remained in office until 1800.[36]

Sir Henry was of age from 5th June 1798, although a month before, part of Bladon Hill was acquired by Abraham Hoskins by exchange for the farm he owned in Egginton. This was facilitated by the Egginton Parliamentary Enclosure Award of 1791-98 which, he argued, had enhanced the value of this farm and made the exchange viable as far as Sir Henry's trustees were concerned. Later, with Sir Henry now master of his own destiny, as it were, a final solution to the estate's problems had

Sir Henry Every, 9th Bt., and Lady Every   *[Sir Henry Every, Bt.]*

to be found, and it was addressed – whether on the advice of the wily attorney Hoskins or not is unclear, although it would appear likely – by the decision to offer no less than 619 acres for sale. This amounted to fractionally over half the estate in Newton Solney plus five closes in adjoining Winshill. Such a course of action, bearing in mind that the estate had been placed in Chancery, had to be authorised by a special Act of Parliament, which was duly obtained. The auction took place on 9th December 1799 at the *Three Queens Inn*, at Burton-upon-Trent and, although not everything sold on the day, by August of the year following all lots had found new owners, primarily Hoskins, who emerged with enough Newton Solney land to create therefrom a new landed estate. Another parcel of 35 acres centered on a messuage called Biddulph's Cottage – not certainly located to date, but probably on the south edge of the parish - was sold to the Earl of Chesterfield. He also obtained by the following year other unsold property (including Common Farm) to a total of just over 78 acres, all for an outlay of £1,876 – 17 – 6d. This presaged later developments, and re-established the link between Bretby and Newton Solney. What remained in the hands of the Every family was everything east of Newton/Bretby Lane, along with a strip on fields and closes on the southern edge of the parish, everything north of Main Street in the village that lay east of Trent Lane, Rock House and its pleasure grounds, the church and glebe, all but two strips in Town Field, and everything in and north of the river. One property on the west side of Newton Lane, the brickworks and Claypits were, as we have seen, also retained with a few slim parcels to its south.[37]

Thus relieved of most of the debt hanging over the estate, Sir Henry was able to settle back into running what remained. He was appointed a Deputy Lieutenant of the County in 1803, and served as High Sheriff the year following. It was because this was the sort of appointment for which one was obliged to have one's coat-of-arms regularised, that in 1803 the College of Arms were asked to conduct a search into the family's ancestry (at a cost of £276), the result of which was that the heralds pointed out that the family were using the arms granted by William Camden to the cognate Everys of Weycroft, from whom Sir Henry was not directly descended. As described at the beginning of this chapter, new arms were therefore granted in 1804. Henceforth, however, the Every family was to take a secondary role in the affairs of Newton Solney, a role that would gradually diminish over the nineteenth century almost to vanishing point.[38]

*

[1] Every family, Visit. *Derbys.* 1662; Visit. *Somerset*, 1623; Cothay, Emery III (2006) 529; d'Ivry, Rietstap (1861) 547; notes of E, M. Every, copied courtesy late Sir John Every, Bt

[2] Settlement, D5236/4/97 of 2/2/1627/8 & PEC of 22/3/1627; rectory purchase, 1530, confirmed by release, 1635, Every Ped.; land in Repton, 2/1640, *ibid.*; right to manor: abstract of title in Carnarvon MSS, Highclere, Estaste Paoers, Vol.l XXI, 57-65, by permission of Rt. Hon. The Earl of Carnarvon.]

[3] Gresley Priory lands, *Cal. Pat. Rolls* 1553, 202-207; Repton Priory land, *ibid.,* 1563-66, 99-100; grange, *ibid.,* 1572-75, 299-300; Boylston lease, *ibid.,* 1578-80, 142

[4] *Cal. Pat. Rolls*, 1555-57, 544-546 & 1560-1563, 257-260]

[5] Duchy of Lancs., Somerville (1972) 18; Curzon baronetcy, BP (2003) III. 3532-3541 – 5 years later Sir John also received an English baronetcy, too; Every baronetcy, *ibid* I. 1358-61

[6] Brighton (1981) *passim.*; Every MS Ped.; Glover I (1831) 74.

[7] as previous note and Fisher, F. N. *The Every Family in the Civil War,* in DAJ LXXIV (1954) 112 -127

[8] Rights and tolls, D5236/27/3 of 21/5/1641; County Committee, Cttee. Adv. Money, 22/7-5/8/1650, 1096-99; Fisher, *loc.cit.*

[9] Cal. Cttee. for Compounding, 2448-2450, 22/6/1652; fine, information courtesy of Sir Henry Every, Bt.

[10] Hearth Tax, Edwards (1982) 119-120

[11] 1758 terrier, *op. cit.*; 1836 sale catalogue

[12] John, D5236/4/52 of 5/9/1563; land at Walton, D5236/19/3 of 16th February; mortgage, DRO D5236/17/9/1-11 of 1720-28; marriage and lease at Overseal, D5236/21/3-4 of 16/9 and D5236/21/2 of 10/10/1696; summons, D5236/29/29-31; sales 1739, 1744: D5236/18/5/1-5

[13] John's commission, Minutes of Commissions for Officers of Foot, I; improvements, Every MS Ped.; 1702 estate, D5236/18/12/4; Woolley, in Glover & Riden (1981) section 1, p. 12 (*sub* Egginton). The acreages probably contain an element of exaggeration.

[14] Every MS Ped.: Sir Henry 2nd Bt., will dat. 21/9/1700; Sir Henry 3rd Bt., settlement on wife D5236/26/20-22 of 1701/2 & will dat. 14/5/1709, pr. 14/3/1710; Sir John, 4th Bt.,. will dat. 10/76/1729, pr. 21/5/1730; Every MS Ped.

[15] Capital messuage, D5236/18/6/1-5 of 1745; Longford mansion, see Ch. II & Beacon Lodge, Fraser (1947) 101; Every MS ped.; Sir Henry, 6th Bt. died 21/9/1754; Every MS ped.; mansion house, D5236/18/6/1-5 & *ibid.* /18/8/1-5; bequest, 15th December 1775, Sir John Every's accommodation book 4/1774 to 5/1776, PEC;

16 DRO, *op.cit.*; William & Samuel Wyatt, Colvin (1995) 1101-1103, 1126; Heath pers. comm.. 2/2009.

[17] D5236/32/3-5, 56

[18] Every MS Pedigree

[19] John Every, Every MS ped.; Hearth Tax, Edwards (1982) 119

[20] 1719 ownership, D5236/18/7/1-21; 1770 purchase, D5236/18/6/1-5 & *ibid.* /18/8/1-5; Fisher, BP (1970) 1011-1012, BLG (1952) 863 & Repton parish registers; William Fisher of London was son of another John Fisher of Foremark; Nathaniel Tench, will, dat. 9/8/1706; Tench family Burke (1838) 522; hall, D5236/18/1/1-7; Harpur, Stone (1992) 97.

[21] Picture by kind permission of Sir Henry Every, Bt.; Every MS Ped., *passim.*

[22] Every MS Ped.; Emes, Craven & Stanley (2001) I. 91, 101, 127-130; Wyatt, Colvin (1995) 112

[23] Knowle Hill, Craven & Stanley (2001) I. 132-133.

[24] Every MS Ped.; Aston, Shardlow & King's Mills, Turbutt (1999) III. 1214 & IV. 1481, 1541

[25] Occupants, directories and census returns; Thornewill, VCH *Staffs.* 192; Wilmot, Bigsby (1854) 352 (& fig. 46), BP (2003) III. 4200; Mitchell, Wain (1976) II; Yates contents sale: *Derby Mercury* 21/1/1846; ex info. courtesy Roger Kerry, Esq.

[26] Run in hand, Every 1758 Terrier; Every MS Ped; Coal Pitt Way, qv. Ch,. I

[27] Hoult, D5236/4/69,81; Lease of 1824, D5236/18/12/19; White (1857) 370; DLSL *Return of Owners of Land 1873*; Bulmer (1895) 789; information courtesy Roger Kerry from Patricia L. Hopkins of Caringbah, Australia (letter 27/3/2009).

[28] Information courtesy Alan Gifford, Esq., of Willington & Philip Heath

[29] Barton, Cal. Pat. Rolls 1405-8, 85; Woodward, 10/3/1346/7: Cal. Pat. Rolls 1345-8, 82; Gilbert, DRO Quarter Sessions, Q/SB/2/1219 of 27/3/1648, lock-up, White (1857) 370

[30] Every MSS Ped.]

[31] Every MS notes

[32] Mary Smith, D5236/32/14-15

[33] 1758 survey; 1789 figures, Pilkington (1789) II. 96-97

[34] Hanson Grange, Lysons (1817) 275; John Leigh had issue, Elizabeth who married Arthur Milward and had James Milward of Egginton, in whom Sir Henry Leigh vested the manors of Egginton & Newton Solney 1632 (see Chapter II). He was ancestor of J. Milward of Egginton, Gent., who sold a house and half an acre there to Sir John Every for £270 in 1767; purchase, D5236/19/13 of 29/9/1772; Hoskins and his letter of 5/1779 to Michael Bass, quoted in Wain (1976) II.

[35] DRO D5762/4; Landlands Lane, D5236/18/10/1-5; the suggestion that Middle and Newton Farms were one and the same was made by Mr. Philip Heath

[36] Financial situation, D5236/32/73; Hoskins, Statement of account: DRO D5236/26/79

[37] Act of Parliament: 39 Geo III; Sale: Staffs. RO D877/196/1/1 & 2; 1836 sale: map; Biddulph's Cottage: Carnarvon MSS, Highclere, Misc. estate papers, Vol. XXI. 41-57, by kind permission of Rt. Hon. The Earl of Carnarvon. The occupiers of the land were James Matthews and Daniel Webster, neither of whose families show up on the 1758 list. One of the trustees for the sale was "Mrs. Elizabeth Darwin, wife of Erasmus Darwin, Doctor of Physick" with her brother, E. S. Pole of Radburne (deed of 4/7/1800).

[38] Every MS Ped.

*

IV

TRANSFORMATION: NEWTON PARK

We have seen in Chapters I and II how there had been a Medieval hunting park at Newton Solney, which one of the earliest de Solneys must have granted to Repton Priory, this being implicit in the confirmation of the park with mill and fishery by the Prior and canons of Repton to Sir Norman de Solney in 1230. We have also seen that it survived to become part of the Longford family portion of the estate and indeed it appears to have had a house on it too, perhaps a hunting lodge, for Henry Longford, the fourth son of Sir Nicholas, was his brother's collector of rents for Longford and Ellastone and was described then (1521) as "of Newton Park". Later in that century, the status of the dwelling there must have declined, for it became the residence of a tenant farmer, for we find William Gardner, Jane his wife and their younger son William being granted a lease for three lives of (amongst other things) Newton Park in April 1569 and thirty years later the area was being referred to as 'Newton Parks'.[1]

Whether this tract of land was co-terminous with the Newton Park of recent times is unclear, nor does there seem to have been any real continuation between the two, for in the Every era we hear no more of a park at Newton and suppose that it was all given over to agriculture. However, with the opening of the nineteenth century, the name was revived (although not initially) for what a sale catalogue later described as a "Derbyshire Elysium", created by an ambitious romantic, Abraham Hoskins, who started out with the laudable aim of setting himself up as a gentleman farmer, using the very latest methods of modern husbandry and ended up creating a carefully planned landscape, albeit one that showed every sign of being an afterthought. Nevertheless, in so doing, he managed to transform utterly the majority of the parish, creating to a large extent the Newton Solney we see today.

Hoskins and his family

With the diminution of the Every influence in Newton Solney, there emerged a new dynasty: the Hoskins family. Abraham's impact on Newton Solney was so complex and far reaching that it merits a chapter to himself, especially as his period left a paucity of written records, least of all of his building activities. Hoskins *pere* has already been made manifest in the saga, starting out as the Every family lawyer, and contriving to acquire portions of their estate for himself from as early as 1772, when he bought almost 300 acres at Hanson Grange (Thorpe) from them, followed by a farm in Egginton. In 1786 he (or possibly his like-named son: the two are often hard to separate at this period, both being active in Every affairs) was appointed, with his partner John Fowler and Daniel Parker Coke, radical Tory MP for Derby and later Nottingham, an Every family friend, as trustees of the estate of Sir Henry Every, 9th Bt. Later, by 1793 he had also become receiver of rents for the estate at Newton Solney, then debt-laden and in chancery during the minority of young Sir Henry. Yet shortly before that minority had expired, Hoskins made an exchange with the rest of the Every trustees by which he obtained some land on Bladon Hill, running to some 103 acres. The deal did, however, omit much of Bladon Wood, which contained valu-

Abraham Hoskins, the younger [*M. J. Sayer*]

able shooting that the Egginton Hall family wished to retain. This seems to have been the first move in Hoskins' successful campaign to build up a viable country estate in Newton Solney.

As the Hoskins family were to loom large in Newton Solney for forty years and considerably transformed the appearance of the village, it would be reasonable to know something about the family's background. They were in fact originally called (or spelt) Hodskins, from Cornwall, but Abraham's first ancestor to come to the Midlands was another Abraham, born to James and Elizabeth in St. Budeaux, Devonshire, in 1651. He settled as a merchant at Stafford, where he was twice Mayor, in 1708 and 1716, and where he died at a good age in 1732, leaving six sons and four daughters. The youngest son, William, managed to get himself appointed Equerry to Frederick ('Poor Fred') Prince of Wales and left a son who settled at Shenstone Park, Staffordshire. The elder son, Richard, a Stafford lawyer, was, by his wife Jane, father of our Abraham Hoskins, baptised at St. Mary, Stafford on 18th September 1728.[2]

Abraham moved to Burton-upon-Trent largely through having made an advantageous marriage, although how the two came to meet is difficult to guess. His bride, whom he married at Holy Trinity, Hull in October 1757, was an heiress, being one of the daughters of Francis Haworth, a Hull Merchant and a member of an old gentry family from Rawcliffe in Yorkshire. More important for the alliance with Hoskins was the fact that Anne Haworth's mother was also an heiress, of George Hayne, a rich Wirksworth merchant who had made a fortune in the lead trade and happened to be the proprietor of the Burton Boat Company. The background to this is that in 1699 William, 6th Lord Paget, owner of most of Burton and keen to improve the trade of the town, managed to secure an Act of Parliament allowing him to make the Trent navigable between Wilne Ferry – opposite, by co-incidence, Kings' Mills, Castle Donington – and Burton. Having done so, he let the monopoly to operate barges along this stretch (and on to Gainsborough thus giving access to the Humber, Hull and the North Sea) to the highest bidder, who happened to be George Hayne, in alliance with Leonard Fosbrooke of Shardlow Hall. The latter operated barges east from Wilne Ferry which he owned, whilst Hayne operated exclusively to Burton. Until the coming of the Trent and Mersey Canal in 1777, the Trent Navigation was a vital artery by which the burgeoning beer industry of Burton could export its products to an increasingly thirsty world. Hayne's Burton Boat Company operated a fleet of barges with 40 ton capacities. He ended up a rich man and, although his brother Henry (1728-1757) took over the Company, its control ultimately came to Hoskins who was, like his father, a lawyer, a trustee of the Trent Navigation, and sole proprietor of the Burton Boat Co.[3]

Hoskins, with a partner, John Fowler, took over the long established legal practice of Isaac Hawkins in 1764 and worked extensively for the local brewers, including Michael Bass, whose son, Michael Thomas Bass the elder, married one of Hoskins' six daughters in 1794, thereby becoming the parents of Derby's long-serving MP, Michael Thomas Bass the younger and grandparents of 1st Lord Burton. Her eldest sister also married Sir John Dickenson Fowler, son of John, Hoskins's partner and his successor in the firm. Abraham was also appointed Deputy Steward of the Manor of Burton by Lord Uxbridge (the Lord of the Manor) a well-remunerated honorific. The legal firm itself, founded by 1649, acted for most of the nobility and gentry of the surrounding area, so Hoskins's contacts were without doubt extensive and helpful; it has survived as Talbot & Co. The temptation to use knowledge gained working for clients to build up a potentially profitable portfolio of land led Hoskins to buy the Hanson Grange and Egginton properties referred to above, although they were by no means his only investments. Unfortunately, he over-stretched himself and in May 1779 found himself owing £17,000 against investments worth (on paper at least) £22,000 and was obliged to allow his former partner, Isaac Hawkins to bail him out of what was a narrow escape from bankruptcy. He was, however, asked by Robert Burdett of Foremark to be his under-sheriff (for Warwickshire) in 1784, which betokens a remarkable degree of rehabilitation.[4]

Building on Bladon

Hoskins had four sons as well as the six daughters, of whom the youngest, Francis, was the only one to marry and have children apart from the eldest son, another Abraham, baptised at Burton on 14th December 1759 and to whom we shall return later. Today, for a trustee to acquire land from a client in financial difficulties would be accused of betrayal of trust, if not corruption, but in 1798 people were less scrupulous. For it was, as we have seen, that in the May that year, just a month before his client was to come of age and take control of his own destiny, Hoskins acquired a 103 acre parcel of land on the side of Bladon Hill in an exchange with his fellow trustees and on behalf of Sir Henry. The acquisition included Underwood Flatts alongside the river, Horns Meadow, Near, Far & Short Bladon (Field), Near & Far Form Beds and Bladon Brook Head (part of which was in Winshill) and the western half of Bladon Wood.

One might reasonably wonder why Hoskins wished to acquire this land. An event the following year explained everything. A design for "A Villa at Bladon Hill…seat of Abraham Hoskins, Esqre." was exhibited at the Royal Academy by the latest member of the illustrious Wyatt dynasty of builders and eminent architects, Jeffry Wyatt, later Sir Jeffry Wyatville. He had probably been recommended to Hoskins by his uncle, Samuel Wyatt, who had worked for the Everys but fourteen years before, and who would by this time have been too busy with Shugborough and Kinmel Park, Denbighshire, in Wales, to accept this commission from his former employer's trustee. Jeffry had indeed served his articles with Samuel Wyatt before becoming an assistant to his more illustrious brother, James, setting up on his own account in 1798, the very year of the Hoskins' acquisition of the land at Bladon. Furthermore, Jeffrey's father, Burton builder and architect Joseph Wyatt (1739-1785) appears to have been a friend of the elder Abraham Hoskins. Indeed, this villa may well have been Wyatville's very first commission, for although he exhibited another design at the RA that year, it was only for a remodelling of a rectory in Berkshire and not a commission for a completely new building. In short, Bladon villa was a piece of direct patronage for the young Burton-born architect from an old friend of the family who suddenly found himself with a promising piece of ground nearby to hand.[5]

The question that arises, was it actually built at that time? Local lore, which may have been transmitted via the late H. J. Wain, had it that it was decided against building a residence on the hill at this time due to the lack of a water source. It continues to the effect that he built the present Bladon Castle as a folly; was forced by village opinion to go and live in it, but after two years of having water brought up to the house "in buckets" gave up and lived in Newton Park. In fact there was never any problem at this period about watering houses on minor hill-tops. After all, even if no source could be located – a doubtful assertion in itself bearing in mind the long-established Bladon Farm half a mile along the ridge – John Whitehurst had invented the hydraulic ram in 1775 and Erasmus Darwin the artesian well the year before, both in nearby Derby and both tailor-made solutions to the problem. Robert Bigsby, writing in 1854, was also no doubt influenced by this imaginary tale when he asserted that the building now on the crest of Bladon Hill, Bladon Castle, was built "in 1801" solely as an uninhabited folly, and most subsequent commentators have taken him at his word. Yet Bigsby is not so reliable in other areas that we may take him as gospel. If we do, the rationale for a folly in this place is lost, as there was, at first, no habitation from which to enjoy the view of it. It seems almost certain that Wyatville's villa *was* built and was subsequently subsumed within the bravura window dressing of Bladon Castle. Rawlins – more reliable and closer to the time than Bigsby and writing in 1816 - avers that it was "only a small house, which was originally raised as a banqueting retreat". This villa was, without doubt, a very compact three bay affair, rather like Wyatville's uncle James's now lost Gresford Lodge, Denbighshire, and almost certainly Classical, with a central bow or canted bay overlooking the meadows to the south east. It is interesting, however, that both of the young architect's next two commissions were for castellated houses; perhaps, then, the villa was classical but crenellated, like a Robert Adam "castle". Subsequent illustrations of the Bladon building after its conversion to an eye-catcher suggest that the central bay, today replaced by a late nineteenth century affair with mullioned and transomed windows, was originally bowed. The likelihood is that this splendidly situated new house was intended for old Abraham to live in or at least to retreat to as the mood took him, for banqueting or more sedentary purposes (see note). The fact that the design was exhibited, though, helps us little, for unexecuted ones were frequently shown at the RA as well as executed buildings.[6]

Gresford Lodge (James Wyatt, c. 1790)

Thus, we shall proceed in assuming that Wyatville's villa (or something like it) was built at about the time the design was exhibited, that the elder Hoskins lived in it or visited it, and that some start was made in landscaping the view to the east, over land that had been acquired by his son from 1798. This view is re-inforced by the way the planting works best when viewed from the hill; it has a lot less cohesion when viewed from the vicinity of Newton Park house, for instance. The grotto mentioned by John Farey may have been part of this, or might have come later, when the pleasure grounds of Newton Park were being laid out[7].

Building Newton Park

The next act in the saga was the sale of 619 acres of the Every family estates in Newton Solney which, as we have seen, occurred on 9th December 1799. Interestingly, a swathe of nine fields and closes immediately adjoining Hoskin's property, on which, as we have speculated, a villa was rising, was withdrawn from the auction, as Philip Heath has demonstrated. These fields were mainly bounded on the east by the brook but may have included property as far to the east as the village end of Trent Lane. The land adjacent and to the east again, included in Lot 7, which later became the site of the present Newton Park House, was not withdrawn and Heath reasonably sees this as an indication that it was not in Hoskins' plans at this juncture. What he was clearly trying to achieve was ownership of a potential small park to go with his new villa on the hill. Lot 7, though, failed to reach its reserve, and it was bought, less a few small parcels, on 9th August 1800. The purchaser was not Hoskins for, as he was still Receiver of Rents for the vendors, the Every estate (which not out of the control of the Court of Chancery until 1801 when Sir Henry finally came of age), it would even then have been invidious for him to be seen to have bought it directly. Indeed, it may be that people had already raised doubts over his acquisition of the Bladon portion of the estate by his 1798 exchange. Consequently, Hoskins' brother-in-law Michael Bass actually made the purchase, rapidly selling it on to the lawyer, which completed the assembly of all 197 acres of the land which would in due course become the new Newton Park. Nearly thirty years later, these doubts re-surfaced when Hoskins was faced with the possibility of having to sell some land, and it was felt in some quarters that his title might be questioned. This led to a deed of confirmation between him and Sir Henry Every, which regularised Hoskins' rather rash earlier dealings. Abraham's new landholdings were later consolidated between 1801 and 1805 (between which dates his land tax had risen appreciably, from £1 – 17s – 0d to £23 – 11 – 21/4d) by the purchase of what had been Lot 8 in the 1799 sale: that is, all the land between Lot 7 and Newton Lane (excluding the brickworks) and extending south to the Winshill-Repton track, by this time falling out of use. Who had purchased this lot originally is not clear; it might merely have remained unsold.[8]

Abraham Hoskins junior was still living at Burton-upon-Trent in 1803, whereas his father was as early as 1800 described as "late of Burton-upon-Trent" confirming by inference his residence in the new villa. In 1806 (by which time the father had been dead almost two years) his son, too, was also "late of Burton-upon-Trent, but now of Bladon Wood." Now, Bladon Wood was almost certainly the name of the Wyatville house on Bladon Hill prior to its later transformation; as to why he was there in 1806, however, this will emerge in due course. It is therefore reasonable to suppose that his father and mother were the occupiers the villa at Bladon and he had temporarily joined or replaced them, perhaps even adding the extension to the NE, where the main living accommodation is today, albeit screened. The question arises, therefore, exactly when the new house, Newton Park, was built. The late H. J. Wain, in a series on articles in the *Burton Mail* in 1976 claimed on the evidence of a statement by a descendant, that Abraham Hoskins "did not reside there before 1801", which is undoubtedly true, but which we cannot take as meaning that from 1801 he *did* live there – far from it for, as we have seen, he was still living in Burton two years later and we have postulated that his father was occupying the villa on Bladon Hill.[9]

Young Abraham was a keen agronomist and it would appear that one of his ambitions was to go down in history as a man who brought modern methods to farming and on a scale that would justify the outlay. This one precept seems to underlie much of what followed. A letter of 25th August, 1805 throws some further light on the sequence of events. It was from Staffordshire builder Benjamin Wyatt (1755-1813), Jeffrey's cousin, to his kinsman Lewis (1777-1853), with whom he worked extensively at this time realizing designs Lewis was making from his father James's office. In it he says that he had just returned from measuring and valuing the new building erected by Mr. [Abraham] Hoskins at Newton, adding, "…there is a deal of it, but of a very Indiferent (*sic*) quality". The fact that Farey later praises Hoskins buildings there "on which no cost has been spared", does not in any way have to affect the lack of quality perceived by Wyatt; merely that a lot was spent, a common dichotomy where new wealth is expended a trifle rashly! Philip Heath has suggested that Hoskins had acquired with his purchases a fairly modern farmhouse on the site of Newton Park - Lot 7 of the 1799 auction - and incorporated it into a new mansion for himself. He also considers this letter to refer to the signing off of work creating Bladon Castle. Yet the evidence deployed is not especially persuasive, especially in terms of chronology.[10]

Newton Park, south front, photographed by Richard Keene, c. 1877 with central three bays stripped of stucco.   *[Brian Appleby]*

The chief reason for supposing that Hoskins adapted an existing farmhouse is the photograph of the south front, taken c. 1877 by the younger Richard Keene (above). The central three bays, which have lost their covering of Roman cement (patches of residue can be seen under magnification) seem to suggest that originally it was a three bay two and a half storey house with a gable-ended roof punctuated by stacks, later extended by the addition of rather cramped end-bays, and small single storey square extensions enclosing the (rear, farmyard) entrance and pulled together with a new cornice. The stucco was almost certainly part of a second phase, because the windows are embellished with gauged brick lintels, an expense that would have been spared had the house been intended to be rendered *ab initio*.

Yet the proportions belie this theory, quite apart from the unlikelihood of the Every estate, long in chancery, having spare money to build rather well proportioned farm houses for 120 acre tenants like the Dicken family (which Heath sees as having lived there prior to the sale). Measured off from the photograph and using the standard 3 ft. 6 in. window widths as a scale, the building, less end bays, was 45 ft. 8 in. wide and 32 ft. to the eaves. If we take the distance between the projecting bays flanking the entrance as the likely width of the hallway and stair well (allowing for a dog-leg staircase) we find that it was probably 8 ft. 6 ins. wide, giving us two symmetrical rooms off, each of which would have been 17 ft. 6 ins. wide and proportionally deep in what was only a narrow single pile house. Ceiling heights on both main floors work out at 11ft. 6 ins., with 7 ft. for the attics – very similar to Pickford's House, Derby, of 35 years before, for instance.

These are without doubt the proportions of the house of a gentleman, not an ordinary farmhouse. Georgian tenanted farmhouses, although usually of pleasing proportions, were generally smaller, especially in Derbyshire, and commonly have remarkably poky reception rooms, with a large kitchen parlour taking up much of one side of the house. A similar brick three bay two and a half storey tenanted farm house of the same sort of date on a neighbouring estate measures up at 36 ft. wide, 22 ft. 6ins. high with 13 ft 3in. wide reception rooms either side of an 8 ft. 3 in. hallway, the room heights being 8 ft. 6 ins. on the ground floor, 7 ft. 6 ins on the first floor and only 5 ft 9 ins in the attics – all much more cramped than Hoskins' new house.

We may, from Wyatt's letter, be fairly sure that this house - which we will call Newton Park (although it may have been called something like Hoskins' Farm originally) - was built around 1804-1805. And it was indeed built as a farm house, but one in which the younger Hoskins - who had, be it recalled, lost his appetite for the law in exchange for an enthusiasm for farming - intended to live prior to his father's death. Behind it, was a double courtyard of offices and farm buildings with stabling. What Hoskins' had built, probably with the aid of a local builder using a pattern book (for the house is a typical pattern-book design and looks 15 years out of date for 1805, which is what one might expect, building from such a source), was a gentleman farmer's house with attached farm, so he could farm in hand. This, surely, is the 'deal of it' that old Ben Wyatt appraised in 1805 – newly finished in advance of the would-be agronomist moving in and showing them all how it really ought to be done. In fact, he had built himself a classic model farm very similar to that provided for the Bretby estate contemporaneously by William Martin, Lord Chesterfield's architect (see plans, below). The position of the farm, at the effective rear of the house, explains why the house's south front faced, not gardens as one might expect, but an office court with a

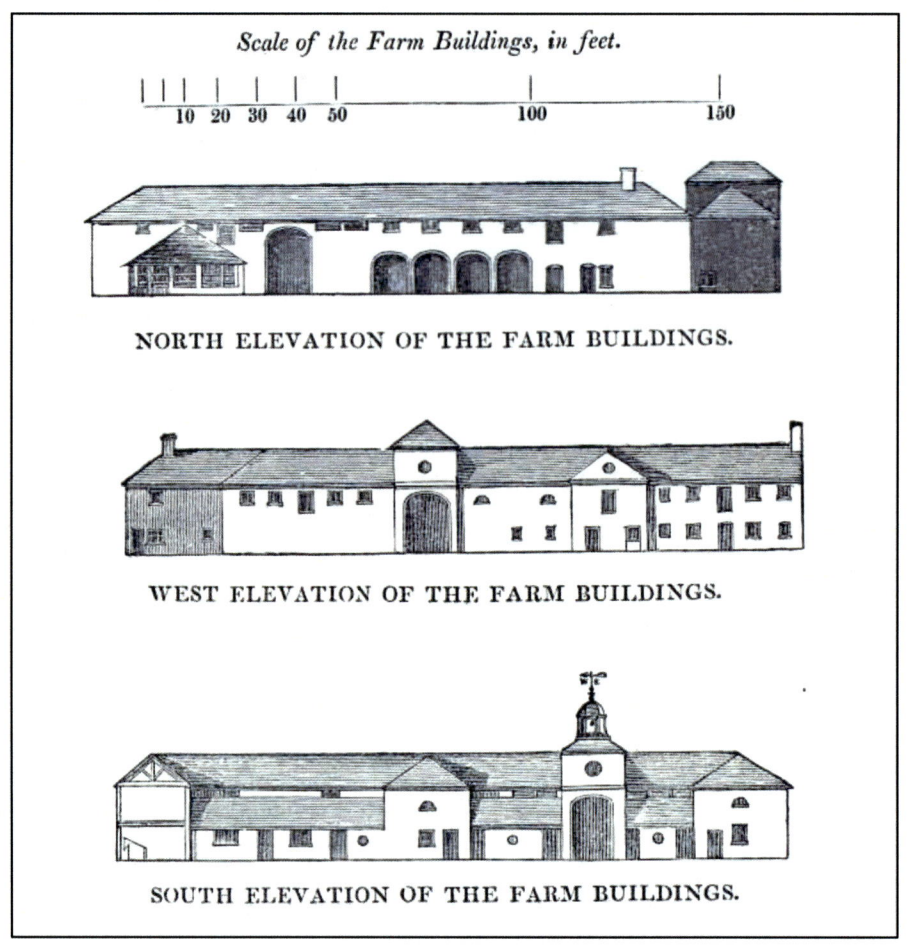

Elevations of Bretby Farm, from Glover   *[M. Craven]*

Newton Park Farm, north range, (as reconstructed 1838 and rebuilt in 1890).
[P. McManus]

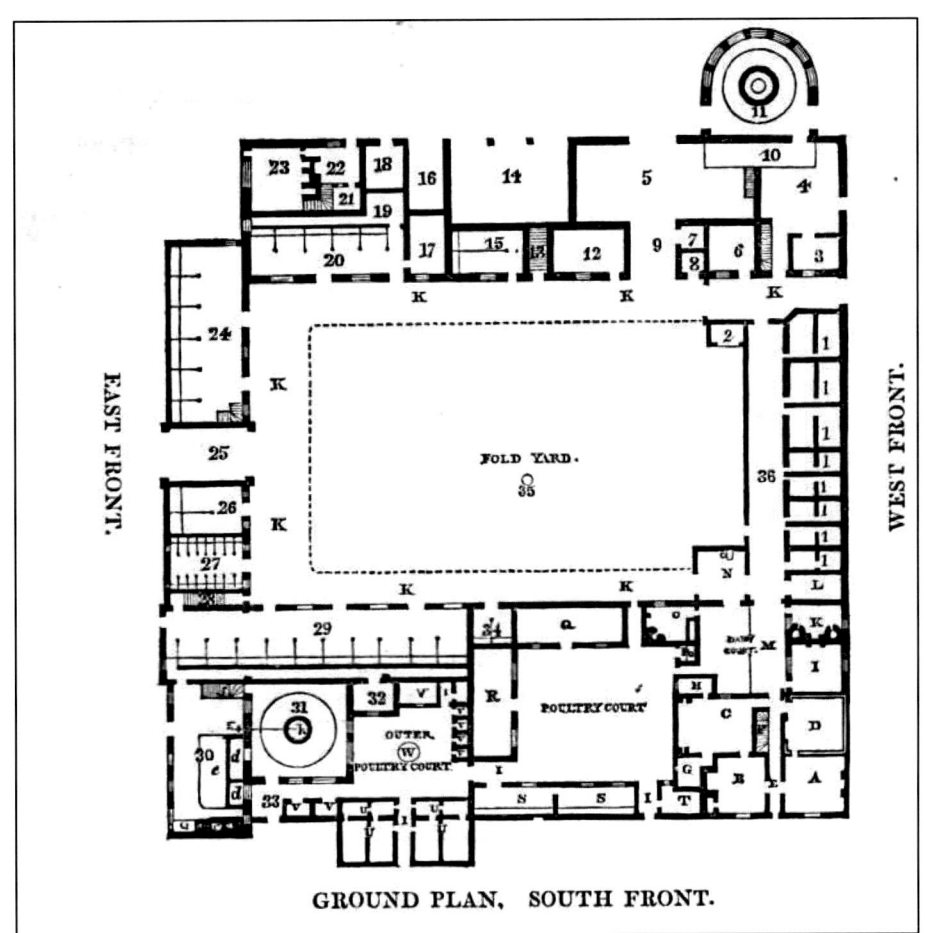

FOLD YARD.

GROUND PLAN, SOUTH FRONT.

Bretby Park, Model Farm, plan, from Glover

* * * * * * * * * * * * * * *

Newton Park, ferme ornee *and house 1836*

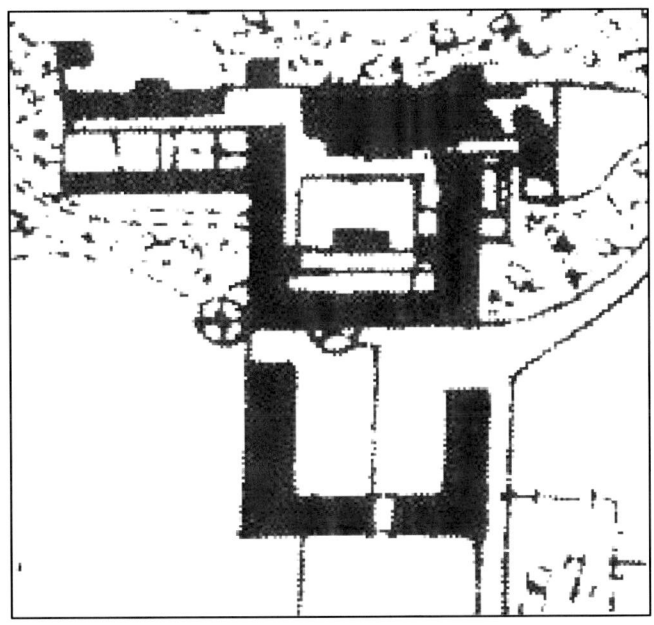

similarly proportioned fold yard and steading beyond with a rick-yard off to the east side, whilst the entrance front faced north and stood at the edge of main street (then not yet diverted away from the house), like most of the other Newton farmhouses in those days.[11]

Hence, of course, the belated purchase by Hoskins of the land SSE of his new house, the former lot 8 of the 1799 sale. This was the natural hinterland for his working farm, referred to at the time of sale thirty years later as a *"ferme ornee…the expense of which has exceeded Five Thousand Pounds"*. After all, he had started work on improving the newly acquired family lands at Newton as early as 1802, when we find him pruning oaks & firs in Bladon Wood. Even six years later, Farey reported that the keen Abraham was still "equipping his farms" and described the buildings and their equipment: "A most convenient and elegant suit [*sic*] of Farm Premises: on which no cost has been spared, to render them most convenient and complete." These included a four-horse threshing machine made by the Burton clockmaker Thomas Noon (an Ashby man originally) - which could thrash 70 bushels of wheat in ten hours simultaneously with 300 bushels of oats – milking sheds for 34 cows, a 153 ft. long vinery, an ingenious cheese chamber and the drainage of 150 acres contiguous to the brook and the use of the water to supply new fishponds and the house. There were three kitchen gardens, and two ranges of dog-kennels, underscoring Hoskins' other enthusiasm: greyhound breeding. From what one can tell from Farey and the maps evidence, his farm closely resembled that at Bretby and indeed, the one may have been modelled on the other.[12]

But, having finished it, and probably having moved in, things changed suddenly. On 27th April 1805, his father died (attested by a memorial inscription in St. Modwen's Burton), quite possibly an unexpected event, despite his age. In his will, proved on 15th August, he left a substantial portion of his estate to his son Abraham and his own house to be his wife's residence for life. This immediately transformed the latter's available resources, the availability of much more money giving Hoskins the incentive and opportunity to re-think his plans completely.

Towards the Elysium

The sale particulars of 1836 describe Hoskins' transformation of the landscape as "this Derbyshire Elysium" which at the time may not have been far from the mark. Hoskins seems to have decided to turn his property at Newton Solney into a seat, rather than just a working farm. This would involve enlarging his newly built house to suitable proportions but retaining the farm, this being its entire *raison d'etre*, after all. Another factor which must have influenced him at this stage was his growing family. His first wife, Frances Somerville, had died, probably in childbirth, on St. Andrew's Day 1798. By her he had two sons, Abraham and Henry (neither of whom made it beyond 25) and a daughter, Frances, who went on to marry Henry Jackson, the general manager of Bass. He re-married, probably in the same year that his new house was built, Jane, daughter of Thomas Smith, and went on to have eight more sons and six further daughters, the youngest not being born until 1822. The new house, therefore, was quickly becoming teeming with offspring; something larger was clearly needed, and the villa on the hill would clearly not be large enough (assuming its present proportions represent what was there then), nor handy enough for the farm, especially as his widowed mother was in residence. Thus it would seem that its enlargement was determined upon fairly rapidly. Furthermore, he clearly had by this time determined to use the land SW of his new house and extending towards Bladon Wood as further parkland, with some kind of pleasure ground along the course of the brook in the central declivity. Probably, too, he then or not long afterwards decided also to transform the villa on Bladon Hill his mother lived in into something more exciting: an eye-catcher. The argument that it cannot have been built to be seen from Newton Park is probably wide of the mark; the fact is that it was to be seen, and once built indeed became a notable landmark from a variety of angles. One of the problems in turning his fairly grand farmhouse into a seat was that it had his precious farm to the immediate south and faced north. Any alterations would have to address the acute limitations of the site. In any case, work probably began before the middle of 1806, hence, of course the reason for Hoskins being "now of Bladon Wood" in 1806 – he had moved out onto the Bladon Hill villa so that the builders could begin work transforming his modest house into a grand seat.[13]

The next stage was to enlarge the house, then, to which end a full height, full width bay was added at either end (affecting the size of the main rooms) and curving quadrant screen walls with accommodation behind up to the height of the first floor sill band were also added. The added bays are not, however, well proportioned *vis-à-vis* the rest of the façade, for ideally in terms of Georgian design practice they should have been wider with the fenestration placed nearer the centre. To disguise any unsightly joins, the whole was covered in Parker's Roman Cement (from a 1796 patent owned by Samuel Wyatt and made by the Brookhouse family in Derby, and just beginning to become popular) which was given a decorative treatment, according to John Farey, by no less a craftsman than Francis Bernasconi (1762-1841), although the way Farey phrased his statement – "very tastefully and well finished with Parker's Roman Cement, executed by Francis Bernasconie" - gives the impression that the *stuccadore* designed the house, too.[14]

Newton Park, North front, photographed by Richard Keene, c. 1877 [Brian Appleby]

Clearly, however, Bernasconi did not design the house for the architectural treatment of this new north front was ambitious, if eclectic (above). The wings and ground floor were rusticated, but unconventionally high, up to the first floor sill band and the windows endowed with skinny entablatures on brackets, whilst quoins marked the angles, not only of the building itself, but also of the three bay centre – Hoskins' original house – which broke slightly forward. The rest was subtly grooved to

85

resemble ashlared stonework. The centre bay, flanked by tripartite windows with rectangular blind panels below, boasted the entrance, protected by a Doric portico supported on paired columns. Above it was a blind depressed arch with keyblock and decorative imposts, which rose over the sill band to enclose the central window on the first floor, almost touching the entablature of the window. The hipped roof rose from a substantial cornice topped by a dwarf parapet. The wings each had two niches above each being a small lunette – Diocletian would be too flattering a term – each topped by a bracketed entablature as the main house, giving an odd effect, to say the least. The wings ended in doorcases parallel with the main facade with blind panels over and again the skimpy entablatures. The south front was similar, but much plainer with no corresponding quadrants. Without doubt, Bernasconi will have enlivened the interior, probably in an exuberant Rococo neo-Louis XV style, then undergoing some thing of a revival in local villas of this sort, although the only interior to survive - showing the drawing room with what looks like 17th century panelling and a ceiling stuccoed in traceried ribs – may be the result of a post-1837 makeover. The internal spaces were completely re-arranged, judging by the room sizes after re-building, although there was an oak staircase and four bedrooms each with a dressing room on the first floor. There was also a nursery, billiard room and *commodite* for the females'.[15]

The overall effect is so strange, with its proportioning slightly wrong almost everywhere but not so wrong as to look disastrous, that the immediate thought is that we are not here dealing with a local builder and a pattern book – far from it; so who was the architect?

The frontispiece of Newton Park (L) and of The Pastures, Littleover (R)

The most striking similarity of this decorative stucco scheme is to that applied to The Pastures, Littleover in 1806, built for another Burton-upon-Trent man, Robert Peel, mill proprietor and uncle of the homonymous prime minister. He would have known Hoskins well, for Peel's solicitor was Hoskins' venerable parent, which strengthens the case for Leaper's involvement considerably. Here one sees the same rustication carried up too high – again to the first floor sill band and a very similar portico (albeit pedimented with single columns) and blind arch above it. There are even *Louis Quinze* interiors with exuberant and first quality stucco, although no record of Bernasconi at work. Another related house was Derwent Bank (originally Darley Grove) Derby, again with rustication carried up to the first floor sill band and, like Newton Park, of two and a half storeys. The architect of both was the amateur, Richard Leaper (1759-1838), a Derby alderman, serial mayor, banker, tannery proprietor and receiver of taxes. He came from a very similar background to Hoskins, and was related to a widespread nexus of local families. The fact that both The Pastures and Newton Park were built in the same year for rich Burtonians is also persuasive, and Leaper would seem the most likely candidate, albeit not the only one

Derwent Bank, Duffield Road, Derby, photographed in 1899

[*Late Mrs. Peter Lander*]

in what turns out to be a crowded field. With all this, the presence of Bernasconi would seem, perhaps, anomalous. Yet Bernasconi – "the most fashionable purveyor of Regency stucco work" - around 1806, when Newton Park was being enlarged, was working at Windsor Castle with none other than Jeffrey Wyatville, and three years before had collaborated with him at Westminster Abbey, where he would surely have met Thomas Gayfere and perhaps, Thomas Greatorex, both, significantly, Newton Solney residents within as decade or so (see below). He was also working at Shugborough nearby in 1806, and worked under Wyatville again, as Longleat. Bernasconi usually worked indoors, the only exterior stucco he is recorded as having executed at this time was for the Duke of Devonshire at Compton Place, near Eastbourne under John Harvey, which has a sophistication entirely lacking at Newton Park and any suggestion that Bernasconi designed the stucco work is absurd. He also stuccoed the gothic house of Lord Ashburnham, in Sussex, much later on. The Wyatville connection my surely have commended him to Hoskins.[16]

A plethora of architects

The Newton Solney of this period was fairly bursting with architects. After all, for instance, one could hardly imagine that an amateur like Richard Leaper would be up to designing a state-of-the-art model farm, and it is quite possible that William Martin, Lord Chesterfield's architect at Bretby - next door – may have been happy to design Hoskins' farm for him. Unfortunately, although we know what its ground plan was like from the two maps of 1827 and 1836, there was precious little of it remaining in its original position when Keene photographed Newton Park prior to Lord Carnarvon selling it in 1877, as it had by then already been re-located, partly to the site of the present Newton Park Farm, so that we are unable to make any useful comparisons. The remaining stable block in 1877 may well have been down to Leaper, for he is known to have designed them elsewhere, at The Pastures, for instance.

Furthermore, there is the mention of "A Mr. Brown (not Capability Brown but equally capable in every respect) once sojourned at Newton, and greatly contributed to the improvement of the estate." Philip Heath reasonably suggested that this might be Samuel Brown of Derby (b. 1756), an architect who worked at Calke, Repton Park and Swarkestone for the Harpur-Crewes, at Derby and probably elsewhere for William Strutt, and is recorded as having become bankrupt in 1811. Now although the remark about Brown appears after a section on gardens, the words 'improvement of the estate' might imply something rather more far-reaching. It is also interesting to note that Brown and Leaper are linked. In 1807-1809 they were working together on turning a farm at Wheathills on the Markeaton estate into a seat for F. N. C. Mundy. It may be that they worked together at Newton Park, too, and that Brown stayed on to supervise what would have been a lengthy assignment, bearing in mind that it involved more than just improving the mansion at Newton Park. One thing is certain, however, he would never have designed a façade like that at Newton Park; rebuilt the house as contractor, yes – but not designed it: he was a seasoned professional and his most similar building, the Derbyshire General Infirmary of 1806-1810, bears none of the infelicities of Newton Park. Yet even then, Newton Solney was not finished. In 1827, the same year that the London architect Thomas Gayfere died in the village (on whom see above and again below), Glover's *Directory* lists Robert Chaplin (1774-1860), architect of the Royal Hotel and Ivanhoe Baths at Ashby as resident in the village. In 1836 he was still there, listed as a tenant of Hoskins in the village, but also residing at his own creation in Ashby, Rawdon Terrace. Gayfere had worked closely with James Wyatt (and, no doubt, Bernasconi) at the Palace of Westminster, where he was Surveyor, from 1805 until 1822, when he retired to Newton Solney. Chaplin is usually listed at Rawdon Terrace, Ashby. In any case, the number of potential architects to hand, not only for Newton Park but for the numerous other projects Hoskins embarked upon, is startling in so small a village, quite apart from the Smith family in Repton, who also worked for the Harpur-Crewes! Nevertheless, on stylistic grounds, Leaper must easily remain the favourite, especially when the transformation of Bladon Wood is taken into account.[17]

A final element of Newton Park as built is the exceptionally pretty and urbane lodge at the east end of the house. This consists of a set-piece of two storey block with superimposed fenestration set in recessed panels, under a pyramidal roof culminating in a stack set at 45 degrees to the building. This all rises between lower wings, beyond which a pair of curved walls, each with a single niche, end in paired pillars with ball finials, all stuccoed over and still grooved to resemble ashlar, like the main house, the side walls un-painted as originally built. The whole concept is almost Palladian, although the treatment is Regency, and the decoration has the same eclectic detailing at the main house once had and The Cedars (see below) retains. Opposite, stands a cast iron gate in equally *retardataire* style between lattice piers topped with flaming torches, very high quality, albeit in desperate need of sensitive repair. It is to be presumed that the lodge post-dates the main house but not by much. Its massing and use of recessed panels rather reflects The Cedars (see below) and certainly presages Burnaston House, across the river (now demolished) and it is possible that both may be ascribed to the same architect – as argued above, Richard Leaper of Derby.

Newton Park lodge, 2009   [*M. Craven*]

The pleasure grounds

One may suppose that the works at Newton Park House were completed by 1809, for in that year, the final touches were made. These included the diversion of the main road from Repton to Burton away from the front door of the house beyond a new ha-ha, as befitted its transition from opulent farm to gentlemen's seat. Furthermore, pleasure grounds were in the process of being created, whether by the hands of the enigmatic Mr. Brown ("not Capability") or not. "Therein," enthused Farey, "The wildness of nature is imitated in the hardy fernery." The 1836 sale particulars amplify this with:

> "The gardens are extensive and have been arranged with great judgement...and of considerable extent and need not dread a comparison

with any in the County... ornamental waters, the rippling cascade, rock work and rural bridge" [18]

Much of this survived to be photographed by the younger Richard Keene, then running an outpost of his father's photographic business at Burton, in 1877. From his record we know that whoever laid out these quite ambitious pleasure grounds had a good grounding in the landscape of the Romantic movement of a few decades before.

The moss hut or rustic summer house and castellated wall (L), c. 1877.

[Brian Appleby]

It is unclear when the course of the brook was densely planted, by the fact that two horns of standing timber shown on the early 19th century maps reach out and embrace Simnett's Flat in front of Bladon Hill, suggests it was originally done as part of the landscaping of the villa on the hill. The brook itself was dammed to form two ponds and a cascade with a bridge crossing the intervening stretch of water. The whole area included a Gothick cottage (almost certainly on the site of the present Museum Cottage), a moss hut, a log cabin, and one walk, created from the former village street, was reached through a stuccoed brick arch with a ramped top supporting the Hoskins' crest, the pillars either side bearing crescents. Wain also mentions that the moss hut or summerhouse in the plantation walks was paved with encaustic tiles removed from an early church refurbishment, although he adds that they were returned to the church and re-instated during the major restoration of 1880-1881. All these structures, excepting, perhaps the arch, look as if they were in reasonably good condition in the 1877 photographs, and there is no reason to suppose that they were anything but part of Hoskins's carefully planned pleasure grounds. Regrettably, nearly all were altered, destroyed or subsequently replaced.[19]

Bladon Castle

Having completed all his works by about 1809, Hoskins was able to move out of his mother's house, which we have assumed was then called Bladon Wood, and into his new residence, although it must be remembered that, for all its refurbishment and eclectic decorations, it was still the heart of a working model farm, the buildings of which obscured the view to the south over the gently rising ground towards the Bretby boundary. The stable block, a linear stuccoed construction with a hipped roof, pediment (on the northern side) with a turret clock within it, and a columned cupola on top (almost certainly of timber), similarly blocked the view to the west. Thus, despite the fact that there was no real view from the new house to the villa on the hill, that villa was about to receive the most dramatic of makeovers. And, whatever order one might like to think this makeover occupies in the complex history of the Hoskins estate, the fact is that even in its new form, it was only ever going to be visible from the upper stories of the house at Newton Park. Its impact was more generally to be appreciated, and it took its place, in due course, as one of the County's wonders.

Bladon Castle: the earliest view of c. 1810/1820, detail from Mr. Hoskins' Greyhound
[*Mellors & Kirk*]

The date of the transformation of Bladon Wood villa into Bladon Castle was probably c. 1813-15, for the 1821 OS map calls it 'Waterloo Castle', a name that appears not to have stuck. What Hoskins did, was to include the original villa - or banqueting house to use Rawlins's expression - and the extension one suspects he added when retreating from his Newton Park builders in 1806-1809, in a long screen wall which was done mainly as a folly or eye-catcher, even though it could barely catch the eye from the Newton Park mansion itself. The style was castellated 'cardboard cut-out' Gothic and the effect, once complete, certainly spectacular. The architect was without doubt, the same man as had transformed Hoskins' Newton Park house, for a *leitmotif* common to both was the use of the somewhat inconsequential blind lunettes found over the niches in the quadrants of Hoskins' mansion. Interestingly, these also appear in William

91

Martin's earlier elevations for the model farm at Bretby, and may well have been repeated in that built in 1805 immediately south of Hoskins' new house. Indeed, these inconsequential openings, which derive from the earlier Palladian movement's obsession with all things Roman and which nearly two millennia ago were found lighting the baths of Diocletian in the Eternal City, re-appear as a conveniently decorative way to light industrial buildings. They are, for instance, used extensively at Shardlow Canal Port built from 1777 to 1782 and may have inspired Martin's designs at Bretby. Hence, if Martin's model farm directly influenced that of Hoskins, the motif may have transferred to Newton model farm, from whence Leaper – perhaps at Hoskins' urging – incorporated them into his designs to embellish the house.

Now, unless Hoskins was personally so obsessed with lunettes – usually called Diocletian or Thermal windows when glazed – that he insisted that everyone who designed for him use them, their presence below the parapets of Bladon Castle, as the new eye-catcher was called, surely indicates the same hand as the house and that hand was almost certainly Richard Leaper. Leaper, although not known to have designed a major Gothic house, did a number of gate-lodges in this simple form of the style, notably that at the entrance to The Pastures, Littleover and the one (now demolished) that once guarded the gates of the generally similar The Limes, Mickleover.

The Bailiff's Farm, Norris Castle, Isle of Wight, by James Wyatt [*NMR*]

The general concept of Bladon Castle's design was akin to James Wyatt's Bailiff's Farm, at Norris Castle, IoW, which dated from only a decade earlier, although Leaper's had a larger and much more dramatic concept. There the role of Wyatville's small villa is taken by the gardener's cottage and the scale is smaller, although it carries a similar impact. Another inspiration might have been 2nd Lord Boston's 18th century folly at Bourne End, Bucks., of c. 1775, or even Ralph Allen's much simpler eye-catcher above Bath of 1762. The centrepiece at Bladon incorporated the original Jeffry Wyatville villa with a central bow, enhanced by a pair of octagonal towers behind, heavily machicolated and crenellated. How else to account for the central bow – essentially a Classical feature – visible in the two surviving early 19th century views of the otherwise Gothic façade? The rooms overlooking the park were also equipped with "elaborate plasterwork" – presumably by Bernasconi - and according to Derrick Pounds, writing of the Second War, were frescoed, as well. The half storey is punctuated by the blind lunettes, which re-appear above lancet windows on the bays either side, linking the centre with two square towers, giving a similar visual effect to the decoration of Newton Park's quadrants. The impression of a further pair of octagonal turrets at the north end is actually given by the side-on view of a fairly massive but thin gatehouse, built at right angles and giving access to the residential part, of which the original villa retains its sill band between the floors but acquired vertical brick strips to give emphasis to the height on Gothicisation. The whole thing, whilst large, striking and extravagant, is architecturally eclectic, to say the least, but in a way, therein lies its charm.[20]

Hoskins' 'Little Folly' with Derrick Pounds (L) & Dennis Adams in front, c 1950.   [*D. Pounds*]

The terraces of the garden that had once lain in front of the villa remain and add to the castle-like ambience, with Bladon Wood to the right, masking the drive, re-aligned after the NE section of the covert was acquired from the Everys at some time before 1827, and probably at this very time, when the whole thing was built, 1807-1809. This drive, replacing one that was originally put in which rose in a series of dizzying zig-zags to the gatehouse, had a lodge built at its foot on the main road. Not content with that, across the road near the edge of the scarp above the river terrace, and north west of the Castle, Hoskins built an extra, bonus, folly: a crenellated tower with two lower walls and an arch facing the river. This was variously called 'Hoskins' Little Folly' or 'Folly House'. The latter name implies that it was originally yet another quirky Hoskins' estate house rather than a proper (useless) folly. Indeed, Derrick Pounds remembers "…that my father told me the Folly House was used in earlier times as a changing place for swimmers and boaters from the family living at the Bladon Castle. In my time it was only used by tenant farmers (Shepherd, Shilton & Brooks) to store animal feed." The meadow in which it stood, Near Underwood, rapidly became therefore Folly Field, although it was also called 'The Kitsons' or 'Kitson Hills', from the un-natural looking uneven-ness of the terrain there. Mr. Pounds adds, in that context, "Many sheep with their lambs were a common sight on the Kitson Hills. I stalked and shot the many rabbits which abounded there with my .22. My father [the Ratcliff's game keeper] also shot and snared rabbits there. He warned me to be extremely careful before shooting at rabbits particularly on weekends since, during the War years, US soldiers barracked at the Castle took their girlfriends there with blankets for hanky panky!" This additional bravura flourish of Hoskins' is said to have been built to catch the eye of the young Queen Victoria, but as he had sold the estate the year she came to the throne, and almost certainly was by then financially embarrassed anyway, this story cannot be true – the more so as this extra folly can be picked out both on the 1827 and 1836 maps. It is not clear when lack of maintenance made this folly ruinous, but Derrick Pounds attests that it was standing and being used as a hay store in 1950, but more recently Wain claimed that it had "quite disappeared", although in fact a single brick stump can still be seen from the road.[21]

It is to be presumed that Bladon (or Waterloo) Castle, as it had now become, remained the home of Hoskins' widowed mother until her death in 1818. It was at about this time that Hoskins was being well and truly hit by the agricultural recession that followed the Napoleonic Wars, added to which his Trent barges were no longer making much money, as the Trent & Mersey canal was taking most of the potential

Bladon Castle, rear elevation, early 1970s. Most of the windows in the main part by this time had been blocked up. [*M. J. Sayer*]

revenue. Thus a fresh income stream gained from renting out the accommodation in the Castle would have been welcome although, if the 1836 sale catalogue is to be believed, his rents were un-commercially low. If he did not enlarge the accommodation of the building in order to move into it temporarily in 1806-1809, whilst Newton Park was re-building, it would have been at this time that the living space at Bladon Castle was almost doubled, with fresh apartments being built behind the northernmost section of curtain wall, between the original villa and the gatehouse. This was all in matching style albeit with larger lancet windows embellished with Gothicky astragals, or glazing bars. It was thereupon let with two acres of ground, the first tenant being William Jenney (1779-1859), who had married the grand-daughter of Sir Henry Harpur 5th Bt. of Calke. The Jenneys lived there until 1835, when they went to live at Drayton Lodge, Drayton Beauchamp, in anticipation of inheriting that estate from Mrs Jenney's kinswoman, Hon. Isobel Manners, who died a year later. The couple were the ancestors of the last three Harpur-Crewes of Calke, Charles, Henry and Airmyne. Jenney's replacement as tenant, but with 16 acres instead of two, was brewer William Wilders, married since December 1833 to Hoskins' daughter Jane, and then father of a son, William Abraham, on a rent increased from £109 – 8s – 0d to £130.[22]

The view from the Castle, according to the hyperbolic rubric of the 1836 sale catalogue,

> "...will not fail to command the warmest commendation. Nothing can
> exceed the beauty of the umbrageous drives and walks through the

plantations, ever and anon catching a glimpse of the Trent; the lawns and pleasure grounds are delightful, and the scenery every where luxuriant to a degree. The offices are well planned and quite simple; and within the castle will be found all the comfort and convenience which even a family disposed to be fastidious would desire."[23]

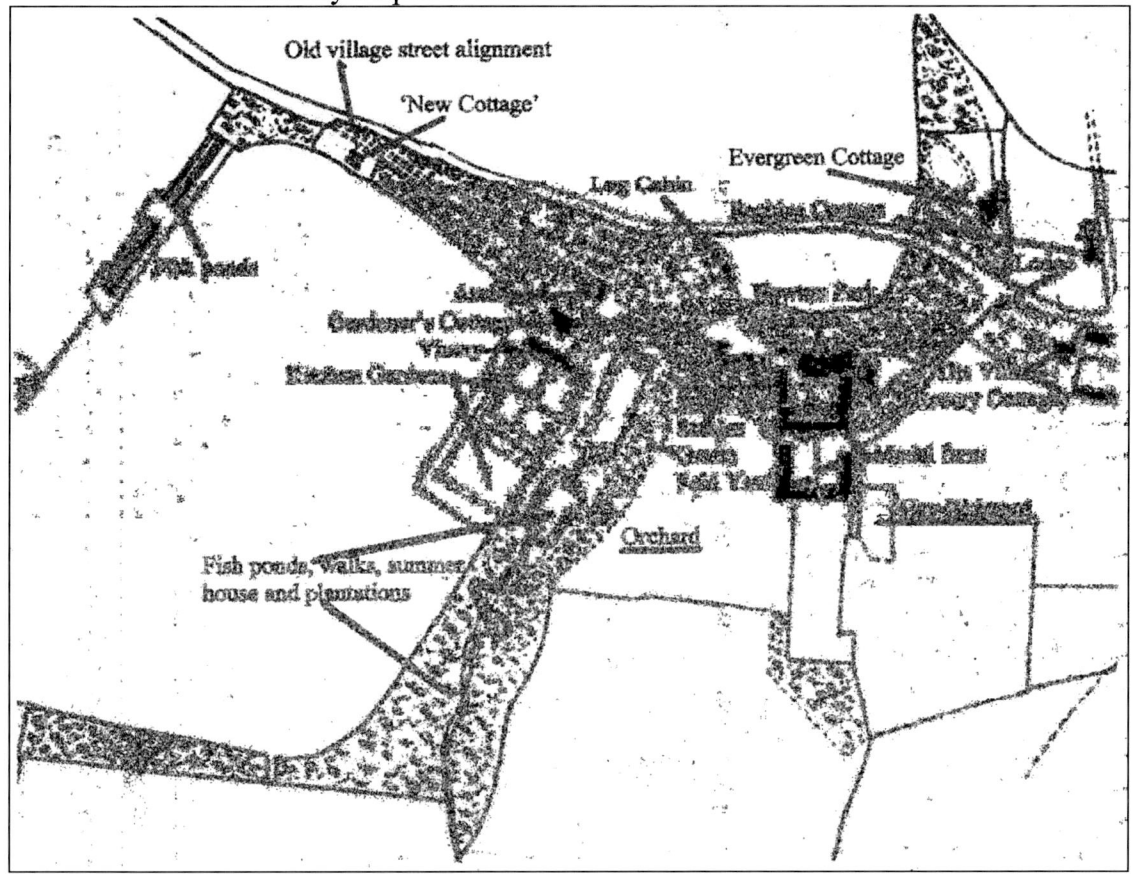

The 1836 sale catalogue map with various features marked

This passage conveys a clue to Hoskins' overall scheme, for the pleasure grounds and plantations not only took in the Castle but also crossed the main road (then little more than a lane) and curved towards the church, in which two picturesque houses were built, Evergreen Cottage and Beehive House. Likewise, east of the main house's lodge, a stuccoed dwelling of almost Soane-like purity of line and proportion, stood another house, called The Villa. All three are buildings of considerable interest, and there may have been a fourth major residence built, too, sold off prior to 1836: The Mount, right in the south of the parish off Knight's Lane.

Evergreen Cottage

Evergreen Cottage stood originally within a belt of planting which swept NE from the mansion in a horn-shaped protrusion towards Rock House (which, of course, lay outside the domain of Mr. Hoskins) and was thus an integral part of the landscape, which explains why it was designed to be as picturesque as possible. Indeed, the way this most northerly sector of Hoskins' planting tailed off almost at Rock House, which was in turn surrounded by its own planting, suggests that he was consciously allowing his landscape to take advantage of this striking building and its setting.

EVERGREEN COTTAGE.

The sale particulars of 1836 describe Evergreen Cottage (later simply called The Cottage) briefly as "…a snug abode, fitted up with considerable taste, both within and without. The gardens and office(s) are in good keeping."

The house, in truth, is eccentric, even today, when extensions have rather lessened the impact of the original design. It was built as a fairly generously proportioned two storey brick box, and the main front faces west. It is marked by Gothic windows, two ogiform ones flanking the lancet entrance and a single tall lancet above, capped by a miniature gable rising out of the coped parapet, the whole being rendered in Roman cement More arresting still is the first floor balcony, supported on four cast iron columns with fan-work spandrels below and a veritable fence of decorative ironwork surrounding it above, punctuated by what resembles a gate with lancet headed overthrow in front of and echoing the matching single window giving access onto it. The roof was originally a depressed pyramid with a central stack. The return elevation provides the giveaway as to the architect, for the upper floor window is a lunette set over a lancet of precisely the sort found on the brick curtain wall of Bladon Castle and similar to the quadrants at the mansion. Clearly, the building was designed by the same architect, almost certainly Richard Leaper of Derby. This engaging structure certainly bears the mark of his amateur approach, unfettered by much of the convention adhered to by his more professional contemporaries.

The only matter that gives pause for thought, is that the occupier, in both 1827 and 1836, was Robert Chaplin, described as an architect in the 1827 directory, and therefore to be identified with Robert Chaplin of Ashby-de-la-Zouche, best known for designing the Ivanhoe Baths, the Royal Hotel, railway station and Rawdon Terrace there, and as a long-term resident of the latter. As noted earlier, he has to be at least a contender for the architect of all Hoskins' works, although his style as it survives at Ashby is not really evident on any of the three buildings boasting the architect's trademark lunette windows. Chaplin's presence in the village ought perhaps to be treated as a co-incidence, and it is probably true to say that he never gave up his Ashby house in Rawdon Terrace, but rented Evergreen Cottage as a weekend retreat, to fish in season.

Richard Keene's photograph of Evergreen Cottage in 1877   [*Brian Appleby*]

Chaplin, who retired to his native Devonshire around 1850, did not stay at Evergreen Cottage for long, for in 1846 it was being rented by Thomas Wilders, a cousin of Hoskins' daughters, three of whom had married various members of this Burton brewing family between 1833 and 1836. This was the beginning of an irruption of brewing families into Newton Solney, for Thomas and his cousin Henry were partners who set up the Burton Brewing Company, Henry being a son of Thomas's brother William and husband of Hoskins' third daughter Charlotte, whom he had married at Newton church in September 1834. Ironically, the Wilders' enterprise was taken over by the Worthingtons, in 1915, before both were swallowed by Bass in 1929. Henry's two brothers, William and John were married respectively to Jane and Rosa Hoskins. Indeed, William had occupied Evergreen Cottage for a time prior to retreating to Bladon Castle. It was probably in Thomas Wilders' time that the Cottage was first enlarged, acquiring a matching extension to the north, incorporating a second staircase where the two parts joined and further lancet windows. In the 1860s to at least 1891 it was the home of William Smedley, described in the directories as 'cashier at F. Thompson & Son, Burton, brewers', and a member of an old Newton Solney family, long freeholders at Waterside Farm. He was succeeded by one William Robinson by 1895 and during the Edwardian era by Herbert Lance who by 1912 was sharing it – as by now 'The Cottage' - with Edward Walters, formerly of The Mount, and indeed it was Walters who lived there subsequently up to and into the Second World War.[24]

A more recent photograph showing the 20th century alterations to Evergreen Cottage.
[Derbyshire Life]

It was probably Walters who further altered the house to incorporate an extra dormer on the right of the balconied section crested to match the original one and equipped with a similarly Gothic window. Mercifully, the ironwork, probably supplied, like the gate surviving across the road opposite the lodge and the railings in front of The Cedars, by Messrs. Weatherhead, Glover & Co. of the Britannia Foundry, Duke Street, Derby, was suffered to remain.

Beehive Cottage

A few yards due east of Evergreen Cottage, an even more eccentric dwelling stands, on the edge of Church Lane. Again fenestrated in ogiform Gothick, the octagonal and exceedingly picturesque cottage rises to a tiled pyramidal roof with a central chimney. In 1836 it stood at one side of a walnut orchard, commended by John Farey whilst bemoaning a great nationwide decline in the cultivation of them, presumably because walnut was out of fashion for furniture making from the 1720s for around 120 years. By 1836, the map reveals that it was equipped with a modest service wing, which probably it always had.

Beehive Cottage in 1979   *[Derbyshire Life]*

It is reasonable to assume that it is, again, the work of Richard Leaper and thus dates from around 1809-1813, assuming that the majority of Hoskins' secondary and ancillary buildings followed on in sequence from the completion of Newton Park which we have supposed to be 1809. The 1836 occupier was a member of an old Newton Solney family, William Shepherd, then employed on the estate, but from shortly after this and through the 1840s the landlord of the newly established beer house in Main Street from 1874 recorded as the *Brickmakers' Arms,* taking its name from the adjacent premises of Mr. Hopkins. As both the ogee windows and the form of the roof echo the arrangements at Evergreen Cottage only a few yards away, the assumption must be that this is yet another quirky little structure designed by Richard Leaper - no doubt at the prompting of the fertile imagination of Mr. Hoskins. During the Ratcliff period it was traditionally the under-gardener's cottage.[25]

The Triumphal Arch & Gothick Cottage

All Hoskins' buildings are, in a sense, garden buildings, as integral parts of his vision for romantic pleasure-grounds around the mansion. And although one couldn't appreciate the landscape to the south and west from the house – essentially Bladon Castle - due to the presence of the model farm, it was well managed to the north. Planting ran out from the entrance front in two curving arms, that to the east containing Evergreen Cottage, Beehive Cottage and The Villa, and that to the west embellished by a log cabin and a triumphal brick and stucco arch.

Looking westwards along the former village street through the triumphal arch; a Richard Keene photograph of c. 1877.   [*Brian Appleby*]

This all enclosed a generous space in front of the north-facing house towards the Trent to the north, mainly of grass, with the public road now hidden below a ha-ha; the miracle was that it was not thought by Hoskins a suitable place for some kind of monument or other *grand gesture,* yet none seems to have been built even if

99

contemplated, although it would have been perfectly in keeping with his grandiose vision.

The arch spanned the former course of the village street after its diversion as part of the up-grading of the mansion in 1809. An unscholarly structure of dubious antecedents, the top was embellished with the Hoskins crest and the side-pillars with crescents, the origin and significance of which are obscure. It was undoubtedly the work of the same architect as everything else, whose amateur status it makes readily apparent.

South of the arch was laid out another belt of plantations, consisting of serpentine walks and two linked ponds, with a summerhouse. Plantations also ran west long the line of the old road, before turning south again to form the termination of the view

Gothick cottage, from the former road, photographed by Richard Keene, c. 1879.
[Brian Appleby]

down the park from Bladon Castle, this last element probably pre-dating the rest by almost a decade, as we have seen. Where this last southerly arm branched off from the planting along the line of the road was another small cottage, an impossibly pretty little Gothick one, called 'New Cottage' on the 1836 sale plan. It had two parallel ranges, one low and plain, the larger, decorative with ogee fenestration, some of it blind, and with a stack at each end - very much in the eclectic and decorative spirit of the rest of the estate buildings.

In 1836 it was tenanted by a man with the unlikely name of John Oose. It was called the 'New Cottage' because, ranged along the former main street between this cottage and the arch, were two other dwellings, both predating the Hoskins era, one being a small farmhouse, thought by Philip Heath to have been one of the former Rennison farms (described as a 'house, yard and garden' tenanted by Peter Caulton in 1836) and the other a reasonably substantial cottage close to the gardens. It would seem that early in the Ratcliff era, both arch and Gothick cottage were demolished, the latter no doubt seeming to the stricter and more liberal standards of that era too poky and inconvenient. It was, as a result, replaced by a reasonably spacious brick cottage with top paned plate glass sash windows, a slate roof and modern plumbing which is today

The Cottage, Newton Park Gardens 1879   *Gardener's Cottage, c. 1879.*
(replaced by Museum Cottage, 1880s)   *[Brian Appleby]*

called Museum Cottage, but was intended to be the gardener's cottage. This appears to contain some vestiges of the previous building, re-used rather than as a retained core, and was intended to serve the re-positioned kitchen gardens. The original cottage for the gardener, built near Hoskins kitchen gardens in a bosky cleft (the only one of Hoskins' buildings erected to anything resembling a plain, workaday design in un-stuccoed brick) was dispensed with. This, it might be added, was also removed by the Ratcliffs.

The Cedars and its residents

This substantial villa, originally called, indeed, The Villa, stands facing north on the edge of Main Street. This suggests that it may contain the core, or was erected on the footprint, of an existing cottage. Nor does it look early enough to date from much earlier than c. 1809/1813. The house is of two storeys and has a façade three bays wide, the flanking bays being tripartite and enclosing a columned portico. There is a projection to the east, considerably set back from the façade and the whole is stuccoed - no doubt, as with the others, with Parker's Roman Cement. At first glance The Villa looks conventional, but closer inspection reveals quirky features. The portico columns, for instance, are architecturally ungrammatical baseless Tuscan, which immediately suggests the work of an amateur.

Furthermore, the horizontal grooving in the stucco below the eaves, suggests Greek revival (rather than the 'Jacobethan' suggested by the cranked hood moulds to the windows), and were a favourite motif of Richard Leaper, especially at his Mill Hill House (of before 1814) and The Leylands (c. 1821), both in Derby.[26]

The Cedars, (formerly The Villa), 2009, north front; there is a modern lift shaft in the angle. [*M. Craven*]

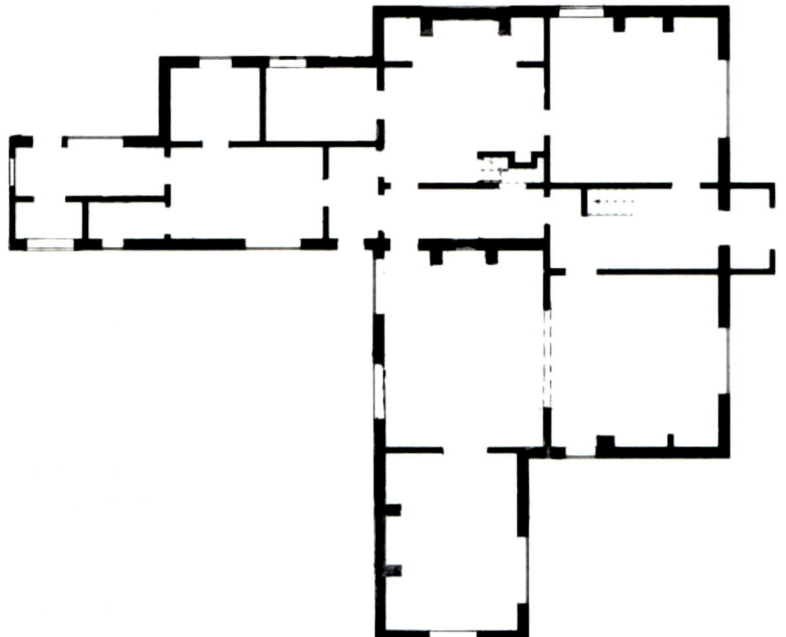

Reconstructed plan of The Villa, as built, west at the top. The room in the extension was where Greatorex kept his pipe organ and music; that on the NW angle, his library, where he had Handel's bookcase and J. C. Smith's MSS of his master.

The house was completed in 1814, when it was let to Thomas Greatorex, a Derbyshire-born musician of considerable contemporary renown who had then succeeded his father Anthony as organist of St. Modwen's church, Burton, a post he held until 1828. Up to the previous year he and his family also shared it with the retired architect Thomas Gayfere. At this point he seems to have retired to London and Charles Yates, who may well have been Greatorex's son-in-law, succeeded him at St. Modwen's, whilst the house was sub-let to Yates's brother, Capt. Richard Yates, on a seven year lease with just over two acres of garden, for which he paid £62 – 10s - 10d per annum. Thus at about the time of the Hoskins sale when Yates decided to move across the road to Rock House, it was re-occupied by Greatorex's widow

Elizabeth, who may have been a local woman, and she was living there with her son Edward at the time of the 1841 census, remaining there over the following decade.[27]

The later history of the house is not without interest. In the early 1850s, by then in the ownership of the Earl of Chesterfield, and following the death of Mrs. Greatorex, it was let to Edward Perks, a brother of Charles Perks of Bladon Cottage (see Chapter V) and after his death in March 1875, by his daughter Rosa, who resided there until the end of the century. In the early part of the twentieth century it was the home of Charles Richardson Harrison, but after the Great War brewery director E. J. Gothard came to live there and changed the name of the house to The Cedars, by which it is still known. He was succeeded by solicitor Harold Argyle (of Talbot and Co., Hoskins' father's old firm) from about 1932, during whose time the house flooded and the Newton Park estate were forced to undertake culverting works round the gardens to avoid a repetition. There was, at that time, a tennis court and a summerhouse on a revolving base there. Later, Harold Argyle's son, Michael (1915-1999), later an eminent circuit judge, lived there. It was offered for sale on the death of Newton Park owner Percy Ratcliff in October 1956, Mr. & Mrs. S. M. C. Jones being in the second year of a seven year tenancy, following the Argyles, but was withdrawn to allow Ratcliff's widow, Olive to live there. She moved in during 1960 and drastically altered the plan of the house, added central heating and a lift and extended the service wing. On her death in 1971, Burton Hospital consultant Hubert de Castella – a member of an ancient and noble Swiss family which had founded the Australian wine making industry in the 1840s – bought the house for £15,600, remaining there until sold to the present owners in 2006, and adding a large conservatory.[28]

Thomas Greatorex, FRS, FLS

Thomas Greatorex of The Villa was probably the most eminent man to have lived in Newton Solney. The family was an ancient one of very minor gentry from Callow-by-Wirksworth and his father Anthony (1730-1814) had made his fortune as a nail manufacturer and had bought half of Riber Hall, although he was living at North Wingfield when his son Thomas was born 5th October 1758. The father was also a talented self-taught amateur musician and became sufficiently competent on the organ to become a nationally known recitalist as well as a bass singer of repute, performing in Handel memorial concerts in London from 1784. Another child, Martha, was also a prodigious talent on the organ, and at only 13 was appointed organist of St. Martin's Leicester, where she quickly earned sufficient money to acquire "a small estate near Burton" on which her father, for a time, lived, having being appointed organist at St. Modwen's in 1771.[29]

Thomas was a younger son, and was initially more fascinated by science and especially mathematics, but also acquired a prodigious talent for organ playing, additionally becoming a bassoonist and competent in a variety of other instruments.

He went to London to train under Dr. Pepusch and later with Benjamin Cooke, before making the acquaintance of the Earl of Sandwich at a concert of his sister's at Leicester, and was soon a member of his household. He assisted the conductor Josiah Bates at the Christmas oratorios at Huntingdon which Lord Sandwich presented and for a time was the Earl's musical director.

Bates was the founder of the aristocratic Concerts of Ancient Music in which Greatorex sang before becoming organist at Carlisle, where he engaged in literary and philosophical discussions and thereafter at Newcastle, before spending two years abroad to deepen his studies starting in 1786. In Rome he was introduced to Bonnie Prince Charlie, who, on his death shortly afterwards, bequeathed him his collection of music MSS.

Back in England he set himself up as a teacher and was soon earning over £80 per week , a colossal sum for any musician in those days. In 1793, when his friend Bates retired, he was appointed to succeed him as director of the Ancient Concerts which he continued for 39 years. About this time he also joined the Royal Society of Musicians and became a co-founder of the Royal Academy of Music – the Prince Regent is said to have said to him, "My father is *rex*, Sir, but you are a greater *rex*!"

He was also elected a fellow of the Linnaean Society and the Royal Society, the latter as a result of a paper in their *Transactions* introducing a new method of measuring the height of mountains. He performed occasionally in London operas and more frequently in oratorios, but composed little. It was thought that he had no underlying 'feel' for music, despite his superb playing. As a conductor, though, and as an organist, he was a riveting performer, Dr. Gardiner writing of his playing technique said:

> "His style is massive, he was like Briareus with one hundred hands, grasping so many keys at once that surges of sound rolled from the instrument in awful grandeur."

He was a friend of Belper born tenor, Samuel Harrison, and together they revived the British music festival as a genre, Greatorex conducting those at Derby, Birmingham and York as well as in London on a regular basis. He had a house in London but "in the country had a beautifully situated house on the banks of the Trent" - an obvious reference to The Villa at Newton. Not content with being organist at Burton (from which post he was frequently absent, Yates standing in for him) he was appointed organist at Westminster Abbey in 1819 and shortly after was made Professor of Music at the Royal Academy. He retired to Hampton-on-Thames after he resigned at Burton in 1828, dying there of a chill caught whilst fishing, another favourite pastime of his, and no doubt one of the reasons why he chose to live at Newton for upwards of 14 years.

Thomas Gayfere

Thomas Gayfere was born in 1755, son of another Thomas, a mason who in 1766 was appointed Master Mason to Westminster Abbey and who was in 1773 elected as Master of then Worshipful Company of Masons. We may safely assume that young Thomas was apprenticed to his father, who had been the contractor for Westminster

Bridge, probably from 1796-1776, but at some stage during the latter process was taught architectural drawing, perhaps at the St. Martin's Lane Academy, for in 1774 he exhibited a view of (King's) Norton Church in Leicestershire at the Society of Artists and a drawing of the ruins of Furness Abbey there three years later. The choice of his first subject may have been because his father worked on this church, a powerful Gothick design by Wing of Leicester, although no records of individual payments survive to attest to the suggestion. The following year, 1778, he exhibited topographical drawings at the Royal Academy and again in the two years following.[30]

Gayfere seems to have worked in tandem with his father thereafter until December 1802, when the two of them were appointed master masons to Westminster Abbey a post he retained solo after his father's death in 1812 and in which he continued until he retired in 1823. In 1807-1808, Parliament voted funds for the complete restoration of Henry VII's chapel, and Gayfere travelled extensively around the UK to find the most suitable stone, deciding on Combe Down stone from Bath. Work began under Gayfere's direction (James Wyatt, as Surveyor to the Abbey was only nominally in charge) in 1809 and lasted until 1822, when a total of £42,000 had been spent. It was the first modern and scholarly restoration ever done on an ecclesiastical building and was unique to his contemporaries, which is why Gayfere is such an important, if neglected, figure. He personally examined every part of the chapel, making drawings and taking plaster casts of the rapidly decaying fabric, and from these he prepared full scale working drawings. He went out of his way to choose the best masons and to instruct them in the execution of what was in those days an unfamiliar style of architecture. It may be no co-incidence that whilst he was working there, Francis Bernasconi was executing stucco work in the Great Tower under Wyatt's direction.

Whilst thus occupied, he also carried out the restoration of the north front of Westminster Hall under the supervision of the Office of Works, an undertaking which also ended in 1822 after three years. He was unmarried and, when he retired in 1823, he was invited to spend his declining years in the household of Thomas Greatorex, whom he had met and of whom he had become "the intimate friend" during the years both men spent working at the Abbey. He died on a visit to Burton-upon-Trent 20th October 1827 and was buried by Greatorex in Newton churchyard under a tombstone – once inside the church (where it surely belongs) but now outside – which reads:
> "His qualities as a man will find their best Memorial in the affection of his Survivors, while the Restoration of King Henry the Seventh's Chapel, and the Hall at Westminster, will prove a lasting Monument to his Abilities as an Architect."

Although he arrived in Newton Solney too late to have been a candidate for designing Abraham Hoskins' buildings, he may, nevertheless have done some work locally. If so, though, direct evidence has yet to come to light.[31]

The End of a Dream

Most accounts of Newton Park tell us that Abraham Hoskins over-reached himself by extravagance in enhancing and embellishing his estate way beyond his means and that he developed his secondary residences only in order to raise rent to increase the estate's income. That the various dwellings were not built specifically for this purpose can be demonstrated by recalling that all, or nearly all, were built in the period 1809-

1813, long before any fiscal pressure was apparent and by the fact that the 1836 sale catalogue includes the following:

> "The several Residences, including the "Castle", are occupied by annual
> tenants, at a most inadequate rental..."

which suggests that income was not a primary concern.

From 1814, of course, there had been a well-documented agricultural recession which got increasingly severe, provoking desperate measures amongst those whose livelihoods were affected, as locally with the so-called Pentrich Martyrs of 1819. Bearing in mind that Hoskins' expenditure was largely laid out by 1814 and that he was no doubt hoping to recoup the money by the flourishing of his modern and efficient husbandry, the impact of this recession may have had a damaging effect on his finances. It would be reasonable to conclude that, by the mid-1820s the only way to ameliorate the effects of the downturn would be to sell some land. To that end, as we have seen, he arranged with Sir Henry Every to enact a confirmatory deed of conveyance of his estate, re-inforcing the acquisitions of 1798 and 1799. The first, it will be recalled, was done whilst Sir Henry was still a minor and Hoskins his Receiver of Rents, and the second was done through Michael Bass as proxy and thus both could be called into question if he re-sold. This deed was duly completed in 1829, and it may be that certain properties were sold off at this time, although there is no proof of this.[32]

When the Everys sold much of their Newton Solney estate - 722 acres in all, with Hoskins buying 103 acres in 1798, and 619 being sold the following year - it is difficult to work out exactly all that Hoskins bought altogether. It would appear, however, that he bought at least some of the land south of the main road and east of Newton Lane, probably Poplars Farm, which bears every appearance of the type of smaller brick building on the estate. Added to which, it sports an extraordinarily architectonic stone portico in Neo-Greek style which looks like a typical Hoskins-ism, although it is said to have come from Cliffe house, the first Ratcliff mansion in the parish, but which is demonstrably untrue: Cliffe House in fact had a much larger Jacobethan portico and that on Poplars Farm is too small and 30 years too early in style, with its Soanian key pattern grooving on the pilasters. If it came from anywhere, The Mount, demolished post-World War Two, is perhaps the more likely source. It may be, therefore, that this farm was sold following the 1829 agreement; unfortunately, the 1836 sale particulars map fails to name the landholder in this area.

The Mount

The same map does, however, name the landowners immediately to the south of the Newton Park estate: 'Thomas Allsopp, Esquire, Mr. Thomas Higgott' and 'Mr. P. Holmes'. The latter was presumably the founder of Common Farm, lying in the SW corner of the estate, but the presumption must be that he bought it from the Everys in 1799; certainly the very workaday farmhouse is not one that one could imagine Hoskins allowing. Higgott's land (which he certainly had by 1811), as shown in this sector and probably also acquired in 1799, but did not directly pertain to his farm, which was still presumably still in the village proper. Allsopp was different. He lived at The Mount, later Newton Mount, a true gentleman's residence. There are several pointers to its having been part of Hoskins' empire. Bagshaw's directory described it as:

> "A neat pleasant house on a rising ground amidst shrubberies and plantations one mile east of the village"[33]

We also learn that it was "stone built", but in all truth, the directory compiler was probably misled by stone-coloured stucco. The biggest problem when it comes to analysing it, is that it was demolished shortly after the second world war, and no photograph of it has yet surfaced.

Thomas Allsopp was the younger son of a Derby merchant, James Allsopp, himself born in 1751, who made sufficient money to be able to acquire Birlingham Hall in Worcestershire. He married into the family of the Burton innkeeper-turned-brewer, Benjamin Wilson, who had established a Burton brewery at the *Blue Stoops* inn, High Street in the 1740s. His elder son Samuel - who inherited the Wilsons' business and built upon it, and whose name was thereafter attached to the company - was the father of Sir Charles Allsopp, created a baronet in 1880 and who entered the "beerage" six years later as 1st Lord Hindlip of Hindlip and Alsop-en-le-Dale. It was Samuel's younger brother who was our Thomas, who married Ann Ratcliff (a name which will loom large in the next chapter), who lived at Newton Mount from before March 1821, when his name and that of his residence appear in the Newton Solney vestry minutes. He was at this date 39 years of age, and was almost certainly a tenant of Hoskins. Again, the house probably dated from 1813/1814, and would have been visible from the gardens at Newton Park on the rising ground to the south, so was probably interestingly designed, like Hoskins' other creations. Although the house has gone, it was surrounded by a model farm, parts of which survive, albeit on a much smaller scale than Hoskins' at Newton Park, but built along the latest lines and with a row of four brick labourers' cottages which, mercifully, also survive. These last are of

The Mount, surviving cottages, 2008   [*M. Craven*]

one and a half storeys and are built in the same style and scale as Poplars Farm, with similar gauged brick lintels and are well proportioned under a hipped roof, very much in the Hoskins mould. By the date of the sale map in 1836, Allsopp is shown as a freeholder in the vicinity of his house, and he is also listed as such in the 1846 directory. Thus it is likely that Hoskins' 1829 confirmation was enacted in order for The Mount to be sold to him, and probably to sell the Poplars, too. In 1841 Allsopp was living with his widowed mother, Ann, then 85, which suggests that both his wife and only son William had died.[34]

H. J. Wain claimed that this house was bought with the rest of the estate in 1837 by Lord Chesterfield, but this is clearly not so. When Allsopp died in February 1855, he left The Mount to his nephew James Drewry, second son of *Derby Mercury* proprietor John Drewry. He was a Burton-upon-Trent solicitor and, having married into the family, was also director of Samuel Allsopp & Sons. He and his family had clearly been invited to move into The Mount by Allsopp before 1851 when they were recorded there in the census, and they were certainly in residence in 1857. Drewry moved to Burton Priory in the 1860s, when the house and land were, it would seem, only then sold to Lord Chesterfield, being contiguous to the Bretby estate, just across Knight's Lane - which is why Wain probably thought the Bretby estate had owned the Mount from 1837. The house was thereupon let to George Mitchell who was married to the daughter of John Faulkner, Lord Chesterfield's agent, George being the spendthrift son of James, the impresario, of Rock House, to which the son moved in 1870. That year it was re-let to one Albert Hoyles and this is the first occasion on which the property is recorded as Newton Mount. Hoyles was succeeded by yet another Burton attorney, Henry Goodger, although he did number the Bretby estate amongst his clients! By 1895 Herbert Lance, who re-appears in the saga as resident of Evergreen Cottage, was in occupation, but in 1898 it was Repton-educated local farmer's son J. H. Barrs. After his departure, early in the decade following, it remained empty until offered for sale by the Bretby estate in 1910, but failed to sell, and remained in a sort of limbo until bought by H. S. Holmestead, the son of a Falkland Islands farmer who had retired to Bedford. He intended to use it as the focus of a nursery enterprise with B. J. Maw as partner. In due course Holmestead was superseded by L. Alec Maw, his partner's son, who ran it post war with G. G. Holmers [*sic*]. It was the younger Maw who demolished the house. The nursery today is a flourishing garden centre.[35]

The Great Sale

The lack of evidence for any Hoskins sales in 1829-1830 suggests that Hoskins was less fiscally constrained than has often been suggested. Yet with a vast number of children – the eldest of whom, it must be admitted, were by the early 1830s beginning to marry and leave home – and the cost of hobbies other than building (which we may safely assume had ended by c. 1814) he was kept busy despite advancing years. His chief pastime apart from husbandry was the breeding of greyhounds, attested to by Bigsby and confirmed by the appearance at a sale in 2001 of a portrait of one particularly fine black and white hound - proudly posed in front of a brand new Bladon Castle - and by the generous kennelling provided at his model farm. If he was racing or coursing these dogs, they may have been as much a drain on his finances as the children.

In 1836, therefore, perhaps with advancing age (he was 76) and failing health playing a much more significant part, Hoskins commissioned George Robins of the London Auction Mart, Covent Garden, to sell the estate, preferably in one lot including all buildings and 490 acres. A lavish catalogue was produced, embellished with four fine stone lithographs of the house, Bladon Castle, The Villa and Evergreen Cottage, and which was rich in hyperbole about the delights of the area, including the

"Quiet , unpretending village of Newton"

and emphasising the quality of the landscape in which
> "This interesting vale appears as one continued park"

and that
> "Its character is, fortunately, so well appreciated in the County,
>   that the observations which follow are necessarily directed only
>   to those at a distance."

Furthermore, Newton Park mansion was described as:
> "An elegant abode…a chaste specimen of English architecture"

and Bladon Castle as
> "One of the commanding features of Derbyshire and the architectural
>   skill displayed will be found well worthy of imitation. From the ex-
>   tended terraced walk, Windsor Castle, and its varying qualifications,
>   will be immediately brought to recollection…."[36]

The sale was to take place on July 21st 1836 at noon, with viewing, including the "plans and drawings" of the estate and buildings – would that they had survived! – available by permission during the preceding 28 days. A notice of completion on 20th May 1837 suggests that the sale went through, but the purchaser clearly failed, on the day, to find the money. Thus the whole thing then had to be re-run, using the same catalogues, the date being 20th July. Bidding started at £40,000 and rose in thousand pound bids until it was secured by the agent of the Bretby estate for 55,000 guineas (£55,755). This acquisition represented part of the programme of George Stanhope, 6th Earl of Chesterfield (1805-1866) to boost his estate at Bretby, to accompany his efforts to build his new house there, designed by Jeffry Wyatville; it was completed by none other than William Martin of model farm fame. Although Lord Chesterfield had succeeded in 1815, he only came of age a decade before the sale. Furthermore, £55,000 was a good result, and indicates that the economy had picked up since the 1820s. The sale was completed on 9th June.[37]

Hoskins, meanwhile,
> "Leaving his beautiful seats and estates at Newton Park, and Bladon
>   Castle, and retiring at his patriarchal age from the fairy scene his
>   own hands had created, reared and perfected"

retired to a spacious and comfortable house, again of his own devising, called Wood Villa, Woodgate, by Uttoxeter, which he had built some time before, letting it to a widow called Elizabeth Brown. There he died on 13th March 1842, leaving numerous progeny and their equally numerous issue. Bigsby, who may have known him, despite his slightly unreliable account of his buildings, supplied his epitaph:
> "Few gentlemen have been more justly noted for the maintenance
>   of a Liberal style of hospitality or for the exercise of a quiet, un-
>   ostentatious course of benevolence."[38]

His connection with Newton Solney was not broken for he was buried in the churchyard there under a table tomb of some size and is commemorated by a tablet proudly bearing his crest opposite the south door of the church.

*

Mr. Hoskins' Hound c. 1810/1820; oil painting sold 31st March 2000 [*Mellors & Kirk*]

[1] Grant of 1230, J. 755-6; Henry Longford, RLC 551 of 31st May & 552 of 9th July 1521; Gardner grant, DRO D5236/4/54 of 5/4/1569; Newton Park, Cameron, *loc.cit*

[2] Family details from Sayer M., in DAJ XCII (1972) *loc.cit.* amplified by PRs

[3] Trent navigation etc., Turbutt (1999) IV. 1542; the Hayne family came originally from Ireton Wood and were later of Green Hall, Ashbourne, FMG III. 1015-16

[4] VCH *Staffs.*, IX 83-4, 87; on Bass, BP (2003) I. 599; bankruptcy, Wain (1976) II

[5] Wyatts: Colvin (2008), 1190 (Joseph), 1193-1197 (Samuel) & 1197-1202 (Jeffry 1128-1130); villa at Bladon, Colvin (1995) 1130.

[6] No water, unattributed note beginning "Local legend has it that…" left by the late Michael Day, cf. Sinar, J. in DLC (4/1981) 50-51; Bigsby (1854) 356, repeated, for instance, in Hipkins (1899) 130 -131. Rawlins (1843) *sub* Newton Solney; The fact that the elder Abraham's will calls him "of Burton-upon-Trent" is not conclusive; these designations were only indicative of a man's primary residence and numerous local examples can be adduced of people of Hoskins' position in society doing this. Indeed, his son, Abraham, describes himself in his 1838 will as "of Newton Park" even though he had sold it the previous year and was then resident in Uttoxeter! (will, PRO Prob. 11/1972). Indeed, the elder Hoskins was described in a deed of Lord Chesterfield's dated 4/1800 as "*late* of Burton-upon-Trent" (cf. n. 9)

[7] Farey, II (1811) 6 – one of only five in the county which he mentions

[8] Auction, Heath (2005) 3; confirmatory deed, DLSL No. 5243. Atr the same time some outlying pieces of land were sold by the Everys to Lord Chesterfield, ther trustees including the elder Hoskins (Carnarvon MSS, Highclere Derbyshire Estate book, 41-110, deed of 4 & 5/7/1800).

[9] Hoskins 'the elder…late of Burton', deed of 5/4/1800, Bundle 18, Highclere MSS; Hoskins living at Burton, DLSL deed 5241 (1803) and 2240 (1806); Wain (1976) *loc. Cit.*

[10] Will pr. 15/8/1805, PRO prob,. 11/1413; Wyatts, Colvin (1995) 1102,1103, 1121-1123; letter, Staffordshire Archives, William Salt Library, Stafford, M96/20; Hoskins was "engaged in building work" in 1805, Farey II (1813) 47

[11] Model farm at Bretby, Glover (1831/33) I. 190-192; on layouts of later Georgian farms, see Robinson (1983) 62-72, esp. 67.

[12] Hoskins' will, pr. 15/8/1805, PRO Pron. 11/1413; Farey II (1811) 11, 47, 53, 216, 281, 392 & III (1816) 60; Noon, McKenna (2002) 254 & Moore (2003) 244; sale particulars, 1836, DRO 2293/1-2

[13] Deaths of 1st wife and sons, MIs at Newton Church; youngest child, Abraham (1822-1913, see pedigree in appendix

[14] Roman cement works, Glover (1831/1833) II. 454: Bernasconi, Farey II (1813) 6]

[15] Sale particulars, *op.cit*

[16] Pastures, Craven & Stanley (2001) II. 304-305; Leaper, Glover (1831/33) II. 602, 604; Bernasconi, Beard (1981) 245; Hoskins as Peel's lawyer, Staffs. RO eg. 3233/1 (1801); Compton Place, Colvin (1995) 457.

[17] Brown, Colvin (1995) 168, DRO D2293/1-2 Sale Catalogue, 1836, 5, Wheathills, DLDL Mundy MSS, Parcel 225; *Derby Mercury* 3/1/1811; Gayfere, Colvin (1995) 395; Chaplin, *op. cit.,* 244

[18] It might be possible to argue for Samuel Brown as designer of the lodge, but if so, he cannot be ascribed Burnaston House, for the late Sir Howard Colvin averred that the writing on the elevations of the latter were certainly not in Brown's hand. Diversion of road, DRO QS/B 9/58; pleasure grounds, Farey II (1811) 6 & sale particulars, *op. cit.*

[19] Keene, Craven (1993) 32, 201; Church tiles, Wain (1976) II.]

[20] Folly, Craven, M. in *Derby Evening Telegraph* 27/3/2000, p.10 cc. 1-5; Bailiff's Farm, Norris Castle, IoW; Jas. Wyatt, c. 1799 Robinson (1983) 39; Headley & Meulenkamp (1986) 30 (Ralph Allen's Folly); 218 (Lord Boston's Folly); plasterwork and frescoes, Pounds (2000) 18.

[21] Second folly, Wain (1976) II; Folly Field, Fraser (1947) 101; Information courtesy Derrick Pounds; Q. Victoria, Sayer, *loc. cit*

[22] Sale particulars, 1836

[23] *ibid.* 5

[24] Wilders family and brewery, VCH IX (2003) 47, 68,80; St. Modwen, Burton and Newton Solney PRs; John & Mrs. Smedley were freeholders of 46 acres at Waterside Farm in 1758 (Every Terrier, qv. Chapter III) and in 1841 (Census) Thomas Smedley (25) was the farmer, followed by his brother Edward from 1845 to 1881 (Directories & Census)

[25] Walnuts, Farey II (1815) 205-206; Shepherd, censuses and directory; usage, Pounds (2000) 42.

[26] Leaper, *Derbyshire Magazine* 3/2007, 26-28; Mill Hill House, Craven, in *Journal* of the Georgian Group, forthcoming & DLC 6/2006, 103-104; Leylands, Craven & Stanley (2001) II. 286-287

[27] Organists of St. Modwen's, VCH *Staffs*. IX (2003), 115, 150

[28] Edward Perks, died 30/3/1875, MI at Newton Solney; Edward Gothard later lived at Mickleover House (Craven & Stanley (2001) I. 154). He and his brother, Sir Clifford were accountants turned property developers; Harold Victor Argyle, latterly of highways, Repton, died 28/8/1965 having married Elsie Marion (Judge Argyle's mother) and Stella Margaret, JP (d. 21/5/2006) mother of Adrian Argyle, recently chairman of Repton Parish Council, *Derby Evening Telegraph* obits *passim*. & DLC 10/2003, 200-201; summer house etc., *ex info*. Mrs. Doris Jones; Mr. & Mrs. Jones had planned to bid up to £5,000 for it, according to Mrs. Jones; H. de Castella moved in 1st December, according to his own account. On his family see Burke (1895) II. 770-773

[29] Greatorex family, *Reliquary*, IV 220; Greatorex, DNB I. 831; home, DLSL NQ 712.

[30] King's Norton church, Pevsner (1960) 129 & Colvin (1995) 1068-69

[31] Gayfere. *obit*., DCR 1/11/1827 p. 3, c. 2 & *Gentleman's Magazine*, 1828 (i) 275. career, Colvin, *op.cit*. 395-396 his friendship with Greatorex & home at Newton, DLSL NQ 710;

[32] DLSL 5243 of 20/9/1829

[33] Bagshaw (1846) 256-257

[34] Allsopp, Foster (1882) II. 7-8 & VCH *Staffs*. IX 66-67; Newton Solney vestry minutes; Bagshaw, *loc.cit*.; census

[35] Allsopp was bur. St. Alkmund, Derby 18/2/1855: his brother Charles (1803-1844) married James Drewry's sister Sarah Emma (d. 1879) in 1836 and she re-married Rev'd William Belcher, a descendant of a Newton tenant farmer from the 1758 terrier; Drewry: White (1834) 322, (1851) 543 & White (1857); Mitchell: Wain (1976) II; 1910 sale: catalogue in National Monument Record, SCO 0193 of 12/8/1910; post 1910: Wain, *loc.cit*.]

[36] Catalogue (1836) 4-8

[37] Revised sale date, *Derby Mercury,* 7/6/1837; Annotated sale catalogue, private collection; Chesterfield, CP III. 180-187; Bretby Hall, Craven & Stanley (2001) I. 53-55

[38] Villa: White (1834) 765; later on the widow's death in 1852 sold to E. Phillips of Burton; epitaph: *DM* quoted by Sayer, M. J. in DAJ XCII (1972) 90; Hoskins MI in Newton Solney church, complete with unauthorised crest; his will pr. 24/12/1842, PRO prob. 11/1972 establishes that he died comfortably off; issue, see pedigree VI in the appendix; Bigsby (1854) 356.

*

V

THE ELITE MOVE IN

The man who bought the Newton Park estate on 20th July 1837 was the neighbouring landowner, the 6th Earl of Chesterfield. For him it represented almost 500 acres of land contiguous to his own in Bretby and therefore an opportunity to consolidate his estate with an accession of land that was served by up-to-date facilities and would thus require little outlay. The purchase did, of course, include two country houses – Newton Park and Bladon Castle – but, like the smaller residences of the estate, they represented a potential source of income. It was also an ironical reversal of the situation in the *Domesday Book*, wherein Newton Solney was the manorial estate and Bretby the outlier. Now they had come together again, but with the pre-eminence reversed!

Bladon Castle after Hoskins

Of the two main houses, Bladon Castle was acquired with a sitting tenant, in the form of William Wilders of the Burton Brewery and his wife Jane, *nee* Hoskins, who had moved there from Evergreen Cottage in 1836 after the Jenneys moved to King's Newton Hall where they remained for eighteen months *en route* to taking over Drayton Lodge in Buckinghamshire. The Wilders had two children, William Abraham (two) and Sarah Jane Elizabeth (14 months) at the time of the sale, and whilst they were in residence at the Castle added Edward Andrew (1837-1838) and James (1839-1841) to their family, albeit for only a short time for both died in infancy. However, in 1841 they moved out and were replaced as tenants by brewery director George MacKenzie Kettle who on 13th October that year had married Elizabeth Grazebrook. Their stay was, however, relatively short, for on 1st August 1846, Mrs. Kettle's brother, Thomas, died unmarried leaving her the Grazebrook property of Dallicott House. Within as year, they had moved to Shropshire to take possession of the estate.[1]

This left the house empty (apart from two short interludes) until 1861, when it was again let, this time to Francis Holbrook (1801-1882) and his wife Marianne. He was the younger son of another Francis Holbrook (1758-1841) of Repton Grange where he owned some 107 acres and a descendant of the builder of the Repton House, Joseph Holbrook, said to have been Lord Mayor of London in 1703, but notably absent from the official list. Francis' elder brother, Charles a lead merchant, built Nunsfield House in Boulton-by-Derby, but Francis was a tanner. In 1870, his eldest son, another Francis had moved in whilst his parents returned to Repton Grange. This was for the son's convenience, for he was at that time a senior manager of F. Thompson & Sons, a Burton brewery company. He was then 34 and married to Emma Georgina, but on his death five days before Christmas 1882, his son Francis George Seymour Holbrook lived there with his mother and they remained there until F. G. S. Holbrook's wife, then widowed for almost a year, died on 7th November 1938, after sixty eight years of unbroken family occupation, there being a sale on the premises the following spring. At that point it was the estate's intention to let the building to the brother-in-law of Percy Ratcliff, the Newton Park heir apparent, a Burton Brewery director called Gilbert Thomson. By the end of the summer of 1939 he had contractors working hard renovating the building, which was at that juncture largely gutted and was about to be re-fitted out. Unfortunately, soon after the war broke out the South Staffordshire Regiment had taken over, and were in occupation before Thompson had had a chance to clear the building. The renovations were never properly finished and, during the war years, after the Americans had taken over, much water got in, and dry rot was rampant by the end of hostilities. The troops were housed in Nissen huts in the grounds, and after D-day were replaced by Italian PoWs. Compensation was paid, but as usual, in insufficient quantity to cover the doing of a proper job - not that such was in any way possible for the first three years of peace, due to the draconian restrictions on building. Eventually repairs were effected and the house re-let to a local family[2].

The Holbrooks had made some alterations during their occupation, blocking some west-facing upper windows and rebuilding the central east facing bay completely, replacing the canted full height centrepiece with an almost rectangular one with large Jacobethan mullioned and transomed windows, greatly improving the view to the east. The rooms behind were also extensively altered and re-decorated. The date of these works was probably a very few years after 1870, when the younger Francis Holbrook had moved in. Traditionally the architect of these works was said to have been William Morris, but this seems unlikely for he is not known to have been linked either to the Holbrooks or their near kin, nor even to the Burton-upon-Trent milieu of the time. Indeed, at about this time he was co-founding the Society for the Preservation of Ancient Buildings, which august body would probably have looked down its nose at Bladon Castle! Furthermore, Morris was by then fully engaged in textile design and related matters and did not undertake architectural commissions, leaving such as came along to Philip Webb especially. Unfortunately Webb's hand is not easy to discern at Bladon Castle and the story probably arises from the interior decorative style, now no longer apparent.

Bladon Castle, NE front, in 1979, showing the "William Morris" replacement central bay   *[M. F. Stanley]*

The house was sold with the rest of the Newton Park estate in 1879 and after a brief period of lying empty following the Holbrooks' deaths, it was, as we have seen, requisitioned by the military in 1939. In due course, it became an observation post -

the views from the building are impressive, especially to east and west – and by 1943 was occupied by the US Army. It was returned to its owners somewhat the worse for wear in 1946. Despite being re-let, the central residential part seems never to have been fully re-occupied, however, probably because the additional accommodation created, in all probability for Abraham Hoskins' occupation in 1806-1809, is more compact and convenient. The Castle was offered for sale un-tentanted by the estate's executors on 17th July 1972, when it was purchased by Mr. J. Shepherd, the retiring farmer of adjacent Bladon Farm and is currently the residence of his daughter Constance. It is statutorily listed II*[3].

Newton Park in the Victorian era

Having acquired Abraham Hoskins' mansion at Newton Park, Lord Chesterfield had no particular use for it, and he therefore set about disposing of it leasehold. The man who took up the lease was following in the footsteps of Thomas Allsopp of the Mount and William Wilders of Bladon Castle, in that he was a brewer from Burton: William Worthington, JP. Indeed, the closeness of the inter-relationships of the various brewing families and the frequency with which they seem to have taken up residence at Newton Solney is remarkable, although it is worth bearing in mind that both the later Grettons and the Ratcliffs had family connections in the village (see Table III below). The place was, after all, convenient for Burton in the days before rapid transport systems, uncommonly pleasant, and had access to fishing.

We do not know exactly when the lease was acquired, but he was undoubtedly in residence by 1839. He was then 39 years of age, the son of another William, who had vastly expanded their company at Burton. His mother was Martha, daughter of Henry Evans of Caldwell Hall, another Burton Brewer (despite being a younger son of a Derby banker) and thus a relative of the cotton spinning pioneers of Darley Abbey Mills and Florence Nightingale, indeed. His sister, Ann had married in 1835 Revd. Roger Bass, younger brother of 1st Lord Burton, and the son of Michael Thomas Bass, Derby's long-serving Liberal MP whose mother was a Hoskins, thus rather squaring the Newton Park circle. William, born in February 1799, married Mary Anne, second daughter of Francis Calvert of Hound Hill Hall, Staffordshire, not far from Sudbury in June 1824, less than a year before the death of his father, from whom he inherited a controlling interest in the family enterprises. By the time they moved in to Newton Park two of their four sons had been born – William Henry and Calvert – and also their elder daughter Catherine Elizabeth, who later married Derbyshire coal owner Charles Denison-Pedder of Kilburn Hall[4].

William Worthington, the first brewer of the family, had moved to Burton in 1744 as a cooper, but bought a brewhouse in 1760 and died in 1800 as one of the major players in the breweries of the town. Henry Evans was his contemporary, having bought a place on the west side of the High Street in 1754, with money put up by his father. He built two malthouses and a brewery and went on to become a partner of the elder Abraham Hoskins in the Trent Navigation. Later, he bought out the Wilson family's brewery, settling it on his elder daughter, Martha, who thus carried it by marriage to the second William Worthington (1764-1825). To consolidate this, William's brother Thomas married Martha's sister Sarah, so that when John Evans their brother died, the entire Evans enterprise fell like a ripe plum into the laps of the Worthington family[5].

TABLE III   *The Newton Solney Beerage*

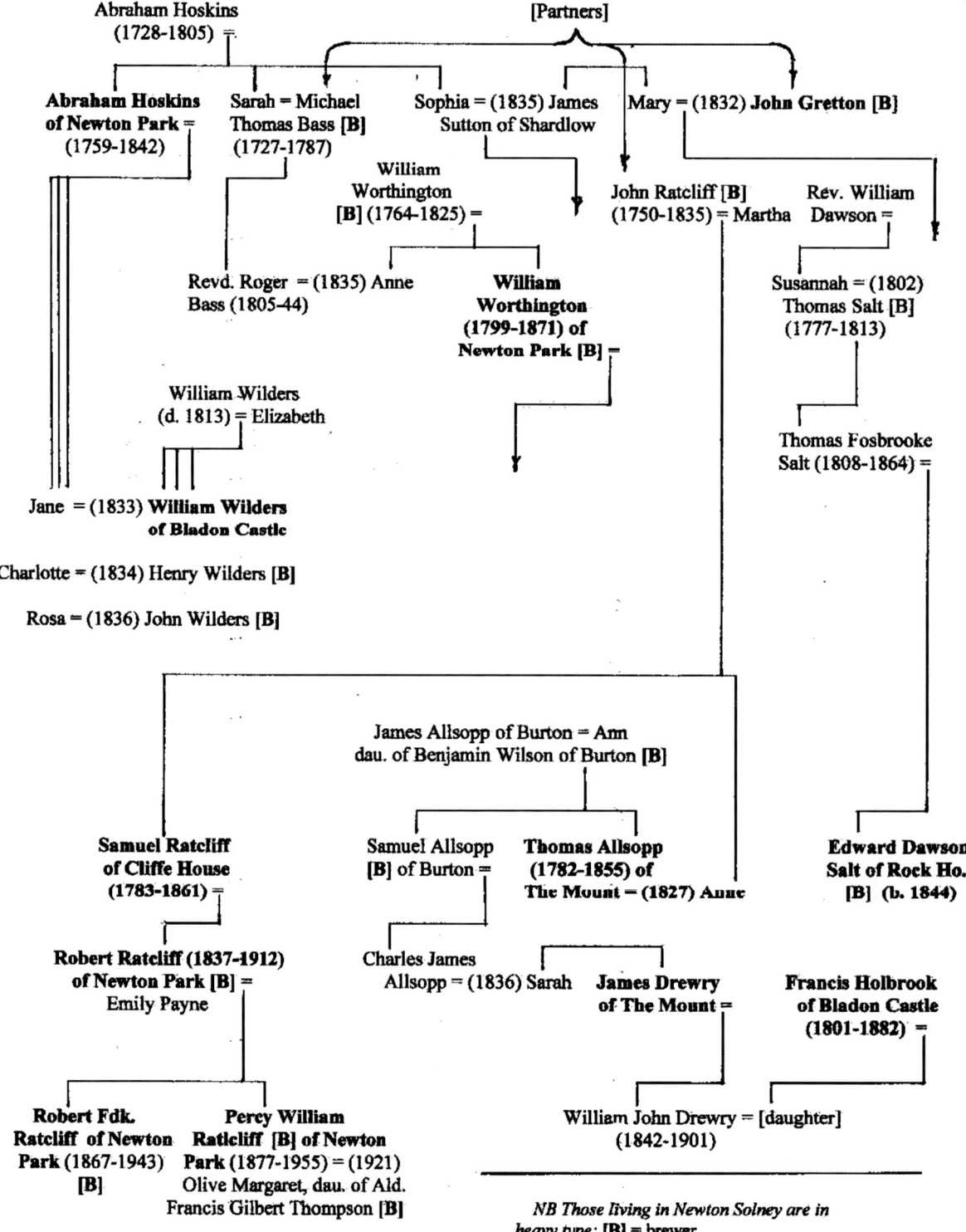

NB *Those living in Newton Solney are in heavy type;* [B] = brewer.

One problem which is not at all clear is exactly how much of the estate was leased to Worthington with the house, for Hoskins had left his model farm, house, pleasure grounds and landscape unusually closely integrated. The records of Lord Carnarvon at Highclere are unhelpful in this respect. The fact that the other houses on the estate were all re-let, suggests, however, that the Worthingtons had only the house and pleasure grounds. This would have been impossible, however, if the very generously sized farm had been suffered to remain where it was, contiguous to the south side of the house. There was, therefore, an imperative to remove it forthwith[6].

The likelihood therefore is that the Worthingtons did not move in until 1839, giving almost two years for the model farm to be moved, so that Newton Park house could have a normal southern aspect without the encumbrances of what was then state-of-the-art agriculture. The farm was thus re-positioned half a mile to the south, where it became Newton Park Farm with 150 acres of the estate. Unfortunately, the 1841 census is too unspecific about where people were actually living for us to be positive that this represents the correct timescale, but certainly by the time the 1850 tithe map was published (it had been surveyed somewhat earlier), the farm had been re-positioned, for Farm Lane appears on the map, although only one building does, but this is because most of the Newton Park estate was un-tithed, and was consequently omitted from the detail of the map, only salient features on it like roads being included on the un-tithed parts.

Newton Park farm house, south (formal) side, 2009.   [*M. Craven*]

Having moved it, a screen of planting was installed east-west to the south of the areas cleared by the removal of the farm, The Spinney, east of Home (Farm) Wood. A recent arboriculturalist's opinion is that what remains of this was probably planted "at least 150 years ago" rather than in the late 1870s. Certainly, too, the farm house at Newton Park Farm is well in the late-Georgian tradition. Indeed, it is an ingeniously contrived and compact multi-purpose dwelling, being at one and the same time farm bailiff's residence, working farmhouse and a shooting box for the occasional use of Lord Chesterfield. Legend has it that amongst several distinguished men, Disraeli attended shooting lunches there as a guest of Lord Carnarvon after 1871 (although he himself did not shoot); certainly their friendship is well attested and the Prime

Minister was a guest at Bretby on numerous occasions. The man who inherited the estate in 1871, Lord Carnarvon served as Colonial Secretary in Lord Derby's administrations of 1857-1859 and 1867-1868, in both of which Disraeli was Chancellor, and later served in the same capacity in Disraeli's second administration. As the 6th Lord Chesterfield's brother-in-law, Carnarvon was long a visitor to Bretby – and thus on occasion in the season to Newton Park Farm – long before he inherited the estate. The brick farm house (now painted) is of two storeys and attics still with traditional Georgian sashes with glazing bars and stone lintels and is a deceptively large and roomy house with two spacious rooms on the south side, a sitting room and dining parlour, for assembling before, and consuming the traditional shooting lunch. The family accommodation is more modest, and there are formal entrances on the farm yard side and also on the south side. There is also a spacious attic accommodation, large cellarage and a kitchen range attached to the west side.

Above: Newton Park Farm: 1838-1890   *Newton Park Farm after 1890*

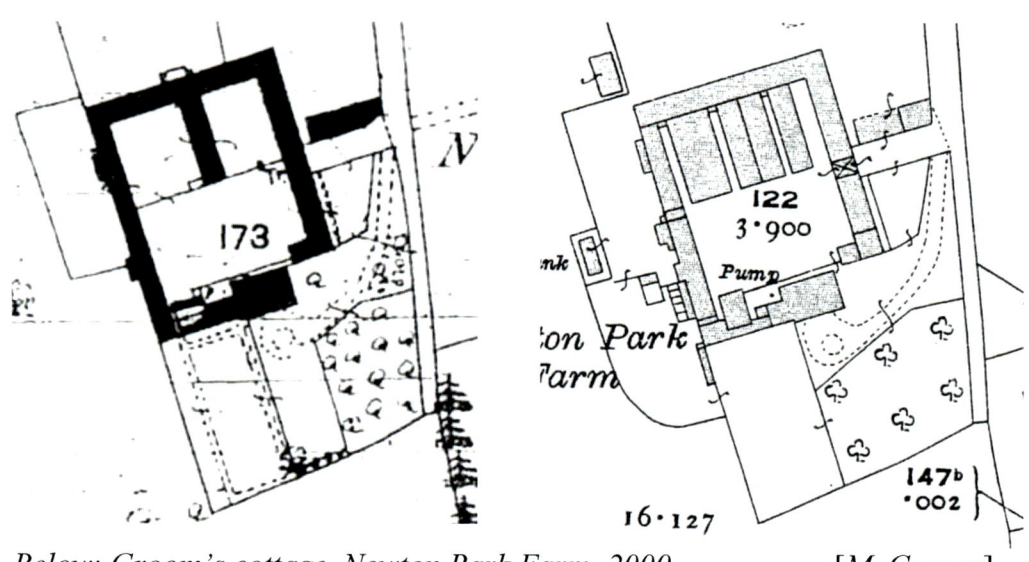

Below: Groom's cottage, Newton Park Farm, 2000.   *[M. Craven]*

118

There would seem to be little doubt that most of the double courtyard farm originally attached to Newton Park house was detached from the office court (which was re-arranged either side of the main house) moved and re-erected; the overall dimensions, when scaled off from maps match almost exactly. Unfortunately, major rebuilding of 1890 carried out to reflect changing practices in husbandry, has obscured the original layout, with only the east (stable) and south ranges of the original still standing and both somewhat rebuilt. Prior to 1890, when four parallel sheds were built across the northern part of the farm, this end consisted of the fold yard and rick yard divided by a single central N-S range of sheds. The rebuilding left the enlarged northern yard spacious enough to parade a company of troops. As first rebuilt, though, it must have still been very much in the mould of Bretby Home Farm of thirty years earlier and a great deal of earlier non-standard bricks remain in the fabric of the two surviving original ranges, the northern one retaining its original square tower topped with a pretty cupola supporting an iron weathervane. The attractive groom's cottage at the SE angle of the farmyard looks as if it is straight out of the pages of Farey's account of Bretby Home Farm (see above chapter IV). The work was probably carried out by the young architect Henry Isaac Stevens (1806-1873), later of Derby, a pupil and later son-in-law of William Martin (1756-1850), who designed the Bretby model farm but who would have been 82 in 1838! A stray reference to Stevens working at Newton Park can only be thus explained; nothing much appears to have been done to the mansion itself[7].

Keene view of re-positioned farm buildings north of The Spinney, c. 1879 [*B Appleby*]

Another group of buildings appear to have been built or re-positioned further round, north of The Spinney, between the mansion and Park Farm, but without a farmhouse, where they were photographed in c. 1879 by the younger Richard Keene (above); one suspects that they were specifically for sheep. Thus the Bretby estate was well served with state-of-the-art set piece farms, the new acquisition serving the 900 acres gained, most of which seems to have been turned into farmland, once the land west of the house had been de-parked. All that was left on the original site, once these fairly momentous changes had been completed, was a series of outbuildings essential to a country house: stable range, carriage house, tack-room, offices and storage.

All that was left on the site of the old model farm by the house in 1877/79 – a cart shed, crudely erected after 1837 against two surviving walls   [*Brian Appleby*]

The first manager of the re-positioned farm seems to have been the 66 year old John Dicken, who was an appointee of Hoskins' long before, but he died in November 1848, and by 1851 was succeeded as farm manager (and estate bailiff) by the picturesquely named Whitsed Laming. He appears to have been especially recruited from outside the area, for he was born in Spalding, Lincolnshire in January 1828, so would have been only 21 when he arrived in Newton. Being young, he probably came on the recommendation of a close friend or near relation of Lord Chesterfield's (or of his agent at Bretby). He was obviously the right choice, and he married a Caulton shortly after his arrival - Peter Caulton had been a tenant of Hoskins in 1836 – and proceeded to bring up a family consisting of a son, Samuel (named after Laming's father and grandfather) and two daughters, Mary and Elizabeth, all born by 1861[8].

With the south side of the mansion now unencumbered, the Worthingtons could take up residence. They seem, from later photographs, to have taken the opportunity to create a parterre on that side of the house, traces of which survived them. In truth there may have been little choice in this, as the former farmyard's gravel surface may well have been left in situ, and covered by a thin layer of soil. The family were obviously happy to allow the various features of the pleasure grounds to remain, and it was no doubt an idyllic environment in which the Worthington children could grow up, Frank and Albert Octavius joining the brood in the 1840s. The eldest son, William Henry – later first Mayor of Burton in 1878 and from 1880 until his death resident in another Richard Leaper-designed house, Derwent Bank at Derby – joined his father in the firm in 1848, but never married. Indeed, in the longer term, only the youngest son Albert married, rebuilding a house on the Pipe estate close to Lichfield – the original family of which we encountered in Chapter II - called Maple Hayes[9].

Fragments of Burton Abbey (L), and (R) in front of the arch of Burton Bridge
[*M. Craven*]   [*Brian Appleby*]

As tenants, the Worthingtons did make some alterations, though In 1863-64 the medieval crossing of the Trent at Burton was finally replaced and demolished after causing acute transportation problems for decades. Its departure was accompanied by much regret in some quarters, and William Worthington seems to have rescued several portions of the ancient structure, re-erecting one complete arch in the pleasure grounds, above the cascades, where it remains to this day. Not that this was William Worthington's first foray into architectural salvage, for there are also fragments of the former Burton Abbey gatehouse to be found scattered in Newton Park's pleasure grounds, too, all now listed grade II. These in all probability were rescued in 1852, when Robert Thornewill, son of the ironmaster Thomas, of Dovecliff, started rebuilding the residence fashioned out of the Abbey's Infirmary in the 16th century. He added a tower, tall chimneys, half-timbered gables and made other alterations and additions which Lord Anglesey's agent, in a letter, described as "fanciful", although his architect for these works has eluded identification. Seeing them today, one gets the impression that Worthington, once ensconced at Newton, was himself not untouched by the romantic notions that inspired Hoskins' landscape. Other architectural fragments were left, seemingly *ad hoc*. The family also acquired some small freeholds which came up for sale in the 1840s and '50s, which the family still held in 1872/73.[10]

The reason why the surviving photographs show most of the estate's buildings looking rather neglected, however, lies with the departure of the Worthingtons. William himself died on 17th October 1871. By this date, the eldest son was running the firm and living elsewhere and Calvert, Frank, Albert and their mother remained at Newton Park. All this seems to have changed, however, by the double tragedy of the death, a month after his father, of Calvert, followed by that of Frank, who drowned whilst on a fishing trip to Scotland on 3rd September 1872. Neither young man was married whereas 28-year old Albert Octavius had married eight months before his father's death and had departed to live at Maple Hayes. Thus by autumn 1872, Mrs. Worthington had nothing but her memories of having lost a husband and two sons within a year. A year later she left the house to go and reside at Craythorne Lodge, Stretton-on-Dove[11].

Almost simultaneously with these events, the landowner himself, Lord Chesterfield died. This was the 7th Earl, who in June 1866 had succeeded his father (who had bought the Newton Park estate), but who was struck down by typhoid along with the Prince of Wales whilst staying at Londesborough Lodge, Yorks., but who, unlike the Prince, succumbed a month after Calvert Worthington, on December 1st 1871. His successor in the earldom was a cousin, to whom the estate had not been entailed, for by his will dated May 6th that year, it passed to his nephew, Disraeli's friend, George Herbert, Lord Porchester, son and heir of his sister Evelyn and her husband, George, 4th Earl of Carnarvon, who was then well under age, having only been born in 1866. Lord Carnarvon, however, rather took to the estate and spent quite a bit of time there, but having lost his wife (an especial favourite of Dizzy's), he re-married on Boxing Day 1878 Elizabeth Howard, a kinswoman of the Duke of Norfolk. This impending further venture into matrimony seems to have occasioned a re-assessment of the Bretby estate's Newton holdings, possibly because the funds released by a sale were required to cope with the expense of the marriage. A local source (quoted by H. J. Wain) claims that the house at Newton Park had lain empty for eight years, and

Arms granted in 1879 to Albert Octavius Worthington

indeed, that seems close. Initially, the Bretby estate tried to let it, an advertisement to that effect appearing locally in 1874, but clearly there were no takers. Thus the house would appear to have lain empty from early in 1873 to 1878, for the sale of the estate (or most of it, for The Mount, more recently acquired [see Chapter IV] was retained for some decades) seems to have been decided upon, and seems to have taken place early in 1879. Richard Keene junior (1852-1899) was brought in to make his invaluable record, presumably in order to make up a suitable brochure to aid the sale, although no copy seems to have survived.[12]

The sale to Robert Ratcliff in 1879 was, unlike the start of the Worthington period, in that most of the estate Hoskins had sold to Lord Chesterfield now belonged to the Ratcliffs. Not only that, but they clearly intended to further consolidate the estate as far as they could, especially as the family had been in residence in the parish since 1860, when Samuel Ratcliff had completed his new residence there called Cliffe House.

Having decided that the main house was to be a seat, and, no doubt, from the evidence of the photographs, from the condition of the building, Ratcliff decided to reconstruct it entirely. In 1879, Robert Ratcliff's address was Stapenhill, and we may reasonably presume that this was because the house at Newton Park was then under reconstruction. Again, there appears to be no surviving paperwork to assist us in understanding this process, but it would seem reasonable to allow two years for the completion of the work – from purchase in 1879 to 1881. The architect of the work is not known unfortunately, although when Ratcliff's brother Richard decided to rebuild his seat at Stanford Hall, Nottinghamshire a decade later he used W. H. Fletcher, working in a similarly Classical idiom. However, unlike Richard, Ratcliff was still fully involved with the brewery as a director of Bass, and may have employed the prolific Reginald Churchill of Burton who had worked on their buildings in the town. On the other hand, Robert Grace, who designed Cliffe House for their father appears to have retired or died by this date[13].

The entrance front of Newton Park in 2009   *[M. Craven]*

The rebuilding consisted of adding a second pile to the house on the south side, but this time of two lofty storeys instead of two-and-a-half (as on the original other side), making for a series of awkward transitions in the levels upstairs. The roof was replaced with one hipped round a central light well which illuminated the new oak staircase, embellished with stained glass representations of the twelve months and four seasons, not to mention the Ratcliff armorial achievement. There are six irregularly spaced bays on the new south front but the sides have only two, paired centrally. The new build was also in brick and the building was re-stuccoed all over to disguise the junctions between old and new work, but this time devoid of the fanciful embellishments required by Leaper and presumably executed by Bernasconi. The effect is largely plain, although there are dressings of Keuper Sandstone: the fenestration has architrave surrounds and on the north (entrance) front, the tripartite windows - suffered to remain either side of a new, balustraded portico with coupled pillars supporting it – were given a mildly Neo-Grec finish. Otherwise, this front retains the slightly awkward proportions of the original, including the three bay breakfront (disguised by downpipes) but now without the blind arch above the portico. The cornice is bracketed, there is a first floor sill band and there are still quoins at the angles. A two storey wing was added to the east side, in matching style, of seven bays, the central one, much wider than the rest, being canted and raised to an attic capped by a pyramidal roof. A further service wing of two linked three bay blocks was built to the east again, but screened by planting. All the windows were renewed as plate glass sashes. The building was also wired throughout for electricity, being right in the van for domestic lighting at this time, the contractor being Crompton of Derby, the firm's proprietor George Crompton having carried out a similar scheme on his own house, Stanton Hall, Stanton-by-Dale[14].

Alterations to the surroundings of the house included replacing the Gothick Cottage with the present Museum Cottage, and the destruction of the Triumphal Arch, log hut, grotto and other features of Hoskins's landscape. The ponds and cascades were re-fashioned to form a single lake and a new, re-positioned, kitchen garden with a garden court was built just west of Museum Cottage, with a turret clock supplied by John Smith & Sons, Derby. The old summerhouse in the plantations, modelled on a moss hut, was dismantled and replaced with a neat brick-and-stone structure with Lombardic style mullioned windows, but attached to an older castellated range left over (but re-hashed) from Hoskins' days and clearly visible on the photograph of the original summerhouse.

Aerial view of the rebuilt house taken in 1956   [*John German*]

Further alterations and additions were made, probably after the death of Robert Ratcliff in 1912. These were executed entirely in stone and in Jacobethan style, consisting of a north facing room with a parapet projecting from the service wing between the canted bay and the main house and a similar, but two storey addition projecting to the south on the other side almost corresponding to the northerly projection and this time with cresting to the parapet. It may well have been at this time when a cast iron verandah was also added to the south side from the new addition to the SW angle, although this could have been a feature of the house from the main rebuilding. Like the main interiors, the spaces provided in these additions were fitted up with much polished timber and ornamental plasterwork to match (in some degree) the style of the new work. A fine conservatory by Messenger & Co. of Loughborough was also added on to the west side of the house, which survives[15].

Garden Court after conversion to residences, 2000　　　　　　　　[*C. Bond*]

Summerhouse as replaced in 1880-81, in 2000　　　　　　　　[*C. Bond*]

125

The Ratcliffs

John Ratcliff, who was born in 1759, had been a commercial traveller for Bass, and such was his success and obvious ability, that William Bass invited him to become a partner on a 25% share in 1797, which was renewed on a more favourable basis between him and the elder Michael Thomas Bass in 1830, and the two families were linked by mutual business interests from that time onwards for well over a century. By his marriage in 1780 to Martha Dawson, he eventually became uncle to Thomas Salt, another Burton brewer, although not part of the Bass Worthington empire. She died within five years of their marriage in childbirth in May 1785. He appears to have re-married six years later, to a farmer's daughter from Aston-on-Trent and by her had his daughter Ann, whose marriage in 1827 to Thomas Allsopp of The Mount brought an alliance with another, separate brewing dynasty.[16] By his first wife, John Ratcliff had two sons, James and Samuel, of whom the younger seems to have been most closely involved with the business, and who from 1860 lived in Newton Solney at Cliffe House. By then however, he was 77 and indeed died within a year of moving into his new house. He had married Sarah Tunley in Derby in 1813, whose sister Susannah later married Robert Grace, the man who would later be Samuel's architect. By her he had eight sons (five of whom survived to have families of their own) and three daughters between his marriage and 1837, when his youngest son, Robert was born. Robert it was who bought Newton Park in 1878.

Robert Ratcliff (1837-1912) [Brian Appleby]

.Arms granted to Robert Ratcliff executed in stained glass at Newton Park [Maxwell Craven]

Again, despite being a younger son, Robert was active in the brewing business being a director of Bass and by the 1870s was indulging in a bit of philanthropy, joining with his elder brother Richard in building Burton's first baths in 1872-73 and adding Turkish Baths a few years later. The architect was Reginald Churchill, which is why his possible involvement at Newton Park is particularly persuasive. By the time he

126

had had moved into Newton Park Ratcliff had been married for 14 years, his wife being Emily Payne (1836-1916). Emily provides a curious link, however, for her father, Thomas Payne, a maltster in High Street, Burton, had been born at Newton Solney in January 1803, son of the Peter Payne who farmed Hall Yard. They had three sons and two daughters, all born before the move to Newton. Richard, the middle son, died young, nor did either of their daughters, Emily and Laura ever marry, but both surviving sons succeeded to the estate in due course. He obtained a grant of arms. His time at Newton he spent improving the estate and gradually expanding it, buying up most of the rest of the Every family holdings (in 1871/72), the patronage of the church, but not the lordship of the manor, which remained with the Everys. His new-found landed status also encouraged him to apply for a grant of arms not long after he had bought Newton Park, the arms themselves being based on the historic coat and crest of the Radclyffes of Ordsall in Lancashire. He also extended the limitation on their use to the descendants of his grandfather and had the achievement blazoned in stained glass in the rebuilt house.[17]

Sir Henry Flower Every, 10th Bt., who sold the family's remaining holdings at Newton Solney and his wife, Isabella. [Sir Henry Every, Bt.]

Robert Ratcliff died in 1912, but he must have been one of those people who always feel they can leave making a will to later, for he died intestate despite being nearly 75, and his affairs took six months to sort out. Nevertheless, he left estate worth £968,413 – 13s – 8d making him virtually one of the super-rich by today's definitions. He was succeeded by his elder son Robert Frederick, who was born in April 1867 and was educated at Rossall and Jesus College, Cambridge. Apart from following his father into the firm, he was a keen officer in the TA rising by 1900 to become to become Lt. Col Commanding the 6th North Staffordshire Regiment, a post he held throughout the Great War, in which he was too old to be expected to fight on the front line.

Col. Ratcliff and two friends, c. 1930
[Brian Appleby]

Nevertheless, his leadership, encouragement and organisational skills got him appointed a Commander of the Order of St. Michael & St. George (CMG) in 1916 and the Volunteer Decoration (then somewhat rashly abbreviated VD) when he stepped down. He was also active in politics, being elected Liberal Unionist MP for Burton-upon-Trent in 1902, holding his seat until 1918. He was High Sheriff of Derbyshire in 1929 and was also elected to two London Clubs, the prestigious Brooks's and the more sedate Devonshire. It was whilst en route back from the former that he died unexpectedly in the foyer of the York Hotel (now the Aston Court) Derby, having just got off a train from London, early in 1943. He never married and in his will left the estate to his younger brother Percy. His estate was valued at £844,527 – 8s – 4d – about £120,000 less than his father's, probably due to the depredations of the great depression and the exigences of wartime. He had, however, acquired other estates, Clatford Mill, Upper Clatford, Hampshire, not far from Andover, Chittlehambolt, Devon, and Dundonell Lodge near Ullapool, Ross & Cromarty, now owned by Sir Tim Rice.[18].

Percy William Ratcliff was 66 when he inherited from his brother, having been born in 1877, also educated at Rossall, but thereafter he went up to Clare College, Cambridge rather than Jesus, like his brother. Again, he went on to become a director of the internationally known firm that bore his name, Bass, Ratcliff & Gretton. A less metropolitan minded man than his brother, he was far more wedded to country pursuits and was a leading member of the Flyfishers' Club. He married in 1921, his bride being Olive Margaret, daughter of Burton councillor (later alderman) Francis Gilbert Thompson, a member of the Thompson brewing family whose firm also eventually ended up in the Bass empire. The couple lived at Newton Park with the Colonel (sharing the same telephone line!) but never had children and he died on February 21st 1955 aged 77. We shall see how their regime affected life in the village later.[19]

Cliffe House

It has already been mentioned that Robert Ratcliff's father Samuel had come to live in Newton Solney, shortly before his death in 1861. He appears to have bought a plot of land called the Cliffs or The Cliffe lying against the border of Newton Parish but actually in Winshill, and sandwiched between the road and the Trent. The plot was one of those sold by Hoskins in 1836 and thus must have been thought by the Bretby estate too distant to fit in with their vision for the expansion of the Earl's holdings and sold on. Whether Ratcliff bought it soon after 1836 or somewhat later is not known. He also acquired, then or later, two adjacent fields, this time in Newton, called Far

Under- wood and Bank amounting to 11 acres in all. By 1857-58 Samuel had resolved to build himself a new house in this impressive site, with hanging woods on Bladon Hill behind and the Trent in front, to the north west. He commissioned his brother-in-law Robert Grace of Burton to design it, and T. Lowe and Sons were the

Samuel Ratcliff of Cliffe House in 1848

contractors who were engaged to build it, using a labour force on site of 170 men. The family moved in during February 1860 and a commissioning party held on 3rd March following.[20] The house itself was of brick with Keuper Sandstone dressings, built in Neo-Jacobean style with the long fronts facing east-west, and the shorter gable-ended, front facing the river. The entrance was on the west side and the garden was terraced down to the Trent where there was a boat-house. A stable block and other outdoor offices lay between the drive and the main road, and mostly survive today, converted into residences.

Cliffe House in 1929   [*John German*]

The two parallel ranges were of seven by three bays, the long entrance front having two square projecting bays each topped with a straight coped gable, that on the left of the entrance (which was via a Gothic portico rather like that at Repton Park) being the wider, with a full height canted bay topped by a crenellated parapet as its centrepiece.

The two gables facing the river also sported similar canted bays, although all the remaining fenestration was of rectangular plate glass sashes. The roofline was embellished by the prominent finials atop the gables and a forest of paired and triple moulded brick stacks. The roof was steeply pitched and tiled. Inside, there was a fine square entrance hall with a well staircase in Hoptonwood stone with a particularly graceful cast iron balustrade, cast at Burton by Thornewill's. The reception rooms were, as one might expect, panelled to excess and the fireplaces were mainly in French taste. The plasterwork was surprisingly restrained[21].

Sam Ratcliff died just over a year after he had moved in, but it remained the residence of his sixth son Richard for some years before he moved to Orgreave Hall on the SW side of Burton, to be replaced by the fifth brother, the bachelor Frederic, who in 1873 held 8 acres 1 rod 36 perches in Newton whilst Robert, then still of Stapenhill, held 70 acres 3 rods 13 perches – this five years before he bought the Newton Park estate from Lord Carnarvon. Frederic died at Cliffe House in the 1880s, leaving his two surviving unmarried sisters, the Misses Sarah and Emma Ratcliff in residence. After the Great War, both ladies moved out to eke out their dotage in more congenial surroundings, and it was let and later sold to Percy Kent Le May, the head brewer at Bass. He moved out in May 1929 when it was placed on the market. Unfortunately, it attracted little interest and was sold to a contractor who pulled it down for the value of the materials in 1930. The site is still vacant, but the outbuildings remain, converted into dwellings[22].

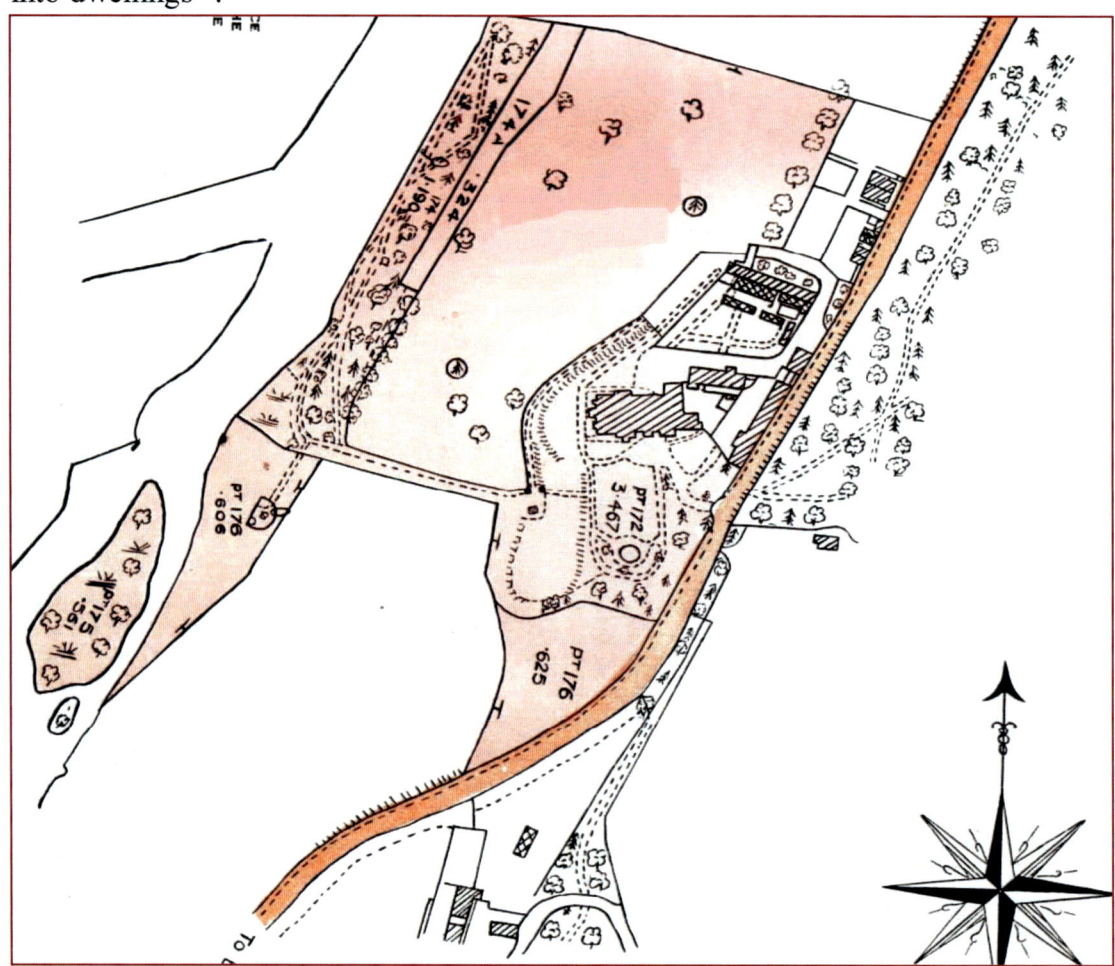

Map of Cliffe House of 1929, re-oriented for clarity with north at the top.

130

Bladon-in-Winshill.

The fact that Cliffe House lay on a plot that was partly in Winshill and beneath Bladon Hill is excuse enough to turn our attention back to that enigmatic eminence. The focus lies in the increasing desire of central government to "tidy up" boundaries, a process which in the end got out of hand and led to the deleterious and unsettling changes of 1974 under the Local Government Reform Act. Thus in 1884, a detached part of the parish of Bretby had been transferred to Newton Solney under Local Government Board Order. A decade later, however, most of Winshill and Stapenhill were transferred to Staffordshire, becoming part of the new Borough of Burton-upon-Trent, of which William Worthington's eldest son, W. H. Worthington, became first mayor. However, the "rural portion of the parish" (of Winshill) was added to Newton Solney – effectively this meant the Bladon House estate, 204 acres of Bend Oak Farm and 13 acres along the Dale Brook but also including land between Newton Road and the river, The Cliffs (Cliffe House). The Bend Oak farmhouse stood in the 1860s on the corner of Hawfield Lane and Borough Road, Winshill. Hawfield Lane runs eastwards from there before turning south to rise up to Common Farm, situated just in Bretby.[23]

Winshill appears in Wulfic Spot's will and means 'the hill of Wyne', a good Anglo-Saxon name. As part of the foundation grant of Burton Abbey it appears in Domesday Book and later became a tithing of the Abbey under the Winshill family, the Abbey's tenants there, for three centuries. At the Dissolution it was part of the Abbey holdings granted to Sir William Paget, and his family was its proprietors for the next three centuries. Of the three open fields, that lying to the east, adjacent to Newton Solney, was called Bladon Field, as was its counterpart over the parish boundary. Unlike Newton, the parish was subject of an Inclosure act in 1771, the award following in 1773, the 50 acres of open land remaining in Bladon Field going to Lord Paget[24]

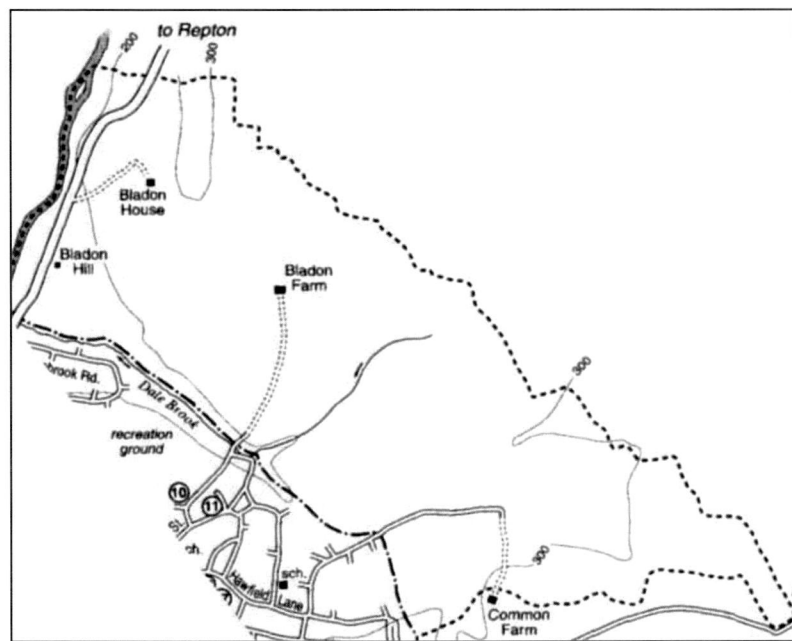

The section of the parish acquired from Winshill in 1894, adapted from VCH Staffs. IX (2003) 197.

The development of the Mills by the river and of Burton generally led ultimately to the break up of the Paget holdings in the parish, and by the 1830s there were a number of freeholds in the portion later transferred to Newton. By 1827 a house called Bladon Hill, was in existence. A dwelling marked on the modern OS map with this name close to the road from Winshill to Repton is presumably part of the outbuildings of it.

The former stable block and Nos. 1 & 2 Bladon Cottages seem to be the remnants and are grade II listed. Who built it seems to have evaded research, but in 1829 a "respectable" school was set up there by a married woman called Clara Bailey. There were 12 pupils in 1833 and 19 in 1841. It was run by Clara's daughters Emma and Maria until at least 1857 when it was listed as a boarding school. Its closure between that date and 1861 would seem to be directly linked to other developments nearby. When the house itself was demolished and what exactly it was like remain unclear.[25]

Bladon Cottage & Bladon House

In March 1836 one Charles Perks died aged 29 in Winshill, at his house called Bladon Cottage. He was the son of Charles Perks, timber merchant of Burton, who lived at Sinai Park from 1818 to his death in 1847, by Anne Edensor, of an ancient family from Tissington, whose sister had married into the brewing family of Charles Hill. Their firm, Charles Perks & Sons, continued until 1913. Interestingly, Edward Perks of The Villa (The Cedars) in the mid-19th century (see Chapter IV) was Charles Perks junior's younger brother[26].

Because Charles of Bladon Cottage left three daughters only, the house and its land were sold. The house, of which no picture has so far surfaced, was probably a later Regency villa erected on the non-Hoskins side of Bladon Hill. probably not so very many years prior to Perks's death; he may well have been its first resident, for there appear to be no earlier references to it. The purchaser was, surprisingly, Capt. Francis Hoskins, eldest son of the second marriage of Abraham, late of Newton Park. Born in 1807, he had been educated at Repton, held a commission in the Staffordshire Volunteers and, living in Birmingham, had at this stage just married a widow called Julia Brooks from Portsmouth. It would have been at Bladon Cottage that their children George Gordon, Walter Hamlet and one other would have been born and brought up. The eldest son, George (1837-1911) settled at Harewood Grove, Yorkshire and became a notable architect in the north east, having been a pupil of W. D. Haskoll of Westminster. He specialised in public buildings after his move north in 1864 and his Associateship of the RIBA in 1867 was proposed by no less a pair of architectural luminaries than P. C. Hardwick and Alfred Waterhouse. He associated himself in practice with his brother Walter, and the youngest brother worked for them as a decorator after the manner of J. G. Crace. George Hoskins married twice and left two architect sons to follow him into practice. One of the reasons he went north in 1864 to set up, initially at Darlington, was the death of his father in 1859, at which juncture, the house was sold. The purchaser was yet another brewer, John Gretton, who also acquired an adjoining piece of land, Haw Field, bordering Hawfield Lane which linked Winshill with Common Farm.[27]

John Gretton was born in 1793, elder son of Thomas Gretton and his wife Sarah Bath. He already had a connection with Newton Solney, as his grandfather – another Thomas - had married Sarah, daughter of Thomas Powis, recorded in 1758 as one of the Every tenants there, with a smallholding of just over 15 acres, a remarkable parallel with Robert Ratcliff's wife, Emily Payne. Thomas Gretton's brother Richard had also married a Powis from Rolleston-on-Dove, a first cousin of Thomas's wife. He seems to have started off as a master-brewer but also became an accountant, for he was working as a book-keeper for Bass in 1834, the year before he joined the partnership, being assigned an eighth share of the profits of the Company, a sixteenth less than Samuel Ratcliff. His responsibility lay with the processes of malting and brewing. Henceforth the firm became Bass, Ratcliff and Gretton, an order of nomenclature which accurately reflected their relative financial involvement in the company.

It would appear that in 1859 he bought Bladon Cottage from Hoskins's heirs – presumably George Gordon – realising that the well drained and gently west-facing slopes of Bladon Hill was an ideal setting for a new permanent country home for his family. Clearly, though, Bladon Cottage itself was insufficiently large or convenient enough for this newly enriched brewer, and what appears from the evidence on the ground, a new start was made. He was also involved with the Trent navigation, although it had by his time lost its pre-eminence to the canal (and was soon to lose out completely to the railways), which means that he would have been acquainted with Hoskins, as well as the Sutton family of Shardlow, who were running boats on both. Indeed, in July 1832 he married Mary, sister of James Sutton of Shardlow who, within three years, himself had married Hoskins' daughter Sophia. Thus, by 1835, not only was Gretton a partner of Bass, but he was also related to them, the Hoskins and the Worthingtons by marriage. Indeed, by the mid-19th century, there had been a whole network of inter-related brewing families living in Newton Solney: Worthingtons, Ratcliffs, Salts, Wilders and Allsopps, with connections to the Bass and Dawson brewing families (see Figure III above)[28].

Gretton's new house, started in or just after 1860 and complete by 1868, was of fine quality ashlar and in institutional classical style; set in a high street, it would pass very well for a fairly opulent bank. Built on a high plinth and of two storeys, the west (entrance) front has seven bays, the central one breaking slightly forward under a stone tablet which interrupts the parapet, set between a pair of capped pillars looking

Bladon House, W. front as it is today   [*Bladon House School*]

like miniature gateposts. Below, a tetrastyle Doric portico supporting a balustrade topped with four equatored stone globes rising from a wide flight of steps which were once guarded by a pair of impressive lions couchant in the manner of Sir Edwin Landseer's in Trafalgar Square. It would be instructive to know what happened to them[29].

Bladon House, E (garden) front in c. 1900   [*M. Craven*]

The garden front is in a sense more interesting. Here there are three wide central bays, slightly recessed with tripartite windows on both floors flanking the pedimented entrance with a simple sash window above it. The ground floor tripartite windows are Doric and sport sarcophagus tops, very similar to those on the entrance front of Newton Park, which might suggest that Gretton's architect was Churchill again, if indeed Churchill was responsible for the Ratcliff's house. The other possible architect is Edwin Holmes of Birmingham, who built the new church of St. Mark, Winshill at Gretton's expense in 1868-69. The house's end bays are wide and have *lesnes*, or rust-

Bladon House: the hall and staircase   [*Bladon House School*]

icated pilasters at the angles, like the extremities of the west front. There is a sill band and plat band right round between the floors which, because of the widely spaced

134

bays on the east front, makes this side of the house look oddly low under its balustraded parapet. There was a segmentally vaulted iron and glass conservatory at the south end of this front which may have been original; it was certainly in place by 1900. The interior boasts well-proportioned rooms, restrained plasterwork and formerly with classical marble fireplaces. The entrance leads into a wide blind arcaded through hall terminating in an imperial staircase with a cast iron balustrade, making the layout of the east side of the house slightly eccentric with the garden reachable only via a short lateral corridor. No doubt, however, it suited the Grettons well enough.[30]

When John Gretton died, it passed to his son, another John, but in 1894 he acquired the mansion at Stapleford Park, Leicestershire, leaving his unmarried daughters Alice, Christine Rose and Muriel Elise in residence, where they remained until their deaths. When he died in 1899, he left it to his second son, Maj. Hugh Frederick Gretton, then renting Donington Park, in Leicestershire, but he died unmarried in 1928, when the property reverted to his elder brother, John Gretton III, who in 1944 was created 1st Lord Gretton of Stapleford, Leicestershire.

Lord Gretton, elevated to the 'beerage' in the 1944 New Year Honours, had served as MP for South Derbyshire 1895-1906, then for Rutland 1907-13 and finally for Burton from 1918 to 1943. His break in Parliament coincided with his service in the Great War, which he ended as a Colonel and received the CBE the following year. After the war, he gave the house with its 23 acres of pleasure ground and park to the Burton Infirmary to be a convalescent home, but what with impending nationalisation of medical provision, the scheme foundered. Consequently it was disposed of in 1947 on favourable terms to the Staffordshire Yeomanry as their HQ following which it took the name of Yeomanry House. In 1968 it was acquired as a special school, reverting to its original name and in 1976 the Honormead Group of such schools was founded there by Brenda Brook. Honormead became part of the SENAD Group for educating autistic children, a role it still fulfils today.[31]

John, later 1st Lord Gretton, 1900 *Frederic Gretton, 1900*

With Newton Park in the hands of as prominent a brewing family and the centre of an improving landed estate, and Bladon House built by an allied family as their country retreat, things were much changed since Hoskins' day. Furthermore, the village itself was affected by the influx of a brewery-based wealthy elite, which boosted its economy and, imperceptibly at first, led to changes and improvements. The time has come now to look at those changes and how they paved the way for the village we know today.

*

1 Kettle, BLG (1937) 964

2 Holbrook deeds, local collection; Ellis (1997) 5; wartime, Pounds (2000) 17-18.

3 Sir John Parsons served in 1703; Nunsfield, deeds, Derby City Council; Holbrook family, deeds & MIs in Repton churchyard, PRs, Bolland (1957) *passim.*, & Derby City Council deeds; Sale particulars, John German, 17/7/1972

4 Worthington family, BLG III (1972) 978; in residence, Register of Electors, 1839/40; chart: note Thomas Saunders, 30 with wife Mary & son Thomas Francis (2) ale & porter brewery living in Newton (and in 1839 when child bp), brewery in Horninglow Street 1837 (VCH 68) but previously cheesefactor, High St. (White (1834) 321

5 Worthington & Evans breweries, VCH IX (2003) 66-67, 71

6 I am grateful to Jennifer Thorp, Lord Carnarvon's archivist at Highclere for her assistance in looking for Newton Solney references.

7 Tithe map, courtesy DRO; Stevens & Martin, Askey (1994) 6-7, 9, cf. Colvin (2008) 680-681.

8 Dicken, census, but not named on the 1836 sale particulars, being an employee as farm manager, not a tenant; his MI in on the west side of the church porch; Laming family: there were two other sons, John Caulton and John Henry, born in 1857 and 1860 but both of whom died within a year. Laming's grandfather had married at Thorney Cambs., in April 1800, the father being born at Spalding in September 1805 (PRs, Spalding and Newton Solney)

9 Derwent Bank, Craven (1987) 107; Maple Hayes, Pevsner (1974) 201

10 Burton bridge, VCH *Staffs.* IX (2003) 26; freeholds, DLSL Derbyshire holders of Land, 1873 & 1872 electoral register; Abbey house, Burton, VCH, *op. cit.,* 53; letter from agent (Landor), Staffordshire Archives D603/K/26/32 of 5/4/1852

11 W. H. Worthington died unmarried in July 1894 three months after his mother, leaving Albert in charge of the brewery, which was taken over by Bass in 1927 shortly after his death (VCH *Staffs.*, IX (2003) 71); Calvert, MI in window, Newton church

12 Lords Chesterfield, CP III. 186, & Carnarvon *ibid.* 48 & XIV 150; Wain (1976) V; letting advert, *Burton Chronicle* 5/2/1874; grant of arms, Craven (1991) 181

13 Stanford Hall, Higginbotham (1987) 57; Churchill (1843-1903), VCH *Staffs.* IX (2003) 41 & n. 4, 42, 95, 127,1456, 151-152, 154; Grace was born in Stafford in 1794 (PR) so was probably dead

14 Stanton, Craven & Stanley (2001) II. 308-309

15 Conservatory, Messenger & Co., *Catalogue*, list of clients, Leicester Museums

16 Ratcliff family, Fox-Davies (1929) II 1622

17 Burton baths, *Staffordshire Advertiser,* 15/5/1875; arms, FD (1910) 1344-45; manor, the directories mainly unite to make him lord of Newton, but the family never exercised any manorial rights prior to their abolition in the 1920s, nor is there trace of it in the sales of 1956 and 1971, and the likelihood is that it remained with the Everys.

18 Robert's will, administration was granted to his elder surviving son 3/2/1913; The VD is now styled Volunteer Reserve Decoration (VRD); Robert Frederick, Kelly (1939) 1527; will proved 29/5/1943; estates, Pounds (2000) 42.

19 Percy's will was proved 5/5/1955, estate valued at £1,079,894 – 8s – 4d; on his career (and sharing the house), Kelly, *Handbook* (1939) 1527; F. G. Thompson was councillor 1926-1949 and alderman from 1949 to 1958; Mrs. Ratcliff's will was pr. 26/5/1971 when her estate was valued at £915,321. Mrs. Ratlcliff was from 1956 of The Cedars, Newton Solney, and d. 11/5/1971 (see below)

20 Cliffs, plot 50 of 2 acres & 3 rods in Winshill, in the auction catalogue of 1836; Far Underwood and Bank amounted to 8 acres 1 rod and 36 perches

21 John German, Sale particulars, 1930, private collection

22 Land-holdings, DLSL *Register of Holders of Land in Derbyshire* 1873; Harrod (1864); Kelley (1891, 1904/1912 – in the latter year only one maiden aunt remained, 85 year-old Emma); 1871/1881 Census

23 Bretby transfer, Kelly (1912) 358; Winshill, Winshill Division, Derby and Stafford (Burton-upon-Trent) Confirmation Order 1894, Local Government Board Order 31969, PRO RG 9/1967

24 Name, Cameron (1959) III 669; Bladon Field, recorded 1597, Staffs. RO D (W) 1734/2/1/104 & D603/A/ADD/1135, 1028; Inclosure, Inclosure Award Stapenhill & Winshill 1773, Staffs. RO D5646

25 School, White (1834) 326, While (1857) 346 & VCH Staffs. IX (2003) 206; Census 1851, 1861

26 Perks, VCH *Staffs.* IX (2003) 169; Perks' death, *Staffs. Advertiser* 26/3/1836 p. 3 (another son of Charles, senior, William, died at Sinai Park 1848, Staffs. RO D4219/1/30 pp. 570/575/652; Perks & Co. VCH, *op. cit.* 81; Perks junior & heiresses, DRO S239 M/T 316 (1835) & 318 (1837)

27 Hoskins, Bolland (1957), RIBA Register & PRs; sale to Gretton, VCH *op. cit.* 200; Haw Field,

137

    Staffs. RO 5081/3/115-124

[28] Gretton was baptised 9/6/1793, his father married 18/8/1790, having been baptised 30/8/1765; his grandfather Thomas, married Sarah Powis at Burton 24/10/1764 (PRs, Burton St. Modwen); book -keeper, White (1834) 321; Bass partnership, VCH *Staffs.*, IX (2003) 68

[29] House complete, *Staffs. Advertiser* 4/1/1868

[30] Winshill church, Pevsner (1974) 88

[31] Death of John II, *Staffs. Advertiser*, 7/10/1899, p.5 & 16/12/1899, p. 8; Infirmary gift, *Burton Observer* 9/8/1945, p. 1; Staffs. RO D5434/9; Yeomanry House, ex inf. Sir Charles Wolseley, Bt.; foundation of school, plaque in hall.

VI

SHAPING MODERN NEWTON

Newton Solney village & farms

The village at the time of the Hoskins sale in 1837 had been improved where Hoskins had had control of it, but remained much as it always had been otherwise, the crofts, cottages and workshops being scattered along Main Street, with a number of farms in between. Chief amongst these were Trent Farm, on the north side of the village street and Grange Farm almost opposite. Waterside Farm, as its name suggests, was situated between Trent Farm and the Trent itself with Hollies Farm still almost integral with the core of the village, being slightly nearer Trent Lane, a little way down Blacksmith's Lane. Brickyard Farm, still in Every ownership in 1836 was also essentially attached to the village a little way up Newton Lane, and was the centre of the brickyard, being run in parallel as a smallholding by the Hopkinses and then the Marbrows who acquired the freehold probably in the 1840s, when the present elegant farmhouse was erected. It was only turned entirely over to agriculture after 1891-92, when the brick-making became un-economic and stopped. It was then re-christened Newton Hill Farm and is now known as Hill Farm, although it is no longer a farmhouse as such. Between 1908 and 1912 the Marbrows ceased farming there and it was acquired by the Ratcliff estate, which installed Joseph Watson Smith there. He was succeeded in about 1922 by Joseph Bailey who was still tenant when it was sold in 1956, when he was farming 171.24 acres[1].

Sometime in the eighteenth century the strip fields of the village were rationalised into discrete blocks of arable by the Every family, probably just prior to the 1758 survey which itself was probably the result of an agricultural consolidation that had the effect of an inclosure without actually having to go through the expensive official Parliamentary process. This re-organisation was almost certainly the result of the succession of the 7th baronet, Revd. Sir John Every, in 1755; the timing certainly seems instructive. These blocks of land were tied to houses in the village as viable agricultural units which in turn allowed the Every estate to let in a much more rational and cost-efficient way. This process was one that Hoskins also used to create his 200-plus acre model farm, and which one or two of the larger post-1799 sale freeholders undertook too.

Two outlying farms created in this way were Dale and Newton Lane Farms, both situated on the thoroughfare from which the latter took its name. The former stands in what was referred to as Dalefields in a charter of 1670, the land so named because the fields ran down to the brook in 'the Dale', which acted as the parish boundary with Repton, although some 300 acres of Newton tenants' holdings then overlapped Repton Parish in various places. Thus, probably in the early 19th century, Dale Farm had come into being as a separate entity and acquired its farmhouse. This is a two storey, three bay affair with superimposed tripartite windows on its north west, main, front either side of a narrower central bay which includes the pedimented doorcase, all very much like a scaled down version of The Villa (The Cedars) but without the deep eaves. This might lead us to suspect that, like The Mount and Poplars Farm (see Chapter IV), it was at one stage part of the Hoskins empire.

Dale Farm, from Newton Lane, November 2008   [*M. Craven*]

The tenant in the 1890s was one Frederick Brooks, who was almost certainly a close kinsman (probably brother) of the James Brooks who was put into Newton Park Farm by the Ratcliffs. We may be sure that, even if it had been sold off by Hoskins between 1829 and 1836, it was back as part of the Newton Park estate by the 1890s. It does not appear to have been included in the sale of 1956 when the Newton Park estate was largely broken up, despite the Smiths and the Jeffords being tenants. Alan Jefford, who ran it in the 1950s with his brothers Tom and Arthur, had a prize winning herd of Friesians, one cow of which set the world milk production record for British Friesians. Indeed, it was eventually sold in 1980, and it still continues as a working farm.[2]

Newton Lane Farm was occasionally known, as was the lane outside, as Bretby Lane Farm and indeed the latter name appears to have been current in 1836 and its immediate surroundings were referred to as Bradby [*sic*] Lane Close a decade later when it appears on the tithe map. The farm seems to have been the creation of Thomas Higgott, an incomer to the village, having been born in Sandiacre in 1781, son of William & Mary Higgott. In January1802 he married Ann Stretton at Newton Solney, and this event may have brought him into the village, although from where he got the money to invest in land in the parish is not clear. He had an elder brother, too, called John, who in 1798 had married Sarah, the daughter and heiress of Aaron Thorpe, an Every tenant holding 63 acres in 1758 who also might have been able to buy his holding at the sale in 1799. This John Higgott, seems to have died by about 1829, so possibly Thomas was the beneficiary of an accumulation of family wealth. He was certainly a freeholder as early as 1811, and the family holdings increased after that date, too. He had a daughter and three sons, of whom one, Thomas, seems to have died young, and the eldest, Samuel, died unmarried before 1860. The third son, John (born 1809), eventually inherited, building his estate up by 1873 to an astonishing 491 acres – slightly more than Lord Carnarvon! This was achieved by buying up much of the remainder of the Every's holdings in the parish, which occurred in about 1870[3].

Higgott's Almshouses, Main Street, 2009.

It was this same John Higgott who, being childless, bequeathed a sum of money to build almshouses in the village in 1876. These were founded for "The poor and deserving of not less than fifty years of age, who were of good character and cleanly habits" of the parish. Preference was to be given to aged agricultural labourers or their widows who had lived in Repton or Newton Solney for at least ten years or more. Those selected by the trustees received 6/- [30p] per week each from them. The row of four almshouses was built of polychrome brick, of a single storey, with lancet doors and windows, each house having a room - one larger than the other – either side of the entrance. A plaque commemorating the donation was mounted centrally. Unusually, the charity was set up before Higgott's death, for he lived on at the farm until after 1881. Afterwards, his holdings were sold, and almost all purchased from his executors by the Ratcliffs, representing the largest single increase in their estate. They installed William Spooner as tenant, but by 1923 he had been succeeded by George Falder, whose family still live in the village[4].

In the village, Trent Farm was run by the Morley family in succession to the Paynes, whom we last encountered renting part of the former demesne of the lost manor house. The Morleys came from Egginton, as was so often the case after the two parishes had become one estate in the later middle ages, William Morley having been born there in 1784. He was living in the village by 1827 with his wife Mary and sons William and Robert, and they were freeholders by 1846 and by 1873 the younger William was the owner of 55 acres (with his mother holding a further 11) and was renting another 20 from another freeholder. By 1895, William had retired to a new house nearby called Trent Villa (now Trent Cottage) and his farm had, once again, been sold to the Ratcliffs, who installed the Upton family there as tenants. Oliver Upton farmed there at least until the Second World War. By the time it was sold with much of the rest of the Newton Park estate in 1956, it was still 78.5 acres of dairy farm, with S. G. Holdcroft as tenant. Subsequently, the new owners demolished the old farm house and replaced it, but suffered the fine statutory listed (grade II) 18th century barn to remain, where it still graces the main road[5].

141

Oliver and Eliza Upton and child, c. 1906   *[From WI (2000) 8]*

.

Opposite was Grange Farm, again with a post-Ratcliff era replaced farm house. In an earlier chapter we saw how this had been granted to Repton Priory by a Medieval lord of the manor, only to end up in the hands of speculators after the Dissolution of the Monasteries in 1536-39. Despite the implication of house names suffixed 'Grange' the homestead is unlikely to have been an important building. Later it was owned by the Holmes family, of which William Holmes had been a benefactor to the village poor in 1703. His grandson John Holmes (who died in 1773) was farming 121 acres freehold there in 1758 and it was his grandson, another William (born 1766) who still had it in the period 1827 to 1841, when he was 75. He retired shortly afterwards, and Charles Hellaby from Scropton was tenant there in 1846. Inevitably it was bought up by the Ratcliffs in the 1880s, who provided fine new farm buildings, with a barn parallel to the main road.

Trent Farm, 2008, with alleged WW2 blockhouse, surviving, right   *[M. Craven]*

Their tenant was A. Hellaby c. 1898 – presumably a relative of the former tenant – then John Bromley during the Edwardian period and between the wars, Charles Upton. When the Newton Park estate was sold up it was in the hands of J. S. Musson who farmed almost 124 acres, barely more than two centuries earlier. Again, after the sale, the farmhouse was demolished and replaced by a 1950s building which, no doubt, was considerably more convenient.[6]

Grange farmyard, 2008 [*M. Craven*]

A large late-Victorian house immediately to the east of the farm, in brick with faux-timber-framed gables, called The Grange, was built for Robert Ratcliff, probably intended for his wife Emily after his death. After all, her father's family had once farmed Trent Farm, opposite! In the event, once built it was let, at first to Burton coal merchant Reginald Blake Barratt, who in 1894 was elected Newton's first district

The Grange, built prior to 1894, as modernised, in 2008. [*M. Craven*]

councillor and also served on the parish council. He moved away in due course and was followed by John Bromley. However, sometime after 1912, it seems to have become the farm house for Grange Farm, which suggests that the original farm house had never been replaced once the Ratcliffs had acquired the freehold and had become too inconvenient to attract the right calibre of tenant. As we have seen, however, after the Second World War, a new farmhouse was built to the west of the farmyard on a close that had been previously used for communal out-door events and the Grange was once again let as a substantial residence, initially to J. Else from September 1951, and it was offered for sale when the estate was broken up in 1956, but it was withdrawn, probably having been sold prior to the auction. It has subsequently been extensively modernised[7].

Another farm was Poplars, well out along Repton Road, which we have discussed earlier as a possible Hoskins property sold off before 1836. This was probably a Dicken family farm. Two brothers farmed 74 and 77 acres in 1758, and these two holdings were probably amalgamated after the beginning of the 19th century, presumably by Hoskins, who surely had the house built. This would have created a farm of 151 acres which that enthusiast for good husbandry would surely have thought more appropriate. The Dickens remained as tenants throughout most of the 19th century, but by the 1890s it was tenanted under the Ratcliffs by Thomas Docksey, senior[8].

The Poplars Farm seen in autumn 2008   [*M. Craven*]

Two other farms lay on the north side of the road, Waterside farm and Hollies Farm. Hollies never seems to have been particularly large and it may well be that the near-50 acre freehold held by John Rennison as tenant (and, as we have seen, formerly as a freeholder) in 1758 may equate to that, although the old farm house to the west of Newton Park house has also been suggested as their holding. Alternately, the farm may have been created by the Everys by the re-positioning of the farmyard which clearly existed in the remains of the manor house when that was cleared away to create Rock House in the 1780s, but Derrick Pounds claims that it was the Wheatsheaf beer house originally. In either case it seems to have been the farm held by the Eaton family from the second decade of the 19th century to about 1878; they bred and dealt in cattle. After 1881 it, too, appears to have been bought up by the Ratcliffs, for thereafter we find Anne and Mary Eaton living at Rose Cottage nearby in the 1890s and 1890s, making a living as cow-keepers, in which they appear to have been succeeded by John and Fanny Eaton in the Edwardian period. Thereafter it seems to have been the farm of Henry Ball and then from the Great War, of George Marsh, succeeded by Harold Upton. Unfortunately, after the Ratcliff sales following Percy Ratcliff's death in 1955, the farm was acquired by a property developer, demolished and only a modest housing development remains in Hollies Close to remind us of its presence[9].

Hollies Close in 2008: a development on the site of Hollies Farm.   [*M. Craven*]

Waterside Farm was not much larger than Hollies. It was served by a good double pile twin gabled (but originally L-plan) brick house, which still exists, now somewhat buried within the Blacksmith's Lane housing development of the 1960s. It is the only Every period farmhouse to survive in the village largely un-rebuilt and there are one or two beams incorporated clearly from a predecessor. In 1758 it was held by John Smedley (1693-1780), a member of an old local family, who ran it with 46 acres of freehold which he had inherited and which had been acquired by his forebear, another John, who bought it from Ralph son of William Walton of Egginton in 1647. The farm was slightly hemmed in by a considerable group of strip holdings remaining from Medieval days to the immediate NE of the farm, and by the fields bordering the road to Repton to the south but they ran right up to the boundary with that parish. It was probably in John's time that the farmhouse was erected. In 1841 the farm was held by his 25-year-old great-great-grandson, Thomas but, within about five years, the tenancy had passed to his brother Edward who appears to have made extensive alterations, enlarging the house and rebuilding the roof. He was there until at least 1881, after which the Ratcliffs bought the freehold, a sale probably prompted by the severe agricultural depression which began around 1873, in which year the family still held a little over 55 acres of land in the village. On Edward's death, the Newton Park estate re-assigned its land to Hollies and Trent farms and divided the house into two

Waterside Farm in 2008   [*A. Ratcliffe*]

separate dwellings. Hence when it was sold off in 1956 it was catalogued as a pair of semi-detached houses, but was later adapted once again and lovingly restored as a single dwelling which, happily, it remains.[10]

Much of Waterside's farmland was sold for housing development. The estate that was built from 1963 to 1967 was called, appropriately enough, the Waterside Housing Estate and it also overlapped the village cricket ground, given to the village by the Ratcliffs before 1895. This field had been set aside for villagers to play cricket, football, and other sports. The developer, Alan Ford (Contractors) Ltd. of Spondon – the proprietor of which was much given to arriving on site in a helicopter - provided a new ground nearby, however. A new road was also pitched west off Blacksmith's Lane to a junction with St. Mary's Close and 64 houses were built. Originally the majority were advertised as being with four bedrooms ranging in size from 15 by 12 ft to 12 by 11 ft., but in the event, bungalows were substituted for many of them, although the basic dimensions for rooms were adhered to. Living rooms were arranged in the fashion, then just coming in, of running right across the house but not being quite as wide as one might like at 22 ft 7 ins x 12 ft. All were, according to the developer's blurb, fitted with 'Scandanavian-style fitted kitchens'. The larger houses were put on the market in the summer of 1966 at £7,500 and smaller ones ranged down to £4,500 in price. One line of them was built to have their rear elevations overlooking the river by the ford (the view being today partly obscured by trees), but with the consequent disadvantage that they face north[11].

Six of the strip cultivations referred to as lying adjacent to Waterside Farm survived well into the 19th century and were only gradually acquired and amalgamated into Waterside and Trent Farms after those holdings had been acquired by the Ratcliffs in the 1880s: a remarkable survival. Between them and the river lay two osier beds, the thin flexible willow strands of which had also been worked since medieval times, although no record of a basket weaver in the village survives, which is a shame. One bed was situated at the edge of the river off Top Meadow, near the Repton boundary, fed by an inlet, with another slightly to the south between Newton and Trent Meadows[12].

The only farm that has escaped notice here is Newton Park Farm, but of course, it did loom large in the previous chapter. Although the road laid out to serve the farm in its new position in c. 1838-39 has been in use ever since, the accompanying footpath from the village to the farm and on to Bacon Lodge (a smallish house demolished in the 1940s) was clearly deemed by the Ratcliffs to be too close to their new house – or else was in the way of the new service wing - and was moved further east in 1877-78, following an order obtained through the County Quarter Sessions, which establishes it as a public thoroughfare, unlike the drive itself, which was then and still is private[13].

We have also already seen how the Ratcliffs, like Lord Chesterfield, installed their own farmer, who was also the estate bailiff, or resident agent as he might be termed today, at Newton Park Farm. In 1890, the farmyard was extensively remodelled with only the north and west ranges surviving more or less intact and the two northern yards being replaced by a four parallel sheds in accordance with revised farming prac-

Newton Park Farm, part of the 1890 in-filling on the former yard, 2009 [*M. Craven*]

tice. The style of the buildings resembles that of Alexander MacPherson of Derby, especially the enlargements of the stable yard at The Pastures, Littleover (1889-1890) and farm buildings at Locko Park (1883). No expense seem to have been spared and even the ranges erected or re-erected in 1838-39 were given make-overs in varying degrees, although the house seems to have been left as it was. It is unlikely, though, that it was ever again used for shooting lunches, with the main house nearby.

New west range dated 1890, looking north, Newton Park Farm, 2009.

[M. Craven]

1890, the date on each section of new-build, is the date that James Brooks was installed as farm manager and bailiff to succeed Whitsed Laming or his Carnarvon-appointed successor. Indeed, 1890 was quite a year for this thirty-year old son of a member of the outdoor staff at Foremark Hall, for it also saw his marriage to Sarah Spooner, whose father, William, was thereupon installed as tenant at Newton Lane Farm where, as we have seen, he preceded the Falders. James was succeeded in the early 1920s by his son Alfred who ran it with his wife Nancy and, like his father, was farm bailiff for the estate – he oversaw general farming policy, received rents, maintained supplies and resolved petty disputes and problems. They farmed almost 300 acres and paid a rent of £500 per annum after the Second World War. Alfred was still farming there when the estate was sold in 1956, but in the end Olive, Percy Ratcliff's widow, retained it and in her will left the Brooks's the option of taking a 'favourable tenancy' (essentially a rent based on £2 per acre, a remarkably generous gesture) under any new owner assuming the farm was sold on her death, which occurred in 1971. By that, time, however, Alfred had died, following a blow on the leg from a cricket ball in a village match, the wound so caused having developed septicaemia. Thus it was his son James who was offered the 'favourable tenancy' in 1971 at the tender age of 21. He, however, demurred, having other ambitions. The farm buildings and a much reduced acreage were sold the following year to ex-Rolls-Royce engineer, motor-cycling enthusiast, dedicated deer-stalker and author Peter McManus and his wife Edna, who in recent years have run a herd of red deer there. This started in 1981 when ten hinds and a stag of pure-bred Scottish deer were obtained by the McManuses, who put them into a pair of paddocks totalling about six acres on the west side of the farm. This required the erection of 6 ft 6 in high tensile steel wire fencing, for deer are notoriously difficult to keep within bounds. It took until 1999 before two hinds managed to clear this formidable barrier![14]

One thing is certain, and that is that with the sale of the majority of the parish to Abraham Hoskins in 1799, the number of farms that existed in 1758 fell, for several must have been run together to form the new squire's model farm. There were 18 farmers in 1758 with acreages ranging from 126 to the 15 farmed by John Gretton's ancestor Thomas Powis (see Chapter III) but, by the mid-19th century, there were only nine, along with some of the fields of three which lay fractionally outside the parish: Broken Flatts (Repton), Common Farm (Bretby) and Bladon Fields, later Bladon (House) Farm (Winshill to 1894).

Feeding the deer, Newton Park Farm, 2009   [*M. Craven*]

Population, pubs and people

In Chapter I it was estimated that the population of Newton Solney was about 118 in 1327, and we have seen such estimates rise to about 165 in 1662 and 165-170 in 1758. There were 41 houses in 1662, 43 in 1758 and 47 in 1789, when a population of 188 can be estimated, suggesting extremely stable population numbers throughout the Every era. It is not until 1801, just after Hoskins' take-over, that one gets an official figure, namely 181, which accords well with previous estimates. Yet in a decade the population jumped by a whopping 76 to 259, although only three houses were added. This must reflect the construction of Newton Park, the model farm and indeed of Bladon Wood/Castle, all of which would require servants and farm staff, many housed under the one roof. Thus one might argue that Hoskins' passion for building and farming had brought not only an increase in the population of Newton Solney but a significant increase in its prosperity. The following decade to 1821 saw just a two-person increase, although the archdiaconal visitation of 1824 estimates the church-going population at 216. By 1831 the population had gone up by another 77 people but had settled back to 311 in 1841, at the beginning of the Worthington-Chesterfield era, when we get a house-count of 73, inhabited by 143 men and 168 women. In this era too the numbers continue to increase until a new plateau is reached in the period 1871-1931 when numbers hover around the 460 mark before the great Depression and the Second World War take it back down to 408, a figure previously seen only in

149

1861 (406). Thereafter the population of the village has recovered slowly to 430 in 1961, then a jump of more than 150 as the two housing estates were completed, to 530 in 1971 and a further jump of similar proportions in the 1970s took the figure to 686 in 1981, since when an ageing population with the concomitant flight of the young, has caused in to decline by about 70 people. In 2009 it has risen again to about 800[15].

The Unicorn, as rebuilt by the Ratcliffs as a tied house, seen in 2008.   [*M. Craven*]

In 1822 the Everys were still Lords of the Manor – which indeed, the present Sir Henry Every still, happily, is – and also patrons of the living, a fact reflected in the name of the only public house in the village at that time, the *Unicorn*, named after their crest. Unfortunately, there is no contemporary record of it prior to 1815, nor even any previous record of an inn, although the likelihood is that it was considerably older. Whether, as one fairly recent account suggests, it was converted from a farmhouse, is difficult to say, however. At this time, William Eaton was the landlord, which he was until about 1840, although he had become a farmer by the year following, probably at Hollies Farm, and we find a member of another old village family behind the bar (as it were) Joseph Shepherd, although he did not last long, being supplanted as landlord by a shoemaker, William Smithard, only 26 when he was in charge in 1846. It was normal practice, both in town and country at this period for pub landlords to have a second string to their bow, as with Smithard. Usually it was bit of husbandry on an attached smallholding. Smithard was in charge for a decade before a few more ephemeral landlords gave way to the Garratts, husband and wife in the 1870s and the Pearsalls, husband and wife during the 1880s and '90s. Between the wars, Mrs. Juanetta Ramsden was landlady for more than twenty years. It was taken over by former Bass cooper Leslie George Appleby in around 1958 when was landlord for fifteen years followed by his son Brian for a further five. Brian Appleby had the foresight to buy the 1878 Worthington/Ratcliff photograph album with its Richard Keene views of the village (many of which grace these pages) at the Olive Ratcliff sale in 1972[16].

The inn was rebuilt after it was purchased by the Ratcliffs from the Everys around 1872, when the building was replaced by the present brick structure with its distinctive canted bay at the west end looking down Main Street, a perfect environment for a drink on a spring evening! The architect is not known, but probably the Bass, Ratcliff and Gretton building manager. In 1918 the two cottages adjacent at

The Meynell hunt meeting at The Green, Wednesday 5th March 1908, from a postcard sent by Pentlow, young son of Unicorn Landlord Alfred Page.   [*Michael Day*]

the east end were built as linked accommodation, when the pub was let as a tied house to Bass. The brewery still had it when it was put up for sale with most of the rest of the estate in 1956 at which time the cottage actually adjacent to the pub was still let to the brewery as the manager's house, whilst the other let to local man William Barnes at £39 – 8s – 4d per annum[17].

The village has enjoyed the facilities of two other inns, although one is long gone. After the passage of the Beer-houses Act of 1830 – one of the things other than the Battle of Waterloo for which we have to thank the Duke of Wellington! – two of these establishments quickly opened, paying £2 to the exchequer for a licence to serve beer but not spirits in the applicant's own home. The earliest was the *Brickmaker's Arms* on Main Street, almost opposite the end of Trent Lane, a listed grade II building. It probably started in one of what was then a single 18th century vernacular brick-built double fronted cottage, but in the 19th century - as a pub - gradually absorbed a separate small cottage attached to one end. It was strategically placed, not only for those who toiled in Mr.Hopkins' brick pit (almost behind it), but for the waggoners who carted the finished product across the Trent to Egginton and all points northwards, not to mention onward consignments of South Derbyshire coal. The beerhouse may even have been tied to the proprietors of the brickworks, but on the 1836 map is separated from it by the close belonging to the wheelwright's father, William Eyre of Vine Cottage, a freeholder. As an anonymous beer-house, the *Brickmakers' Arms* is first recorded in 1835 but not before 1874 under the name it has borne ever since, although it would be reasonable to suppose that it always *had* borne it. The sign today shows the arms of the Worshipful Company of Tilers & Bricklayers, albeit not wholly accurately painted!

The Brickmakers' Arms in the 1980s when still a Bass house.
[*Derbyshire Life*]

In 1835 the *Brickmakers'* was run by its first landlord, Samuel Bull who also doubled as a shoemaker. like Smithard at the *Unicorn.* In the 1840s the Shepherd family took over for some fifteen years, transferring from the *Unicorn* and the son, John, doubled as the village baker. From 1855 to 1878 Harry Coxon was landlord, probably as the tenant of the Marbrows but, at the termination of his reign the Ratcliff family bought it and, like the *Unicorn*, it eventually became a Bass tied house

Phyllis and Dick Cooper behind the bar at the 'Brickies', in 1985. [*Norman Ellis*]

until similarly, 1980s legislation against too many ties houses caused it to be sold off. After 1880, then it had a fairly regular turnover of landlords until the inter-war period when it was run uninterruptedly by Reggie Wilkins, whose term also included the Second World War and the crash-landing of a stray barrage balloon. During the 1908s, the inn was run by Phyllis and Dick Cooper, who were extremely popular hosts and remained behind the bar for many years, building up a wide and appreciative clientele.[18]

The other beerhouse was the *Plough & Harrow*, commonly *the Plough*, where John Adams was the first recorded licensee in 1857, but shortly afterwards Luke Gaskin had taken over and remained there for over two decades. H. J. Wain tells us that Adams's son Jack was caught poaching salmon from the Trent in the 1880s - using a shotgun! After his time it seems to have become merely an off-licence under his successor John Langford, who also moonlighted as a grazier, in the 1880s. Derrick Pounds's claim that Hollies Farm had once been an inn called the *Wheatsheaf* has been difficult to substantiate.

One of the earliest trades one can trace in the village is that of wheelwright, George Smith being recorded in a deed of 1749, already mentioned in connection with his daughter's apprenticeship in 'housewifery' in Chapter III. The next one we hear about is James Eyre in 1827, who was also the parish clerk and whose father William, a freeholder, was actually a shoemaker. James was born in 1801 and worked until his death in the 1860s, when his son John succeeded him, also working as a joiner. He lived at Vine Cottage, Trent Lane, which may well have adjoined the wheelwright's workshop back at least into his father's time. He was also made coffins and was said to have begun selecting timber as soon as the church bell was tolled to mark someone's passing! His assistant (and probably son-in-law), Thomas Garratt was also a joiner but succeeded to the business in about 1870, running it until the work dried up in or just after the Great War. His son, William carried on, but again only as a joiner, in the inter-war period along with Frank Shorthouse who also kept the hardware shop, but who in the 1940s was the Newton Park assistant estate foreman.

Forge Cottage, today, lightly modernised. It once was thatched. [*M. Craven*]

Vine Cottage, which is in Trent Lane, is of 18th century date, as is the cottage (if not the forge) of the village blacksmiths. These are still situated on the NW side of Blacksmith's Lane – the name of which is surely a guarantee of some considerable continuity of smithing hereabouts - just down from The Green, which is the name of the place where the lane and Newton Lane converge on Main Street. In 1758 Thomas Smedley, a cousin of Thomas Smedley of Waterside Farm, was the smith, aided by his son young Thomas.

The latter's widow Elizabeth was listed as the smith in 1827 and 1835 but was succeeded by John Ratcliff, who is not known to have been related to the brewing family! He served nearly two decades, the longest continuous stint as village blacksmith until the Leedham family, James and Arthur, took over, from the 1880s through to the Great War. The forge lasted at least until the 1950s, for J. Higgins was the smith in occupation (on a rent of £26 per annum) from the Ratcliffs when the estate was sold in 1956. Both wheelwright's and smith's cottages have since become private houses[19].

Round the corner from the blacksmith's cottage west into Main Street lies a row of cottages, effectively two semi-detached pairs. The nearest are earlier and may well have been built by the Everys in the 1840s or '50s, but beyond are a slightly more spacious gabled pair, part of the estate improvements which the super-rich Ratcliffs embarked upon as soon as possible after taking over.

The village centre of which these cottages constitute a part was designated a conservation area in 1982. Beyond the two pairs of cottages is a range of three gabled cottages, the eastern-most the largest, all built in the 1880s by the Ratcliffs. The largest one was intended to be the village shop and post-office, a role it fulfilled until 2007 when it was peremptorily closed. The shop was also a grocery and behind, a further gabled range, set back, older and today white stuccoed, contains the bakery. The Post Office had been established, probably on the same site, in 1870 and was run by Joseph Garratt, father of wheelwright William. By 1891, Thomas Taylor had taken over as sub-postmaster and grocer being additionally also a baker, re-establishing the village bakery. He ran it until the end of the Edwardian period when his widow, Mrs. Mary Taylor became Mrs. Whysall and kept it going well into the 1940s, to be succeeded by the Wrights, father and son, still tenants when the property was sold immediately prior to the 1956 sale.

There seem to have been few other shops in the village in the 19th century, however. In the 1820s and '30s there was a butcher, successively James Brown and Nathaniel Chinn, and one can trace a second shop right through numerous tenants in the 19th and into the last century without being entirely clear what it sold; probably it was

154

hardware and durables. It was situated in the row of houses beside the *Brickmakers'*
Arms. Frequently, too, the pub landlords are listed as 'and shopkeeper' and there are
shoemakers (who would have worked from home) listed right through to the dawn of
the 20th century, again several of them landlords: Smithard and Coxon especially. In
the first part of the 20th century Mrs. Mabel Snell was trading in the village as a
confectioner.[20]

*Shop & former post
office and two
cottages, seen in 2008
[M. Craven]*

There was a smattering
of other, non-retail
trades, however. The
Adams family acted as
carriers, mainly to
Burton, in the first half
of the 19th century, and
a descendant, Robert
Adams was probably
similarly involved in
the 1890s although he
had himself listed as a
coal dealer; possibly
he acted in concert
with Councillor Bennett of The Grange. There was also a dressmaker, not to mention
a builder who, in the early part of the 19th century, was William Holmes of the Grange
Farm family, and from the 1850s to the 1880s William Wilson was in business as a
tailor, as well as acting as parish clerk, a man who, before parish councils were
brought into being, had to arrange burials and act virtually as the curate's manager. In
the 1870s Thomas Burrows was trading as a timber merchant and three decades
earlier Thomas Hart had been the village's only upholsterer. Perhaps he got so much
business furnishing Abraham Hoskins' houses that he decided to stay!

There were also four gardeners in the
village in 1895, two being described as
head gardeners: John G. Bedford, of West
Lodge, Newton Park, Head Gardener to
the Ratcliffs, and Edward Osborne,
presumably to the occupiers of either
Bladon Castle or Rock House. West
Lodge was the original name of Museum
Cottage. Then there was James Upton, a
member of a prominent local farming
family, described as a 'foreman gardener'
(presumably to the Ratcliffs, perhaps at
Cliffe House) and one further man listed
without qualification, Francis Kelham.

Wesleyan Chapel of 1851, closed 1919.

Probably all but Osborne were employed on the gardens at Newton Park, in which by the 1930s twelve men worked. There were nine men working in the gardens up until Percy Ratcliff's death.[21]

Behind the houses on Main Street, west of the *Brickmakers' Arms* and off an enclave called The Square, is a single court – a row of cottages facing south with their backs to the houses in main street. They are said to have been built by the Hopkins family early in the 19th century to house workers in their brickworks, and al-though there seems to be little docu-mentary evidence to support such a con-tention, it would ap-

pear plausible. They are called (for reasons that seem as obscure as Derby's Canary Island) Canary Row. At their west end is a building which was put up as the Wesleyan Chapel in 1851. It does not seem to have flourished for more than two of three decades before going out of use; it was secularised for dom-estic purposes after 1919.[22]

Canary Row, south side, 2008.   [*M. Craven*]

Private residents

There were other residents of the village listed in directories or in the census, but about whom much less is known. At any one time from the 1830s, there were at least three middle class residents to whom it is difficult to assign a house. One, a Hoskins tenant in 1836 was 'John Lees, Gent.' who was, in fact the landlord of the most opulent inn in Burton at the time, the *Three Queens*, where, indeed, the sale of Every lands was held in 1799. He then rented Rosary Cottage, with stable, coach house and garden and may have even have been a Catholic (Staffordshire being the second most Catholic County in England) to have bestowed such a name on his house, although against this is the fact that he is buried in Newton Solney churchyard. His house's name certainly did not last, nor is it clear exactly which house it was, although the number key to holdings in the sale catalogue of 1836 suggest that it was on part of the plot which also contained Thomas Greatorex's house, The Villa, which suggests that it may have been the Lodge.

There was another substantial house in the village, called Fairfield, which appears to date from the 1820s or 1830s. Lying on the north side of Main Street, it is a three bay two storey villa coated in Roman cement and with a relatively high eaves between upper floor windows and cornice. Indeed, despite having been altered somewhat in Edwardian times, with half-paned sashes (subsequently altered to casements) and ground floor canted bays, it bears at least some of the hallmarks of Hoskins' creations.

Fairfield, nearing the end of a restoration, 2009.   [*M. Craven*]

If so, it must have been sold off prior to 1836, for it fails to appear on the sale catalogue which, as we have seen, is quite plausible, even if irritatingly poorly documented. The only thing which gives pause is that it seems less sophisticated than, say, The Villa (The Cedars), less eccentric than Evergreen Cottage and was probably built later, under the direction of a builder aping the general style of Hoskins' earlier buildings.

Nor is it easy to disentangle the sequence of its residents, but in all probability the brewer Thomas Saunders lived in it during period from before 1839 to not so long after 1841. He seems to have been the only brewer (to which trade he was a late-comer, having previously been a cheesefactor) to have lived in Newton Solney without being related to the Hoskins-Bass-Ratcliff nexus. His successor by 1846 was Elizabeth Somers 1846, who was also a freeholder in the village. Born Elizabeth Gascoyne in Derby in 1788, she was the widow of Thomas Somers of Repton 'Gent.' (1779-1838), corn miller at Milton, and who probably bought the house as a widow, her husband having died aged 59 in 1838. Her family seem to have retained a connection with the village, as her 12-year-old cousin Joseph Gascoyne Somers drowned whilst swimming in the Trent off Newton weir on 11th July 1870. By 1857, though, she had moved away, probably to Derby, where her brother had built Fairfield House, Littleover and where her unmarried nephews lived alone. That the two houses shared a name can have been no co-incidence. Nevertheless, she then still retained her freehold in Newton[23].

Thereafter things relating to Fairfield are less clear. Her tenant in 1857 was probably a commercial traveller called James Redfern but, by 1870, a year after Mrs. Somers' death, the house was sold to the Ratcliffs. They let it; by 1895 William Lobb, was tenant succeeded very shortly by William Joseph Oliver. By the time peace had been restored in 1918, it had been taken by a doctor, Francis Lionel Pickett, who went into general practice there until at least 1956, when the house was put up for sale, by which time he was paying a rent of £50 per annum. Probably he then purchased it.[24]

Sir Henry Every, 10th Bt., was the man who presided over the gradual sale of the family's remaining land in Newton Solney, culminating with the sale of the patronage of the living to Robert Ratcliff in 1871 along with further land, including the glebe or church lands. He had succeeded his grandfather, the man who sold so much to Hoskins (and others) whilst quite young in 1855, and the estate was still trying to catch up financially. At the same time Rock House was finally sold, George Mitchell's bankruptcy probably being the cue (see Chapter III). The buyer was again the Ratcliff family, the clue being that Robert Ratcliff, subsequently the purchaser of Newton Park, was then living at Stapenhill but in 1873 held 70 acres 3 rods and 13 perches of land in Newton Solney, which surely represents a major purchase shortly beforehand. John Higgott bought more land, mainly arable.

Rock House seen from the terrace at Cliffe House (from a post-card)
[*M. Craven*]

Following its purchase, Rock House, was mainly dismantled and completely rebuilt as a conventional mid-Victorian villa, perhaps again to the designs of Reginald Churchill of Burton. The only concessions to the picturesque original was the replacement of the oriel window overlooking the Trent by a full height canted bay with an ornamental crest and the flanking walls either side, which were crenellated in the same rather predictable way that one finds on Bladon Castle. This section of the house appears to embody at least some of the original structure. Beyond it, a relatively ordinary two storey L-shaped brick villa with a verandah facing south west was set amidst re-landscaped grounds lavishly endowed with shrubberies, as was then the fashion and which today in its maturity provides excellent security. The work seems to have been completed by 1873.

These works were carried out for the house's new owner, Edward Dawson Salt, predictably a director of the family brewery, T. Salt & Co. His grandfather Thomas had married Susannah, the niece of John Ratcliff, who was first taken into partnership by Bass, and the name of his father, Thomas Fosbrooke Salt (1808-1864), acted as a reminder that the family descended from a marriage with a daughter of Shardlow based canal transport pioneer (and friend of Abraham Hoskins, senior) Leonard Fos-

Rock House when newly rebuilt, photographed c. 1878 by Richard Keene, junior.
[Brian Appleby]

brooke. Once settled in, Salt was elected a churchwarden. On his death, in the Edwardian period, Rock House was sold to the Ratcliffs and let to another brewer, albeit one whose firm was of much more recent foundation, J. T. C. Eadie, JP, who remained there until the end of the Great War, when he moved to the hall at Barrow-on-Trent. His successor for over twenty years was Mrs. Cox, who changed the name of the house to The Rock, and her successor was M. F. R. Moreton who in 1954 took a 14 year lease from the Newton Park estate at a rent of £120 which included nearly five and a half acres. Maurice FitzHardinge Reynolds Moreton (184-1976) had married the daughter of Edward Charlton, rector of Tatenhill, on the other side of Burton, and held a number of local directorships. His other local connection was that, although a great grandson of Thomas Moreton, 1st Earl of Ducie, his mother had been a Thornewill of Dovecliff House. As with a number of properties offered for sale in 1956, Rock House was withdrawn prior to the auction on Mrs. Ratcliff's instructions and seems to have been sold to Moreton in advance of the sale going ahead. The Moretons lived there until 1974 when Arthur Bostock acquired it and lived there for five years before it was re- sold to Roger F. Kerry who still lives there.[25]

The Ratcliffs were keen to be seen as benevolent owners, and at the same time as they provided a sports ground in the 1890s, they also furnished the village with five acres of land off Newton Lane, portions of one eighth of which could be had on lease to the 'cottagers' of the village as allotments at a rent of 7/6d per annum (37.5p). The Ratcliffs also provided annual prizes for the best exhibits at the village show grown on the allotments. After the Great War, it was necessary to provide somewhere in which to hold such shows, and the Ratcliff family again rallied round by building an especially fine Arts-and-Crafts village hall, called the Institute, on Repton Road roughly between Trent Farm and the *Unicorn*. This was completed in 1926. The site had first been allocated during the preceding war to form a firing range for the Volunteers (practice trenches were dug, too), but presented an ideal site for the new Institute. The building, with its hanging tiles and catslide roof was designed by Derby architect's firm of Arthur Eaton & Son, the style being very much that of his son, George Morley Eaton (died 1940), later President of the RIBA. This has since hosted flower shows, WI meetings, lectures, drama group productions and formal dances in

The Village Institute of 1926, photographed in the 1980s   [*Derbyshire Life*]

the days up to the 1960s when such things were still valued. Beside it was laid out a bowling green, where flourishes the bowls club, which enjoyed its annual dinners in the hall, along with the cricket teams and the tennis club, all of which flourished mightily before and after the Second World War. With respect to cricket, the annual clash between teams from the *Unicorn* and the *Brickmakers'* was and is to be relished. It might be added that Mrs. Ratcliff was perpetual president of the local WI – founded in 1931 – in succession to her sister-in-law, and would make the house available from time to time for functions[26].

Nos. 1 & 2 The Green, in November 2008   [*M. Craven*]

The Ratcliffs continued to build from time to time to accommodate estate workers and retired staff. A particularly stylish semi-detached pair of houses, conjoined at right angles and overlooking The Green on the SW corner of Newton Lane and Main Street was built in 1918 and the architect was almost certainly George Eaton, who shortly

160

afterwards designed The Institute. They are of two storeys and designed in an Arts-and-Crafts style. The intention was probably to provide housing for the families of local men killed in the Great War, which conflict resulted in eight fatalities of Newton men: Frank Bailey, Charles Chandler, Hugh Greaves, vicar's son Francis Jansen, John Mead, John Vivkers, George Vine and John Wootton, all commemorated on a tablet in the church. In 1956, when these houses were sold, they were occupied by Messrs. Walter Pounds (the Ratcliff's retired game-keeper) and Frank Shorthouse, later of Trent Lane, who had been estate joiner after the Great War, son of Henry and Emma Shorthouse, who had run the hardware shop at the turn of the century.

After the Second World War a similar act of philanthropy impelled Percy Ratcliff to erect 'Sunnyside' a group of four cottages this time, to be run along the lines of an almshouse, again set enclosing a green space, in this case facing SW on the north side of Main Street on a bank near Evergreen Cottage. They were to be for the elderly of the village, with preference to old retainers of the family. The intention was that they should constitute a war memorial for the village, but one with a positive and beneficient use rather than a new village green with a prominent monumental memorial as had been originally envisaged. They were completed in 1951. Their sequestered garden is centred on a fine square section baluster sundial, which may have originally been supplied to Abraham Hoskins for Newton Park; it is certainly of that sort of vintage in origin, although the maker's name is no longer readable. The sundial itself does, however, carry a secondary inscription:

'Sunnyside Cottages built to the glory of god and the comfort of the aged by Percy W. Ratcliff and his wife January 1st 1950'

Sunnyside Cottages and (L) the sundial, seen in 2008   [*M. Craven*]

Shortly after the construction of the two houses on The Green, Col. Ratlcliff also commissioned a further pair of semi-detached houses, on Main Street, immediately East of the former vicarage (see below, Chapter VII), now called *Nofwen* and *Lindisfarne*. Of two storeys and enclosed by gabled projections, the central portion again has a catslide roof forming the shelter over the entrance doors, with hipped tiled dormers above, and the theme is echoed in miniature bracketed and tiled shades over the ground floor windows in the gable ends. The tall chimneys complete what once more is a convincing Arts-and-Crafts ensemble of much charm, and the architect again was in all probability G. M. Eaton of Derby.

Official life

Whereas in the previous centuries, village life was largely regulated by the lords of the manor holding jurisdiction over their property, modified from the 17th century by the Poor Law Act which gave parish vestries the responsibility for the relief of poverty, in the 19th century great changes began to be made. Beyond the parish, general oversight and provision was made by the County magistrates through the Quarter Sessions until the 1888 Act, which set up County Councils. In 1894, however, a second tier, the Rural and Urban District Councils, were set up in England and Wales, and Newton Solney thereafter came under the jurisdiction of the Repton & District RDC until 1974 when larger district Councils were set up to replace them. From then on until the present, Newton has been in the jurisdiction of the South Derbyshire District Council based on Swadlincote. Under the same 1894 Act, every parish or township with a population of over 300 could elect a parish council yearly (later every three, then four years) in April; the Newton Solney one first met in December of the same year. The franchise was wider than the parliamentary one, too, women being eligible to stand. The RDC laid main sewers, enabling village houses to be connected to it and dispense with septic tanks. Indeed, the Newton Park estate over time ensured that all their properties were connected.

Nofwen *and* Lindisfarne, *Main Street, in 2008*   [*M. Craven*]

Parish affairs were regulated by the church vestry meetings, which had assumed the responsibilities of the manorial administration of earlier eras. Whilst they had always been empowered to appoint a parish constable, to exercise law-and-order and collect local and national dues, under an Act of 1842 the vestries were empowered to appoint a parish constable with what might be termed full police powers, although ratification by the bench through the Quarter Sessions was expected. In Newton, the first appointee under this Act was Edward Smedley, youngest son of William, of Waterside Farm. He was also farming in a small way at this time, for he had leased a close in the village from the Everys in 1832. The parish clerks wielded considerable influence too, and although we know little of John Saint, the first in the 19th century, he was succeeded in the later 1820s by Edward Dicken of an old local farming family, a dynasty which, indeed, produced a second parish clerk at the beginning of the last century, William Dicken, who was *en post* to the Great War. In the 1840s and early 1850s, when the lock-up was built by the parish (probably by The Green – it seems to have disappeared by the end of that century) to replace the stocks, John Adams, the carrier, was clerk. He was succeeded about 1855 by wheelwright John Eyre, and he by tailor William Wilson, who served through from about 1878 to 1900 when the second Dicken preceded Sydney Garratt, the 27-year-old son of Thomas, the last village wheelwright.

The first parish council of Newton Solney met on 15th April 1894, consisting of Rev'd Francis Jansen in the chair, with Robert Ratcliff of Newton Park, William Marbrow, still then a freeholder, but shortly to sell out to Ratcliff, Reginald B. Barratt of The Grange, who was also the village's representative on the newly constituted district council and a coal merchant, E. D. Salt of Rock House, James Brooks, of Newton Park Farm, and H. J. Hudson was the clerk. Bearing in mind that by this date the patronage of the living was in Ratcliff's hands as well, that Brooks was his farm bailiff and that both Barratt, Salt and, quite possibly by this time, Marbrow were his tenants, the entire parish council looks like a Ratcliff stitch-up! Indeed, it rather set the tone for the following sixty years, although it did ensure that village affairs were well-ordered. Modern commentators tend to dismiss such arrangements as hopelessly feudal, but in the days before the welfare state, it almost always worked well, being usually beneficial and humane, with none of the faceless bureaucracy and delays that one tends to experience today. In such circumstances, being 'patronised' by an individual one knows (for good or ill) seems infinitely to be preferred to the cumbersome and often inadvertently and discriminatory 'patronage' of the state! Yet, it may well have seemed to those outside the loop as it were, to be a practical extension of the absolute sway previously enjoyed by landowners from Medieval times![27]

Peel Cottage, glimpsed from The Green, 2008   [*M. Craven*]

Although the Quarter Sessions were empowered to appoint uniformed police officers from 1856, official law and order did not really reach the village until 1894, probably as a result of the Parish & District Councils Act of that year. Without delay a resident constable was posted to Newton, the first being David Pugh who, from his name, might have been of Welsh descent if not birth. In the Edwardian period James Bennett succeeded him, followed before 1912 by William Hancock. Both these last two constables are given in the directories as at the "Police Station" but it is not clear where this was situated, nor what exactly it consisted of – probably a cottage given official status and allocated to the village constable as accommodation, but with a ground floor room adapted as an office. By the 1930s PC Smith's police cottage was in Trent Lane, however and this may well have been the one of two or three decades before, too. The next mention of a village PC was to John Thompson in 1941, following Jack Hallam, about a decade before a new police house was built as The Green on the east corner of Newton Lane and Repton Road which remained in commission until modern day operational requirements – a euphemism for 'cuts' – caused its closure and disposal by sale in the 1980s. It is now, appropriately, called Peel Cottage[28].

Some children of the village school, photographed in 1923/24   [*From WI (2000)15*]

In around 1840, a National School was founded in the village by Sir Henry Every, 9th Bt., the first (and only) teacher being Harriet, daughter of the widowed Joanna Ordish, who kept a shop in the village at the time. There is no indication of the whereabouts of the schoolroom, unfortunately. A decade later, Eliza Monk was the school-mistress but in 1860, the school was re-founded in a new building built on a plot at the NW angle of Trent Lane and Main Street and again financed by the Every family, in this case by Sir Henry Flower Every 10th Bt., who appointed Eliza Oakden as headmistress. Twenty years later she was followed by Miss E. A. Cope who had 75 pupils in 1895 and in 1897 by Mary Gallimore, whose assistant was Miss Jones.In her time the school was enlarged further, having been taken under the wing of the local authority as a Public Elementary School, although it is today styled Newton Solney

Church of England (Aided) School. Mabel Wilmot and then Jane Drackley followed after the turn of the century, joined by one assistant teacher on £50 per annum. By the Second World War Mrs. Tunnicliffe was in charge of 69 children who were taught in two rooms divided by a folding timber partition. Post War, the school underwent a complete rebuild by the County Council, during which all trace of the 1860s building seems to have vanished and only the Edwardian extension remains in evidence. A century after the re-founding of the school by Sir Henry saw the retirement at 70 of Miss Garnham, a much revered figure who had begun to teach at the school in 1919 and died aged 100. When Derrick Pounds was a lad in the 1940s she shared duties with Miss Adams. Happily, despite there being fewer children in third-millennium Newton than in the immediately preceding period, the school still flourishes, boosted by a very favourable inspection report from OFSTED in 2004.[29]

Gas lighting reached the village, fed by the Burton-upon-Trent Gas Company, in the early 1890s, and was not replaced by electricity until the 1950s. A regular 'bus service was running from 1922, operated by Messrs. Tailby & George as Blue 'Bus Services

Ltd., initially from Repton, but which moved fairly soon afterwards to a depot at Willington. The service continued for just over fifty years, but it was taken over by the Derby Corporation omnibus operation after a bidding war with Burton Corporation (which was also keen to acquire it) in December 1973 for £210,000. Unfortunately, the depot and all but two of their stock was destroyed in a disastrous fire on 5th January 1976, after which Derby City 'buses operated the service through the village until de-regulation in the 1980s.[30]

The fingerpost on The Green was removed for the duration of hostilities during WW2. Note the 'Bretby' arm: much older than the others.
[M. Craven]

One intrusion of the Victorian age which Newton Solney was spared was the railway. The Birmingham & Derby Junction Railway's line via Burton was opened in 1839,

165

but kept to the north side of the Trent. Trains could be heard, especially at night, when the wind was in the NW, but to catch one, it was necessary to travel to Burton or Derby. Nevertheless, in 1854 the village had a narrow escape, for in that year the projected Burton-upon-Trent and Nottingham Railway was proposing to link the Midland and North Staffordshire lines at Burton with the Great Northern Railway at Sneinton, Nottinghamshire via Newton Solney, Repton, Ingleby, Stanton-by-Bridge and King's Newton. This would have had the effect of running two lines down the then unspoilt and delightful Trent Valley, one on either side of the river. Fortunately, it never got further than the planning stage.[31]

Last years of the Ratcliffs

From the death of James Brooks of Newton Park Farm, the Ratcliffs had employed a resident agent, as well as a farm bailiff. Thus from 1923 until the sale of the estate the agent was Arthur Cyril Riley AALPA who lived at Cromer Hide, formerly the Lodge. He was a man who clearly gave satisfaction for he was left the house in Olive Ratcliff's will, although by the time Mrs. Ratcliff died in 1971 Arthur had predeceased her, although his wife, Winifred, benefited from the bequest.

In the Second World War, evacuees from Ward End, Birmingham, were taken in by the Ratcliffs and housed in the service wing of Newton Park, in the charge of the housekeeper, Mrs. Glenn. The gardens were, however kept up, seven full time and two part-time gardeners being employed right up to the 1950s. After the war, masses of cut flowers were arranged in the house regularly, carpets of buds burst out in the grounds in spring and the public were permitted to enjoy them on two occasions each year at the cost of 6d [2.5p]. The gardens were also the scene of Mrs. Ratcliff's celebrated village treasure hunts. The conservatory, which was added by Messengers in the 1880s contained a large water-garden constructed mainly of tufa which was another attraction of these occasions. If one heard the distant ringing of a hand-bell in those days, it was the staff calling the Ratcliffs to the house when one or other of them was out in the gardens, for both were keen horticulturalists, hence the employment of nine garden staff even in the lean years following the Second War. The family also provided the ingredients for the pancakes, the making of which preceded the annual Shrove Tuesday pancake race in Main Street, a tradition which survived the Ratcliffs by quite three decades. No doubt health and safety zealots would have stopped it by now had it not ended before! Likewise, at Christmas, a large tree was put up in the house and carols for the villagers were sung round it, led by the choir from the church.

Apart from the housekeeper's staff, the family continued to keep a large workforce even during and after the War. The butler was Norman Gaskin, the chauffeur Frederick Waite – a local man and presumably a representative of a phenomenally ancient village family and – and his assistant was Jack Shorthouse, whose father Fred we have already encountered. The estate foreman was Arthur Astle, assisted by Frank Shorthouse, no less, and Walter Pounds, Derrick's father, and the son of an estate gardener, was game-keeper to the end, having started out helping the Holbrooke's butler at Bladon Castle in his schooldays. He started work properly as a stable lad in 1908, and was gamekeeper and woodsman for over 50 years, often travelling with the family to their other estates and learnt stalking from their Highland ghillie.

166

Were anything untoward to occur with the candles, however, the house had its own fire appliance and it was the staff trained to use it who helped found the village fire fighting team, which was set up concomitantly with a unit of LDVs, later Home Guard, in 1940. Despite these last two admirable moves the war rather passed the village by, despite the dropping of a number of incendiary bombs, one of which hit the roof of the church but which did little damage. Another struck the vicarage, then empty, but this time considerable damage to the library ensued, chiefly because the old boy who kept the key could not be woken. Even then, most of the serious damage was done by the water used to extinguish the flames. More serious was the loss, killed in action of two villagers, Samuel Adams (a descendant of the family that were carriers in the early 19th century) and Cyril Brown. The only lasting topographical result was the erection of a concrete pill box on the northern part of the parish, beyond the Trent, to guard the ford from invaders. Other wartime changes included US troops at Bladon Castle, who were followed by Italian PoWs. There were, of course, ARPs patrolling the village, and Derrick Pounds recalls that the Argyles at The Cedars got into hot water for showing a light during the blackout. Derrick's father Walter, the Ratcliff's long-serving gamekeeper, was a sergeant in the special police, with Ernie Simmonds, Jack Cowley, Wilfred Marriott (the haulage contractor) and his brother 'Snowball' Marriott were special constables. Sgt. Pounds was awarded two police medals for his (unpaid) efforts.[32]

The Break-up of the Estate

Percy William Ratcliff of Newton Park, died aged 78 on 21st February 1955, leaving a widow, Olive (*nee* Thompson) and left all his significant estate to her in his will, which was proved on 5th May 1956. His estate was valued at £1,079,894 – 8s – 4d and it was decided to sell the majority of it, saving for a suitable house for Olive to live in. All estate staff, irrespective of their length of service were awarded a year's pay (none of the posts were pensionable in those days), senior staff like Walter Pounds getting £390 gross per annum at the time – along with a house, of course. The family solicitors, Talbot and Co. – successors to Hoskins' firm – entrusted John German & Co. with the sale which took place at the *Queen's Hotel*, Burton on Thursday 25th October 1956. Newton Park house, with Park Farm and five houses with 347 acres, comprised the first lot, called for some reason, Lot A. The odd name of Museum Cottage, is explained by the remark in the catalogue, "A detached brick cottage used as a Museum and Workshop..." although exactly what was exhibited therein – 'curios' in one account - is not known; Derrick Pounds called it a place for hobbies.

The sale included the shooting rights, for the Ratcliffs were keen on shooting and were able to draw on an enthusiastic band of beaters from amongst the lads in the village and round about. The shot birds, after the traditional distribution of a brace to each participant, were hung in the game larder which survives as room 5 of the Hotel. The remaining lots were: Grange Farm, The Cedars, The Grange, Brickyard Farm, three building sites in the village and on the main road, Fairfield, Hollies Farm, Rock

Two of the six Rural District Council's houses at The End, 2008.   [*M. Craven*]

House, the Post Office and Stores with adjoining house and cottage, Beehive Cottage, Vine Cottage in Trent Lane (which fetched £945) with two building sites of a third and half an acre respectively adjacent (which went for £450 and £1,260), Trent Farm with 78 acres, the Blacksmith's Cottage and forge, a pair of cottages behind the *Unicorn* with the two cottages added to its east, the two houses, 1 & 2 The Green, with two pairs of semi-detached cottages close by, two further cottages in Trent Lane along with a pair of semis, formerly Waterside Farm, Ivy Cottage in Main Street, a pair of cottages in Bretby Lane (more usually Newton Lane) and a building site off that road, on the north side of The End[33].

Several properties on offer were withdrawn prior to the sale, either having been sold by prior agreement or because Mrs. Ratcliff wished to retain them for the time being, They included Newton Park and Farm, The Cedars, The Grange, Rock House and the Post office and its two cottages. Mrs. Ratcliff moved into the Cedars in 1959, following the alterations mentioned in Chapter IV and the main house was finally sold by private treaty in 1960. Sotheby's sold some of the surplus contents over three days when she moved out; local legend has it that several of the local dealers conducted their own *après* sale negotiations in the bar of the *Brickmakers' Arms* afterwards!

The building sites were soon built upon, almost all with houses of excellent taste and which fitted into their surroundings harmoniously. The land on The End was acquired by the RDC in order to build a row of three pairs of semi-detached council houses. The larger plot on Trent Lane was bought by Mr. & Mrs. Norman Ellis, who built a low very modern single storey house with a monopitch roof to an innovative plan in brick, glass, stone and timber orientated to the south west, called *Primavera*, named as the project was in the 'springtime of their lives' as well the season in which the large thoughtfully landscaped English garden was designed to look its best. The house, which was essentially designed by Mr. Ellis himself, owes more than a little to Frank Lloyd Wright in its geometrical plan and separation of bedrooms and reception rooms in opposite parts of the building. Interestingly, the design and plan of the house presaged the style of the Newton Park housing estate built in the following decade[34].

Primavera from the west, 1999.   [*M. Craven*]

As we have seen, Hollies Farm gave way to a building development as did most of the farmyard and some of the land of Waterside Farm, where Cricket Close marks the site of the former Cricket field. This had actually been left to the village for this purpose in Percy's will and should have been left un-developed, but some rapacious attorney spotted that a developer could get away with preserving only the playing square and not the outfield which, Derrick Pounds avers, killed local cricket stone dead, at least for a time, until alternative arrangements could be worked out. The housing estate built in the mid-1960s on the land of Waterside Farm has already been described. Lastly most of the estate's building plots along the north side of Repton Road - opposite The Grange and along as far as Poplars Farm - were gradually built upon, mainly with detached houses in as variety of reasonably unobtrusive styles.

Newton Park mansion and its 18 acres of gardens were sold in June 1961 to W. F. Gospel of Stainsby Manor. Consequently, on 22nd March 1961, the fixtures and fittings were sold, raising £7,600 and the house was then re-sold to a consortium of local businessmen, which announced in the June of the year following that it was to become the *Park Hotel*. Work started that same year, the contractors being Ward & Goodbehere of Uttoxeter, and it finally opened at Easter, March 1966, under the ownership of Solney Hotels, Ltd., of which Robert Leighton was the managing director, leading the consortium. It was provided with 25 en-suite rooms[35]

At the same time the housing development to go in the park was being planned as a separate venture. Unlike most developments today, a real effort was made to achieve excellence and to ensure that the whole did little or nothing to compromise the incomparably delightful and interesting landscape, largely a legacy of Abraham Hoskins' very personal vision. Thus the concrete-bottomed lake, entirely re-landscaped by Col. Ratcliffe, was to become the focus of a new sylvan development. The new owners, who acquired the land and the 11 acre field behind the hall for

169

£38,000, were the Newton Park Development Company, which was based at 92, The Hollow Littleover, Derby, presumably the address of Leslie Bass Gardner, the promoter of the scheme. They engaged a Nottingham firm of architects, Messrs. Bestwick, Bowler, Hogg who developed a scheme in 1963 to build 24 new houses of one and two storeys in park-like setting (no more than four houses per acre) of 23 acres. In the end 18 houses were built between 1966 and 1974 to a luxurious standard, all but one being of a single storey, with geometrical floor plans – each house artfully positioned so that it had the maximum exposure to the sun - and using much glass in construction, as well as innovative systems of domestic economy, heating, cooking, and similar. The planning authority required the houses to be built as low as possible, and this led to eight planned two storey houses being reduced just to one. Indeed, their discrete layout and low appearance, interspersed with trees and landscaping, might appear to the layman to have derived not a little inspiration from Mr. Ellis's earlier *Primavera*, in Trent Lane. The minimum floor space of the houses (both single & two storey ones) was intended to be 1500 sq. ft., but in practice most have 1,800 sq. ft. Before completion, their cost was estimated to be around £8000 each, with £100 worth of kitchen equipment to be thrown in although an MS calculation based on information from the contractors suggests that a price of £12,820 was nearer the mark at the time. The contractor was R. Guilford of Derby[36].

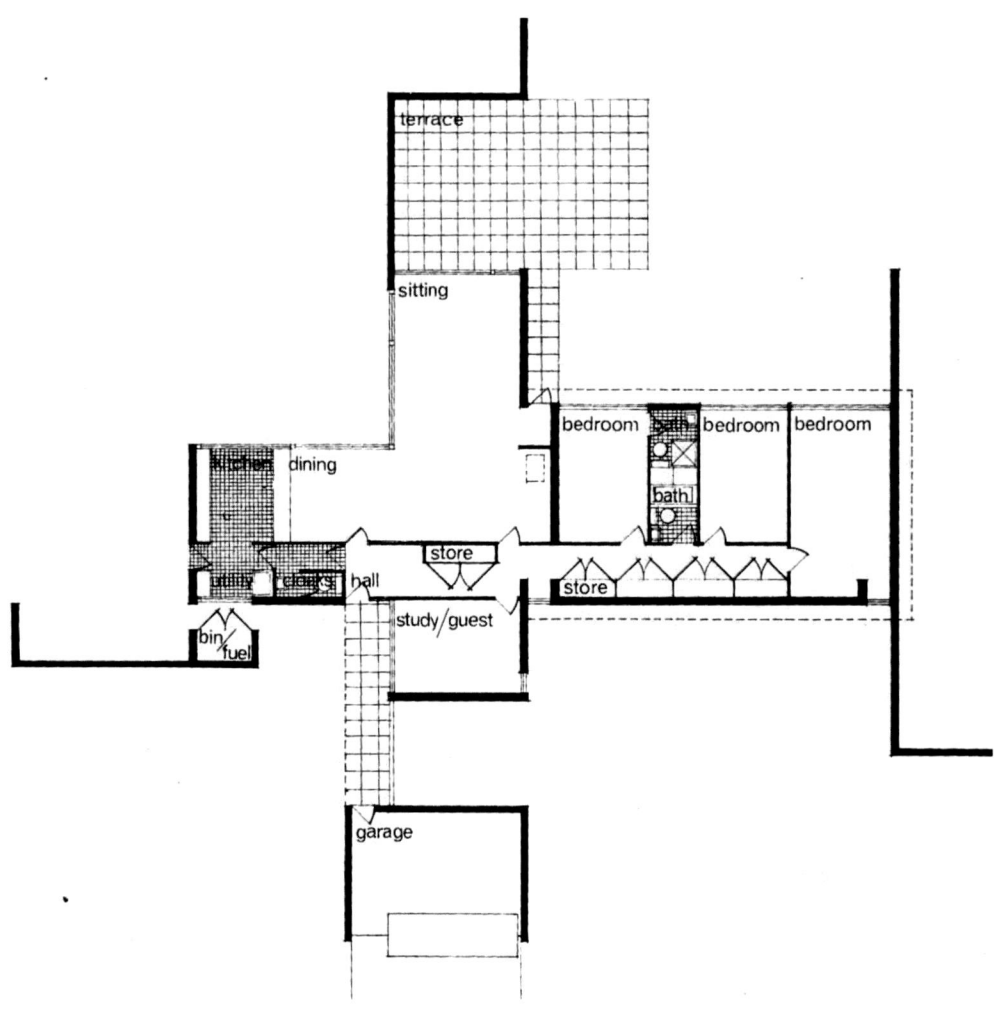

Ground plan of a typical Newton Park House, 1964, from the sales brochure.

What the Newton Park Estate client was getting: artist's impression of the new single storey houses, 1964.

The idea was to incorporate these houses into the landscape, or, as the prospectus said, "The old red brick walls, forest trees and undulations suggested that the houses should 'grow out of the landscape' rather than impose themselves upon it – should be grouped to frame the views within and out of the site – should in fact be subsidiary to its natural beauty." To which end the lake was drained, cleaned and re-stocked (with rainbow trout and golden orfe), with its surroundings landscaped. Around it and its feeder stream the wilderness garden was to some extent retained as a communal space, with the summerhouse as its focus.

The Brochure cover for the Newton Park Estate, 1964.   *[Michael Day]*

The remains of Burton Bridge and those of the Abbey were suffered to remain, too, although the latter stand remarkably close to one of the houses, to reasonable effect. The stables and garden court were converted into mews accommodation, too, with four houses in the former kitchen garden, the walls of which were retained. The two access roads were un-adopted, so that the estate remains a private one. Newton Park Residents' Association was also set up in order to maintain and care for the common spaces and act as co-ordinator. The prospectus claimed that:

> "The drives and paths will be made…to County Council specification but will be retained as private roads. These, together with the lake, northern beechwood and the grassed areas will be owned by the Residents' Association. Each purchaser will be a member of the Association and will be required to pay a Rent charge of £60 per annum towards the upkeep of the amenities. The Company will be non-profit making and will be controlled by members in accordance with the Rules and Articles of the Association."

A view in the estate, 2001   [*C. Bond*]

Today, it costs owners £1,200 to belong to the Association but residents still have to covenant to abide by the terms of the Association when buying their property. Not only that, but a self-catering service was planned for those purchasers of these houses who couldn't face cooking at any time: residents could order meals to be delivered to their door from the adjacent hotel or even request a full party catering service; this service lapsed in 1968. In 2000 there were 64 residents of this estate.

To the south of the estate, however, on rising ground, was subsequently constructed the ranch-style brick two storey mansion of the proprietor of an extensive contracting firm based in Drakelow, Roger Bullivant, who had acquired just over 11 acres of the park. The house, called Park Manor, is irregular, of three wings in Y-plan joining at the entrance hall under a small cupola. The gabled and jettied porch is enclosed by the

Park Manor pictured in 2009   *[Savills]*

dormered and half-timbered flanking wings ending in gabled crosswings of different sizes, that to the right boasting a Gothick tripartite canted bay window. Inside, the rooms are relatively low-ceilinged, although the plasterwork in two rooms is ribbed in a simplified Neo-Jacobean style, and the staircase is trifurcated and exotic, carved in red hardwood and galleried at the upper landing. The drawing room, with its Gothick lights boasts what the agents' charged with selling the house in 2009 termed a minstrels gallery. It was offered for sale in April that year with an asking price of £2,600,000. Unlike the earlier dwellings, it makes less of a concession to the landscape of the rest of Mr. Hoskins' surviving Elysium.[37]

Park Manor, dining room, 2009.   *[Savills]*

Mr. Fellowes, the manager of the Newton Park Hotel, who had set up the rather posh meals-on-wheels option for the residents, launched the new estate with a champagne reception, but his owners moved the hotel on, selling it in 1968 as a going concern – appropriately, perhaps given its history – to a brewery. Unfortunately, this was not Bass but Allied, which incorporated the former Ind Coope & Allsopp (once Samuel Allsopp & Co.), but which still completed a connection to the past history of the estate. Allied later had a change of policy and sold the establishment on to Jarvis Hotels Ltd. in December 1990. This firm became a public limited company six years later and still owns the hotel. They removed many of the William Morris style soft furnishings of the original hotel and dumbed it all down, with a rather anodyne revamp of the interior. Much Victorian panelling was also lost (despite it being a grade II listed building) although modern replacement timberwork was brought in to replace it. Some of the lesser pieces of stained glass found in the house were then corralled together to decorate the bar. The tall first floor on the garden front was also divided horizontally to increase accommodation from 25 to 40 rooms in the main house, thus at last resolving the height disparity between the front and back of the building. This was clearly not thought to be sufficient accommodation by Allied Breweries' accountants and, in 1983, a further extension was added to the east wing,

Newton Park Hotel showing the 1983 extension, left.   [*Jervis Hotels, PLC*]

running north from it but executed in an approximation of the style of the original albeit far too bulky and unsubtle. A further extension to the west was, mercifully, refused consent by the South Derbyshire District Council. There were also changes in the gardens, too. The statuary fountain, surrounded by its large pond and once populated by koi carp was done away with – no doubt out of fear of legal action should some hapless child fall in – and is now a rose garden[38].

Mrs. Ratcliff died on 11th May 1971, when the remainder of the estate was sold, including Newton Park Farm and The Cedars. The auctioneer for John German was Adrian Argyle, who had co-incidentally been brought up at the latter house. Her death heralded further expansion of the village. Whilst the close- knit ambience of the estate village was inevitably lost by the break-up of the Newton Park estate, cohesion has been preserved despite the near-doubling of Newton's population since that event. Even with the present number of around 800 souls, it is not too hard for people to pull together as a community, whether it be through the agency of the WI, the sports teams or the church, or winning 'Britain in Bloom' and 'Best Kept Village', both achieved in the 1980s, and both of which required enormous community effort. Indeed, the former contest spurred the village on again in 1998 when Newton came first in the regional finals and 1999 when it was second nationally overall, an exceedingly creditable record[39].

The present chapter has attempted to give a sense not only of what has gone before in the life of the village at large, but what aspects still thrive to make it a special and notable place that its denizens both today and in the future will enjoy, cherish and appreciate the life it offers. After all, Newton Solney is perhaps a rarity now in the vibrancy of the life of its community. This is without doubt aided by the presence of the two thriving hostelries (the *Unicorn* now with bead and breakfast), the fine village hall, the primary school, an active church congregation and a good many residents who are prepared to contribute enthusiastically to the many events held throughout the average year. There is a WI and a Tuesday Club (the latter for those getting on in years) both of which organise frequent excursions. In addition there are clubs for shooting, bowls, snooker and tennis. Ploughman's lunches are held at the village hall, and there are monthly village walks. Events are advertised in a newssheet delivered regularly to every home. The parish council even has a website.

For those is search of more luxurious accommodation than that on offer at the *Unicorn*, the Newton Park Hotel – Hoskins' Elysium, if much changed – which is a popular place to hold a wedding reception or host a large family event. Sadly, some regular events have had to be set aside for various reasons, 'health and safety' being one. For instance, until recently there was a pancake race up Main Street on Shrove Tuesday and also a 10 kilometre run around the local lanes. Furthermore, people used to dance in the street on New Year's Eve and race around the village and the playing field the following morning! It is, however, gratifying to record that the annual cricket match between teams from the two pubs still takes place, along with a tug o' war. Other events which get people together regularly include a bonfire night party on the banks of the Trent, the start of the raft race to Willington, a well-attended garden produce show, beer festivals with music, concerts in the church, the school fete and other events that take place as of course in almost every rural village throughout the realm.

The one aspect of village life not so far set out in any detail is that of the church. To end this history, therefore, we may now turn, to trace its origins, progress and present day position in the affairs of the village.

*

1 Every MS; Directories & 1956 sale catalogue
2 Dalefields, Cameron III 47; Sale of farm, Aug. 1980 by Eaton & Hollis of Derby; Jeffords, Pounds
   (2000) 51.
3 1836: 1in. OS 1st edn.; 1846, Tithe Award; freeholding, directories and DLSL *Derbyshire Return of
   Holders of Land;* Every MSS notes
4 Charity, Bulmer (12895) 789 & WI (2000) 4
5 DLSL, *Return of Derbyshire Owners of Land;* 1956 sale catalogue
6 Directories; lease, was for 14 years for which he paid £85 p. a. (sale catalogue)
7 Bulmer (1895) 790; Directories, census, 1891, 1901; 1956 sale catalogue]
8 See above and Every Terrier, 1758; Directories & Census
9 Rennison, 1758 terrier; Rock House, see Chapter III; *Wheatsheaf* & H. Upton, Pounds (2000) 9;
   censuses & directories
10 Walton-Smedley sale, PEC no number; DLSL *Return of Derbyshire Holders of Land.*
11 Housing: DLC Vol. XXXI No. 8 (8/1966) 67-68; Cricket ground Bulmer (1895) 789; house divided,
   WI (2000) 11; information courtesy Mr. & Mrs. Tony Ratcliffe.
12 strips: 1836 sale and 1846/50 Tithe Maps
13 DRO Quarter Sessions, Q/SB/9/249
14 Directories, 1956 sale catalogue; pers. comm. from Mrs. Brooks to M. Day; McManus (2002) 383
   -388
15 Early population, see Chapters I & III; 1789 figure, Pilkington (1789) 97; 1811 figures, Davies
   (1811) 372; churchgoers, Austin (1972) 129; 1841, Bagshaw (1846) 256-257 & directories, passim;
   recent figures, census statistics, COI
16 Everys, DRO D5236/26/87; *Unicorn,* directories, censuses; Applebys, pers. comm.. B. Appleby,
   14/4/2009.
17 German (1956) 16
18 Directories & Census returns; Wilkins, Pounds (2000) 48 - his successor was Dick Cooper.
19 G. Smith, D5236/32/14-15 of 2/1/1748/9; Wm. Eyre, 1836 map; rest, directories & census; Smedley,
   Terrier, 1758; directories and censuses; German (1956) *loc. cit.*
20 This & preceding two paras., Directories, census & German (1956) 21, 22, 24
21 Bulmer (1895) 789; Ellis (1997) 3; gardeners, Pounds 2000) 42.
22 Chapel, White (1857) 370
23 Mrs. Somers' niece Frances (1819-1888) married her cousin William Somers (1822-1885), landlord
   of the *Boot Inn* at Repton in the 1850s & their son was Joseph (BLG (1952) 2359 & MIs at Repton);
   Fairfield Ho, DLC (2/2007) 109
24 Directories, census
25 Rock House, Every MS notes; Directories & Census; 1956 sale catalogue; Moreton, BP (1970) 940
   when his address is still given as Rock House; information courtesy R. F. Kerry, Esq.
26 Allotments, Bulmer (1895) 789; Institute, village trail, no. 13 & WI (2000) 36; Arthur Eaton,
   descended from the Etwall and Sutton-on-the-Hill family that had produced George Eaton, the man
   who built Derby's Shire Hall, had died in 1924
27 First parish council, Bulmer (1895) 790
28 Edward Smedley, DRO D5236/17/27/90 of 27/4/1832; Police, Directories & WI (2000) 21
29 Bagshaw (1846) 256; Bulmer, *loc.cit.,* WI (2000) 6, 47-48; school, Pounds (2000) 49.
30 Gas lights, Bulmer (1895) 789; Kelly (1912) 358; 'buses, Edwards (1993) 168-169, Heath (1985) 3
31 Railway proposal, DRO Q/RP 2/47
32 Evacuees, WI (2000) 22, 25; bombing, Pounds (2000) 20; Ellis (1997) 3; other WW2, Pounds *op. cit.*
   19-21. staff, *ibid.* 42-43.
33 German (1956) *passim.*; shooting etc., Pounds (2000) 46-47, 71.
34 Ex. inf. courtesy N. Ellis, Esq
35 Gospel is quoted by Michael Day as being 'of Thoresby Park, Hucknall'; Ownership, DET
   16/12/1960, p. 11, c. 1; Sale of furnishings DET 22/3/1961 p. 17, c. 6 & DET 23/3/1961, p. 16, c. 3;
   Hotel, DET 28/6/1962 p. 26, c. 1; opening etc., DLC (1/1966) 47
36 DLC, *loc.cit*; TPOs revised 1982; price, contemporary MS pencil note tucked into prospectus.
37 DLC 1/66, 45-51, including specimen plans; Brochure, 1964, *passim.*; M. Day, MS notes; Park
   Manor, Savill's brochure, April 2009.
38 Ellis (1997) 4
39 WI (2000) 49

*

VII

THE CHURCH

No one knows when Christianity first flourished in Newton Solney. There is evidence for the faith having come to these islands by the middle of the second century AD, and Britain still had a century or so to run as part of the Roman Empire when the Edict of Milan legitimised Christianity throughout the empire. Yet, as no evidence of Roman settlement has yet emerged at Newton, we have to postpone the juxtaposition of the two until the tenth century, when Newton makes it debut in the charter of that year quoted in the first chapter.[1]

By that time, the former kingdom of Mercia had been Christian for just over three centuries and, with the postulated presence of a colony of Britons lying just over the ridge at Bretby, we might reasonably suppose that the faith had much deeper roots in the parish or its immediate environs than one might suppose from a tenth century charter.

Furthermore, there had been a royally-sponsored Mercian double monastic house of considerable importance at Repton from the later seventh century and, as we also saw in the first chapter, there are grounds for thinking that Repton was the centre of a much larger polity – perhaps quite ancient - which actually included Newton. According to his eleventh century biographer, Rhygfarch ap Sulien, the first monastery on or near the site had been founded by St. David towards the end of the sixth century. This is perhaps not quite as far-fetched as it may seem, for there was a British principality centered on *Letocetum* (Old Welsh *Luitcoyd*) or Wall, on Roman Rylknield Street in Staffordshire until the middle of that century. Such a sacred location on the future site of Repton may perhaps have been suffered to remain under the early Mercian Kings (who were, until the death of Penda c. 655, all pagan) for purposes of prestige or as part of the acculturation of the British population of the area, whose existence appears to be embodied in the name Bretby. Indeed, such a survival may have been the rationale behind the choice of Repton as the destination of the first apostle to the Mercians, St. Diuma, sent on Penda's death. Against it, is the lack of dedications of churches to David in the area, except, oddly, for two in Nottinghamshire. A subsequent land grant from the Mercian Prince, Friduricus, to the earlier Saxon monastery of Breedon-on-the-Hill, probably in the 680s, may have been used to finally establish the double house at Repton in the form it has come down to us.[2]

Thus there was an attested presence of Christianity in the Newton Solney area from at least the later seventh century and it may be that the first Christians in whatever settlement formed the nucleus of the later settlement of Newton met for simple everyday worship at Spellow Cross. Although the name is Norse, the use to which the feature was put, preaching the Gospel, could well have been something hallowed by antiquity even then. No doubt, though, villagers who were by that time Christian, would have also used the monastic and Royal church at Repton for important acts of worship, like mass and festivals.[3]

Pre-reformation growth

The coming of the Vikings in 874 and the destruction of the monastery at Repton was followed only by a very modest recovery. Repton church seems to have been rebuilt as a minster, with two priests (mentioned in Domesday Book, one of only two Derbyshire churches therein with two) whose purpose was to re-evangelise the pagan Norsemen settled in the country round about, just as the minster church of St. Alkmund, Derby had been built before the Vikings came to evengelise the still-pagan Saxons. Then, in the twelfth century, came the re-founding of a monastic house at Repton, as Priory, settled from the earlier foundation of Calke, which thereafter became subordinate to it. There is, however, no mention of a church as such at Newton Solney until the thirteenth century, when it occurs in a deed datable to 1271/1279. In 1304 the topographical name *Le chirchesty* appears, followed in 1317 by a mention of *Le chapelhous*, which confirm the existence of a chapel-of-ease, or subsidiary church to the monastic one at Repton. Thus, well before the opening of the fourteenth century, there was in the village a pig-sty belonging to the church as well as a house in which the priest could live.[4]

The Norman north doorcase.   [*M. Craven*]

In fact, the church itself still retains elements of Norman architecture in its fabric and indeed, a chapel could possibly have existed before the writing of the *Domesday Book* for, as was pointed out in the first chapter, *Domesday* is not all-encompassing and, if something was not germaine to the King or taxable on his behalf, it was omitted. The later attested chapels of Bretby, Foremark, Ingleby, Measham, Ticknall and Newton – all subordinate to the mother-church of Repton – could, therefore, have pre-existed 1086, but escaped mention by owing duty only to Repton. What one sees today – a doorcase in the north wall and fragments of another built into the wall of the tower on the same side – are too plain to really date closely, but the safe presumption is that they are earlier 12th century and that this may be taken for the date of the first stone church on the site[5].

Indeed, the existence of a church can certainly be established from 1274, by means of a charter that confirms the name of the chaplain of the time as William son of Alfred de Solney (V) 'curate of Newton Solney', who was given lands in the village with a fishery at the confluence of the Trent and Dove, confirmed to him by his nephew Alfred de Solney (VII) in 1304 when he was granted a further ten acres. He seems to have lived a long life in the job, for he recurs in 1316 and lived on to pay poll tax in 1327 – thus a 53-year plus incumbency, by no means unique in the annals of the

English church (nor even Newton, where Father Jansen managed nearly 55 years), but probably relatively exceptional in those days when life expectancy was fairly low. The alternative is that there were two men of this name, but certainly the same man was serving in 1274 and 1304. At this stage, too, some priests were still marrying and having children, and it may be that the Richard de Solney who witnessed a charter at Newton Solney in 1354 and was referred to as a chaplain was certainly William's successor and quite possibly his son, too. He probably died or moved on to a new cure in that year, however, for one Thomas de Balderton, who had granted land to Richard the year before, re-appears the same year as holding a house and bovate of land in Newton from John de Saveney, possibly the de Solney family steward. As a house and a bovate seem to recur as the portion of the chaplain throughout this period, we may be pretty sure that Thomas had taken over, albeit only for a short time, for William de Measham also occurs at this time and would appear to have been his successor.[6]

Indeed, a relatively complete succession of pre-reformation chaplains of Newton church can be reconstructed from the charters:

PRE-REFORMATION CHAPLAINS
OF NEWTON SOLNEY

1274-1327+ : William de Solney
+1330-1352 : Richard de Solney
1352-1353 : Thomas de Balderton
1353-1354 : William de Measham
1354-1368 : William Hayward
1368-1380+ : Adam Thorold
+1380-1397 : William Taylor
1397-1420+ : John Neem (ie., Neame)
+1438-[   ] : Adam de Bladon

To which one might add that a William de Newton, chaplain, a witness to a charter concerning Newton in 1375, was probably a canon of Repton Priory but not chaplain at Newton, and in the same year, another chaplain, John de Bellowe, although holding lands, fishing rights and so on in Newton Solney, 'formerly held by Richard de Solney', was probably a rector of Egginton, as was William Taylor, in view of the fact that he was chaplain to Sir Alfred de Lathbury. The latter on the other hand may merely have had a domestic chapel at his house in Egginton. Adam de Bladon may also have fallen into this category, as he was also attorney to John de Lathbury under the terms of John's will of 1438, but he at least is attested as chaplain at Newton too. The fact that one or two of them might also have been either domestic chaplains to the Lathburys or vicars of Egginton might go some way to confirming Cox's statement that the parish boat was originally to enable the chaplains to cross the river to take Divine Service.[7]

The row of conjoined lancet windows along the north wall of the church presumably relates to a first rebuilding of the church, but most of what survived to be recorded in the 19th century and what survives today is mid-14trh century work, notably the nave arcading with its squat octagonal piers, undoubtedly paid for by the de Solneys – probably Sir Alfred VII – in the incumbency of their kinsman, Richard de Solney, perhaps in thanksgiving for the passing of the Black Death which the chaplain seems to have survived.

As we saw in Chapter II, **a** perpetual chantry for two priests was to be established within 20 years of 1391 in memory of the Solneys as part of a settlement of the manors of Pinxton and Normanton (which the de Solneys had bought) with a yearly rent of £12 from the manor, payable by the two sisters and co-heiresses of the last Sir Alfred de Solney who had just died, Alice Stafford and Margery Longford. It is to be presumed that this arrangement survived until the Reformation, but in fact we hear no more of it. Its location in the church is presumed by most commentators to have been in the north aisle.[8]

The church itself is dedicated to the Blessed Virgin Mary, and Cox aptly says of it:
"The picturesque little church contains an admixture of almost every style of architecture, the work of succeeding centuries being plainly written upon its face."

Newton church in 1789

The Norman work, indeed, has already been noted, along with the lancet windows adjacent and the 14th century arcading, with what Pevsner describes as "…low octagonal piers, [with] double-chamfered arcading". The spire looks taller in the surviving pictures than it does today; it was probably added and the tower rebuilt at the same time as the nave was rebuilt, in the mid-14th century. The font is also 14th century, as is the small piscina on the S. side of chancel. The chancel arch was probably removed in the 15th century and in the same era a Perpendicular straight-headed clerestory and chancel windows were added, but thereafter little change affected the church for some centuries. Also probably in the fifteenth century, the interior surfaces were decorated with painted biblical scenes, some of which were revealed at the rebuilding of 1880-1881, along with some later ones, with verses from Genesis, added in the early 18th century.[9]

[*Sir Henry Every, Bt.*] Although we may be sure that the de Solneys paid for the earlier re-buildings and beautifications of the church, their patronage was purely secular, the Priory of Repton being the patron at this stage. The fifteenth century rebuilding was the only identifiable alteration made before the Everys took over before the Civil War, for the lordship was divided between the Lathburys and the Longfords, and both had interests elsewhere. The Priory, indeed, might have made the alterations we can discern, merely imposing a subvention on the two lay owners of the manor to help pay for them. As time went on, however, the tithes – the local tax levied on the agricultural produce of the parish-

Wall paintings on the west end of the church 1880, photographed by Richard Keene the younger. [*Brian Appleby*]

Wall paintings and inscriptions on the south wall of the church, photographed by Richard Keene the younger 1880 [*Brian Appleby*]

ioners to support the church and its chaplain due to the Priory of Repton - were leased out to lay people in return for a rental. This saved the Priory – never a very large institution – from having to arrange the collection and assessment of these themselves, but allowed the lessees of the tithes to make themselves a bit of profit, either from efficient collection or from imposing a slight increase in dues. For instance, in 1528 the corn ('great') tithes, tithe barn and adjacent yard were let by the Priory to William Dethick of Newhall – later father-in-law of Sir Thomas Leigh of Egginton the joint-lord of Newton - for 20 years at a rent of £10 per annum. This arrangement, however, did not last for more than a decade for in 1538 the Priory was dissolved by the Crown and the tithes were sold, along with the patronage of the church, to the highest bidder. That highest bidder, it emerges, was Dethick, and from him the tithes descended through the Leighs to the Everys.[10]

After the Reformation

With the Priory gone and its conventual church destroyed, only the adjoining parish church of St. Wystan remained at Repton, and this had no real claim to be Newton's mother church. This meant that Newton became independent, a parochial chapelry: in other words it was not officially a parish church (and was therefore thus still technically a chapel rather than a church) but did minister to a parish. Henceforth the incumbent was styled a perpetual curate, paid for out of tithe income by whoever had acquired it, for these were disposed of by the Crown in exactly the same way that the Priory had, by fixed term lease. Thus in 1588, fifty years after the Dissolution of the Priory, the tithes of Newton Solney and other property was sold on a 21 year lease to George Cure and his brother-in-law John Brereton of the Inner Temple, and forthwith his half was immediately sub-let by Cure (who was also of Lavertye, Sussex) for 21 years to Brereton. But this was a valuable commodity, so changes continued. Within less than two years for instance, George Cure had passed his share to his son-in-law, George Boleyn of Petworth, who obtained a new lease for 40 years in 1591 at a very favourable rate which he then immediately re-sold at a profit to another Inner Temple lawyer, Yorkshireman Edward Stapleton, for £60. He, however, decided to "asset strip" the tithes, by selling the church properties that went with the lease to the then lord of the manor, Sir Henry Leigh of Egginton, whilst moving the tithes themselves on, yet again, to a London fishmonger called John Cooper in 1610.

However, by 1618, Sir Henry had managed to acquire all the tithes and church property at Newton from these busy entrepreneurs, having, as we have seen, already acquired the Longford half of the lordship. Indeed, as Chapter III showed, this seems to have left him out of pocket, and so in this year he sold a sixteen and a half year lease of the tithes (plus those of Repton itself, which he had acquired as part of the job lot that had included Newton Solney) to Godfrey Thacker of Repton Hall for £80. Thacker, of course, was the senior descendant of the man who had acquired the Priory of Repton and whose son, on the accession of Queen Mary, had destroyed it with enormous alacrity declaring that he "…would destroy the nest for fear the birds should build therein again." Thacker's aim was to recover the tithes and rectory of Repton from whoever had acquired it - clearly not part of his family's own job-lot acquired when the monastery itself was dissolved. Needless to say, nine years later, he and Thomas Hammond of Derby sold the reversion of the Newton Solney tithes back to Sir Henry, having retained those of Repton. Sir Henry's finances had clearly recovered as he paid them £200 with the reversion, extended to his son-in-law Simon Every and, in due course, it all came to Sir Simon who later consolidated the lease.[11]

In Edward VI's reign an attempt was launched by the Government, keen to capitalise on the effects of the Reformation, to ascertain what ecclesiastical property remained in church hands. One of these took the form of a visitation by a group of commissioners looking into and recording church goods. On 6th October 1552 they visited Newton Solney and their report included mention of 3 sets of vestments, 3 decorated albs, 3 altar cloths, 4 towels, a cope of St. Thomas made of worsted, two shrouds with painted linen cases, two brass candlesticks, two altar cruets, a silver chalice, three bells in the steeple and an altar bell. The cope was presumably embroidered with an image of the apostle Thomas, or possibly St. Thomas of Canterbury. Miraculously, of the three bells, one survives, the second in the peal, of fifteenth century date, marked in Lombardic lettering, "Sancte Maria ora p[ro] nobis" (Holy Mary, pray for us). The other two are replacements of seventeenth century date, one by the famous maker Henry Oldfield inscribed "God Save Our Church 1615" and the other, anonymous, marked "God Save the Church 1635". The hanging of the latter bell probably revealed structural problems with the nave roof, because two years later this was renewed or drastically repaired, for a beam (removed in 1880) was found marked with date and W. H., W. D. & E. I. These initials stand for William Hepworth, the incumbent, William Dicken, a churchwarden and local farmer, still alive when the Hearth Tax return was made almost thirty years later, and an anonymous churchwarden, whose surname began with an 'I' or 'J'. Unfortunately, no name beginning with either letter appears, either in the Hearth Tax Return of 1662 or the Terrier of 1758.[12]

Dicken headstones re-positioned against the churchyard wall   *[M. Craven]*

Despite all the lettings and re-lettings of the tithes and patronage of the church, Sir Simon Every managed to inherit them all intact, for at the beginning of the Civil War he was able to grant the tithes for 99 years in trust to finance the education of his younger children, as we saw in chapter III. As he was subsequently adjudged a 'delinquent' due to his support for the King in the Civil War, an Act of Parliament of 1643 disqualified him from disposing of his estate (including the tithes) except by sale, thus preventing him vesting any part of it in further trusts - allegedly to benefit his family, but in reality to protect them from sequestration by the County Committee. Eventually, as we have seen, Sir Henry, the 2nd Baronet, managed to be emollient enough to the County committee to convince them to allow him to keep his estate after a relatively light compounding. By this time, however, another Parliamentary Committee, set up to look into the working of all livings, had reported on Newton. It found that the income was £75 – not a great deal even by the standards of the day – and that the Everys were the patrons and had the tithes – that is they owned the right to the great tithes (those of corn and hay) through their annexation long before, by the Priory of Repton. The committee also were of the opinion that the chapelry be combined with Winshill parish which latter they describer as "…belonging to Burton upon Trent but remote and may conveniently be united to Newton Solney." Needless to say, nothing came of this proposal to unite the two during the following nine years of the Commonwealth, nor ever later. [13]

The Everys did their bit in keeping the church in good repair and occasionally embellishing it. Sir Henry, 2nd Bt., gave a fine silver paten (the shallow dish used for holding the consecrated wafers in the Eucharist) about 1670 – unfortunately the assay marks are too faint to be read, hence the imprecise date. His successor, the third baronet in his will left a fixed sum of £20 per annum as a stipend for the curate, "in order that the Church of England service might be held there every Sunday", which clearly (also Sir Henry) implies that services up to that time were somewhat sporadic. This reinforces the supposition that when services *were* provided, they were taken by the rector of Egginton (or his curate), who no doubt made his way across the Coalpitway Field and over the Trent by the Newton Parish boat - especially in view of the incomplete list of incumbents available for the post-Reformation period.[14]

It was, Sir Henry, the third baronet – who lived most of his life in the Great House, on Burton High Street – the Every's town house there – who is remembered by the very high quality recumbent effigy still in the church, carved by Thomas Carter the elder in around 1734 and installed by Sir Henry's youngest brother, Rev'd Sir Simon Every, 5th Bt., who had succeeded in 1729. Originally, this effigy, very much in the taste of the so-called 'Augustan Age', with the be-sandalled baronet draped in a toga, rested against the north wall against a suitably Classical pyramid of Chellaston alabaster set against Black Marble from further north in the county, all under a carved timber – probably fruitwood – canopy, but which disappeared when the church was restored in 1880-81 and the monument moved to the base of the tower. Thomas Carter (c. 1707-1795) was a carver of great distinction and worked mainly in partnership with his brother Benjamin from a yard in Piccadilly (London). They also took Roubiliac as a pupil in 1729. The 5th baronet probably commissioned Carter having met him through friends made during his long cure in Lincolnshire at Nauntby and Somerby, Sir Cecil and Lady Wray of Glentworth, for whose house at Branston, Carter made chimney-pieces at this time. Tastes changed radically in the century and a half between its being completed and the compilation of Cox's *Church Notes* of 1877, for the good Canon is very sniffy about the monument, saying that in comparison with the late 14th century de Solney effigy, Sir Henry "makes a striking contrast…in every way to the advantage of the latter." To wind up the Every family's benefactions, it is important to mention the fine silver chalice and paten cover presented in March 1758 by Revd. Sir John Every, 7th Bt., marked London, 1757.[15]

We can only presume that there was a sequence of curates appointed by the Everys from the 1709 bequest of a stipend, although the only certain name we have is that of a Mr. Woodcock who on 22/1/1774 sought an augmentation to the curacy in order to increase his stipend – presumably Sir Edward Every 8th Bt was a trifle pushed at this time. Needless to say this attempt failed. In 1730 Rev'd Sir Simon Every who, as an ex-Lincolnshire parson himself well understood these things, put the Newton Solney great tithes into trust in order to secure the £20 which his father had so nobly opted to bestow; previously the money had been paid out of pocket. Another name from the sparse 18th century may be that of the Mr. John Newton of the 1758 terrier, being a freeholder (which the incumbent technically was) and correctly addressed as 'Mr.' Nevertheless, the continuous run of Curates and, later, vicars, does not begin until 1814 when John Hare was appointed by Sir Henry, 9th Bt. after the estate's affairs had been brought back into tolerable order. He duly was to serve for the next 46 years, during which time he received another £10 per annum from Sir Henry Every sometime between 1846 and 1857.[16]

It was in Mr. Hare's time that the Archdeacon of Derby undertook a visitation of all the churches in his care, and his report gives us a most helpful snapshot of St. Mary's affairs in the Regency period. He came on 9th July 1824 and his report starts by confirming that the church is a donative curacy under Sir Henry Every, the patron, the curate himself confirming that it is outside the jurisdiction of the bishop by this status. He goes on to say that the church itself is an

> "…ancient building consisting of nave, side aisles and chancel; seats for 250 and moderately well attended, but [with] no accommodation for the poor. Timber roof, lead covered; stone walls, stone floor, level; good windows with casements; good doors, pulpit, books and seats. A gallery at the W end; no organ, stone font; no chapels; no benediction tables nor charities; new vestry (qv above); middling surplices; new cloth and napkin; silver chalice and patten; there are [sic] a chest for papers and an iron chest for registers which run to 7 volumes beginning in 1633, although the first volume imperfect. Brick porch covered with tiles; no vaults made lately; cleaned inside regularly and not much damp."

Arising from this one might add that the pews were all held on rentals by the parishioners; most churches at this period with such an arrangement had a section of free seating set aside, but clearly this was not the case at Newton Solney. Indeed in 1829 a dispute arose over a pew in church between Abraham Hoskins and Sir Henry Every. This was allegedly part and parcel of the freehold of an 86 acre farm which Sir Henry sold to Hoskins in 1812 for £8,676 and subsequently occupied by the tenants. Sir Henry denied that the sale included the pew and objected to Hoskins's tenants using it. The matter had clearly gone un-noticed for some time, but was ultimately amicably settled, with Sir Henry retaining the ownership of the pew and the tenants having free use of it.

The lack of organ meant that musicians had to be persuaded to provide the music of the services that were not actually said. In fact, even fifty years before, in 1774, "a large Choir, sixteen of whom come from Stapenhill, filled the Gallery of the Church, numbering among their Musical Instruments 2 French Horns, 2 Hautbois [oboes], 2 bassoons". Eleven years before that, "the Burton singers, for performing the anthem on 5th November 1763, received a guinea from Sir John [Every (7th Bt.)]." These efforts to provide music in church were amongst the evidences deployed by Rev'd Mr. Woodcock to obtain an increase in his stipend from Queen Anne's Bounty, to which body, he tells us, a previous application had been fruitlessly made "thirty years before" in 1744. Bearing in mind that by the time of the visitation Thomas Greatorex had been living in the village for seven or eight years, it is astonishing that he had not

185

pulled strings to get an organ put in; perhaps indeed, he had tried and failed to persuade either or both Sir Henry Every and Abraham Hoskins to stump up. As we do not know exactly when the first instrument went in, one can only speculate as to whether his efforts met with any success before he moved away not long after his friend Thomas Gayfere was buried under a slab in the nave, where it was reported still by Cox (it has subsequently been moved outside, which is unfortunate). Certainly there was such an instrument by 1874, when F. and W. Drewry, relations of that James Drewry who earlier had lived at The Mount, are recorded as the joint organists of the church. Mr .Phelps came in to do duty in the 1940s, when the instrument still had to be hand-pumped.

POST REFORMATION INCUMBENTS
OF NEWTON SOLNEY

Curates

+6/10/1552+: Nicholas Sambull
    +1560+: Ralph Clerk (a pensioned former canon of Repton Priory)
    +1637+: William Hepworth
    +1650+: Mr. Bryan, "a man disaffected" (Probably ejected in favour
              of a Puritan by 1652).
    +1662+: Mr. Wiseman
    +1758+: (?)Mr. John Newton
    +1774+: Mr. Woodcock
1814-1860: John Hare.
1860-1862: J. Wilson (died 1862, MI in church)
1862-1872: George French

Vicars

1872-1878: George French
1878-1891: Robert Walter Hurd
1891-1947: Frederick Charles Theodore Jansen
    +1965+: Canon Sidney William Bazalgette
     +1969: Canon F. S. Fairclough
    +1970+: Canon White
1975-1989: Wolfgang A. R. K. Werwath

Priests-in-Charge

1989-1990 : Michael J. Diggle
1990   : G. Goodwin
From the 1990s, the benefice was united with that of Repton.

No mention is made, however of the vestry, but in fact one had just been completed on the north side of the church, in December 1821, which took William Holmes, of the Grange Farm family - the village builder - nine months. The cost was £26 – 0s –

7d, paid in December 1821. A final point arising relates to the porch, which was put on about 1744, the year in which Newton's blacksmith William Ashmore fashioned (for 9/-) and mounted a fine gilded wrought iron weathercock on the church spire. 1744 was also the year in which an un-named incumbent apparently applied (unsuccessfully as it transpired) to Queen Anne's Bounty for a pay-increase. [17]

The archdeacon then went on,

> "Dimensions: church 33ft long 40 ft wide; chancel 28 ft long and 18 ft. wide. Altar a plain table; repairs done by Sir Henry. Tower: with spire about 90 ft. tall, in reasonable repair, with three bells but no clock. Churchyard: Hedged around and with low wall; gates in good repair, no drains but none wanted; no graves within 4 feet of church; rubbish regularly removed; two footpaths across it and no cattle; normally moved on."

Services were held every Sunday plus Christmas day and Good Friday, with Holy Communion celebrated four times a year, usually attended by six or eight communicants; catechism was, as was then and is now, normal, done in Lent.

The incumbent in 1824 was, as we have seen, John Hare, a bachelor of Arts, but who did not live in the parish, but in Repton two miles away, where he was still living in 1827/29. He conducted all the services with no assistant, on (as we have seen) an income of £20, later rising to £30. The other fees he was eligible to receive were very limited. There was no church school, but only a Sunday school, "at present failing through want of funds". The church roll stood at 216 – most of the inhabitants of the parish – the churchwarden was William Higgott of Newton Lane Farm and the parish clerk was John Saint who was appointed by the parish and paid £1 – 10s – 0d for his pains.

The "fine old monuments" referred to were the present three stone effigies of recumbent knights, all de Solneys. All three were noted by William Wyrley, a herald who visited the churches of Derbyshire in 1596. There are two knightly effigies of local sandstone (one decapitated, one partially legless) and another in alabaster. The headless one – which stood upright near the entrance to the church until 1880 - is not considered, either by Cox or Pevsner, to be later than c. 1275 therefore perhaps Sir Alfred de Solney IV who was dead by 1262. The other stone effigy, legs crossed, is a generation earlier, and therefore may be Sir Alfred de Solney III, who died c. 1230. The alabaster figure, which is particularly fine - although it has lost its sheen and polish through damp at some time in the past - was once sited beneath an arch on the north side of the chancel in the de Solney Chantry presumably, but by Cox's visit of 1877 was in the south east chancel angle, near where it remains. It seems generally agreed that it was carved locally, at Burton. John Leland in the sixteenth century wrote: "At Burton are many marblers working in alabaster", and similar remarks are to be found attributed to William Camden in Gough's edition of his *Britannia*. Cox, probably with every justification, thinks it "more highly finished than any other in the county" and suggests a date of c. 1375/1400 which would make it an effigy of the last de Solney, Sir John, who died c. 1390. Sir Nikolaus Pevsner, however, considered it c. 1375, which would make it Sir John's father, Sir Alfred de Solney VIII, who died in 1379. [18]

In 1833 further repairs were carried out to the church at a cost of £138 – 15s - 2d and, despite the breaking of his links with the village in the 1837 sale, Abraham Hoskins was buried in a large chest tomb in at Newton churchyard in 1842 and commemorated by a Gothick memorial facing the entrance, above one of the de Solney effigies. In 1862 a new east window to the chancel was inserted, the tracery of which Cox scathingly thought "a poor imitation of Perpendicular work". This was done as a memorial window to Mr. Hare's eventual successor as curate, J. Wilson, who died that year after only eighteen months. Seven years later, glass in a window at the west end of the south side of the church was put in and dedicated to Sarah, widow of Samuel Ratcliff of Cliffe House.

East window of church, 2009
[M. Craven]

Four years after that again, in 1872, a further window was decorated with stained glass to the memory of Calvert Worthington of Newton Park who died the year before. [19]

The archdeacon's report of 1824 makes it clear that John Hare, the incumbent, was living at Repton and indeed, he lived there throughout his life, dying in 1860. It would appear from the census that Mr. Wilson, his successor, also lived outside the parish. The first curate to live in Newton Solney was George French, appointed by Sir Henry Every 10th Bt. in 1862 to succeed Mr. Wilson. He was a son of the Rev'd. Peter French, the first incumbent of Holy Trinity, Burton (a commissioners' church) from 1824 to 1871. George French's brother, Thomas Valpy French, his father's curate at Burton, went on to be Bishop of Lahore. It may be that Sir Henry found it necessary to provide a house in order to attract a new parson, for even by this date the stipend was only £30, Sir Henry's father having put it up from £20 for Mr. Hare c. 1850. [20]

Abraham Hoskins' memorial tablet on the wall of the church.   [*M. Craven*]

One of the crucial questions relating to the adaptation of the vicarage is when the Ratcliffs purchased the patronage of the living and the great tithes from the Everys. As we have seen in the previous chapter, the Everys sold most of their holdings in the village around 1870/71 and it was almost certainly then that Robert Ratcliff bought the patronage. Most sources claim this happened when he bought Newton Park in

189

1878, but White's Directory of 1874 names him as patron four years before, although Sir Henry was still named as patron in 1870. The adaptation of the vicarage may have tied in with this event, especially as Ratcliff raised the stipend to £150 from his own pocket on acquiring the living, and raised it to £250 in 1878 in order to secure the services of a worthy successor to Mr. French; certainly the initial rise must have transformed Mr. French's incumbency no end![21]

Thus it would appear that the house now called the Old Vicarage, in Main Street, an unremarkable two storey, three bay brick house, was converted by the Everys from a farm house, probably of Regency date. The story that the vicarage was provided by Abraham Hoskins thus cannot be true – after all, he was not the patron, for Sir Henry Every, 9th Bt. was in Hoskins' time. Thus the relatively modern farm house there was subsequently adapted as a parsonage with the addition of a reasonably substantial rear wing.

At the same time as Robert Ratcliff bought the patronage of Newton Solney, he seems also to have obtained from the Diocesan authorities (then still Lichfield) the status of vicar for the incumbent, so that Mr. French, from having begun his cure in Repton as curate of Newton, ended it in 1878 as vicar, in a vicarage in the village. Ratcliff's motives may well be that he was seeking to neutralise the influence of the Methodists, who had opened a miniscule chapel in The Square (right beside the house then adapted as a vicarage) in 1851. Incidentally, this is the only traceable mention of Dissent in the history of the village. If so, he was successful, for by 1891 the congregation seem to have vanished and the building was later - ironically – included within the curtilage of the vicarage.

The Former Vicarage on Main Street, now harled and re-fenestrated   [*M. Craven*]

With a new vicar in post, Robert Hurd, Ratcliff's next move was to improve the church, a process which began towards the end of 1879. His architect was Frederick Josias Robinson of Derby, one time partner of the County's most prolific church designer, Henry Isaac Stevens (1806-1873). He was born at Clitheroe Castle, in Lancashire, 18th October 1833, third son of cotton magnate Dixon Robinson and, having been educated at Preston Grammar School, served articles in London with Sir Gilbert Scott from 1850 until 1855, after which he worked as assistant to Stevens who then had an office in London, coming to Derby to be his partner in the early 1860s. He was commissioned as an ensign into the 5th Derbyshire Rifle Corps in 1864, becoming Captain a decade later. Her married late in life, on Trafalgar Day 1881, just after finishing work on Newton Church, his bride being Emilie, the daughter of one of his father's friends, J. F. Armistead of Blackburn. On the death of Stevens in 1873, Robinson took the practice, by then at 45 Friar Gate Derby, over and continued as a church architect, restoring Parwich church in 1872 and designing new ones, like St. Luke, Derby (impressive) and St. Susannah, Horsley Woodhouse (rather modest)[22].

Robinson was a careful and relatively scholarly restorer of churches, and his interventions at Newton Solney were entirely beneficial. The south aisle was taken down, and extended eastwards to meet the chancel, a new porch was added and Perpendicular style windows of good design inserted. The baptistery was opened out, and the north aisle was cleared, which resulted in Carter's monument to Sir Henry Every, 3rd Bt. being re-located to the tower base, a position which does this glorious piece of Baroque carving no favours at all. This made way for the installation of a new pipe organ for the Messrs. Drewry to play. A number of medieval encaustic tiles were re-

Newton Parish church (L) whilst rebuilding in 1880 and (R) afterwards, in 1881, both photographs by Richard Keene the younger.   *[Brian Appleby]*

laid, having been repatriated from Mr. Hoskins' summerhouse, and the church was re-pewed throughout. It was at this stage that the grave-slab of Thomas Gayfere was unfortunately moved into the church yard; a man of such eminence surely ought to have his memorial in the church. The interior was then re-painted and on 10th April 1882 the church was re-dedicated with some ceremony.[23]

The cost was £5,000, of which £2,000 was given by Ratcliff and £1,000 by his sisters at Cliffe House. The other two substantial donors to the fund were Edward Salt of Rock House and John Higgott. The result is a small church, largely original, and extremely pretty. It is now statutorily listed grade II* and was restored a second time throughout fairly recently, ending in 1995. It is of interest to note that at one stage during the Second World War, German prisoners of war held at Bladon House enjoyed the benefit of Lutheran services read in German by retired Sheffield steelworks director Len Ward, of Cokhay, just across the Repton parish boundary.[24]

The first vicar of the newly-rebuilt church was Robert Walter Hurd but, in 1891, after a short interregnum, the Rev'd. Frederick Charles Theodore Jansen was appointed, and enjoyed an incumbency of 56 years, dying in office, much loved and admired by his flock, having seen them through two world wars and all the vicissitudes of the earlier twentieth century. His life was touched with tragedy, for, as we have seen, his son was missing, believed killed in action in the Great Wear, and his name is on the memorial at Thiepval. He did leave three daughters, though, and also wrote the church guide book, revised and re-issued two decades ago.

The old vicarage was hit by an incendiary bomb during the Second World War, luckily when the vicar was away, but less luckily because it took some time to effect an entrance to extinguish the flames, the key-holder being very soundly asleep (perhaps from the effects of a good night in the pub) and impervious to the frantic knocking on his door! The damage, in the end, was not too extensive, but the most harm was apparently caused by the vast quantities of water enthusiastically disbursed

The Rev'd. F. C. T. Jansen surrounded by the choir attired in their very best, around 1895. [Newton Solney WI]

in the fire-team's efforts to extinguish the blaze. Thereafter, the ground floor windows were rebuilt as bays, connected by a porch roof and the entire edifice harled in white-painted pebble-dash in order to remove the signs of the fire, to its aesthetic detriment.

The short-lived new vicarage, as subsequently rebuilt. [*Maxwell Craven*]

It was eventually sold off by the Church after the Patronage had passed to the Diocese, and a new one was built in St. Mary's Close being sold on after the departure of the last incumbent to serve only Newton parish. It was then re-built in a Neo-Classical style with re-constituted stone lintels to its windows and with a recessed centre, all under a low hipped roof. Subsequently, incumbents have lived out of the parish and at the time of writing, the vicar of Repton, Peter Payne – a name with plenty of local resonance - acts for Newton Solney.

Today and since the 1970s, the benefice has been united with Bretby, not Winshill, as the Parliamentary Commissioners had suggested in 1650, that place having become part of Staffordshire and thus remains in Lichfield Diocese. After Mrs. Ratcliff died in 1971 the patronage of the living remained with her executors until the 1980s, when it was passed to the Diocese, whereupon it has proceeded to alternate between the Bishop and the Diocesan Board of Patronage, although now with a priest-in-charge of the parish, with Bretby, rather than a vicar. The life of the church is still flourishing, both liturgically and socially; a loyal congregation continues the spirit of church music we know to have been flourishing since the 1760s in a Christian community that may have been flourishing for over a thousand years. Long may it continue.[25]

*

1. Page 5 above

2. Page 4 above; on the double house itself, excavated by Professor Martin and Dr. Birthe Kolbye -Biddle for 18 years, the most accessible account is in Turbutt (1999) I 284 ff. Interestingly, he Biddles found two substantial timber buildings, which pre-dated the Monastery. St. David's foundation, James (1967) 33 & DWB 107-108; Principality of *Luitcoyd*, BL Harl. MS 3859. but note that a Celtic monastery of that period was a very different thing from a Saxon one but, nevertheless, if the story about David is true, then it re-inforces the arguments for the presence of enclaves of Britons in the area, as at Bretby and Walton. Frithuric was probably a kinsman of Frithowold, a South Mercian Prince who married Wilburh, sister of King Wulfhere of Mercia (PASE Frithuric 2, Frithowald 4).

3. See page 6 above.

4. Decline and re-foundation of Repton Priory, Turbutt, *op. cit.,* 291; deed, quoted in Cox (1877) III. 450; toponyms, Cameron (1959) III. 648

5. The chapels-of-ease of Repton are itemised in a charter of confirmation of the Bishop of Lichfield & Coventry to the Prior of Repton in 1271 (Cox III (1877) 425)

6. 1274 charter, DRO D5236/4/4; 1304 confirmation, J. 1758 and FF 519; further 10 acres, PEC LXV; 1316 confirmation FF 624; poll tax, DAJ XXX (1908) 52-53; Richard, PEC LII as Rico Sulny; Balderton, PECs XIX (1353) & LII (1353) also D5236/4/24 & grant by William Hayward, chaplain of Newton to Adam Thorold of a house held by him with a bovate in 1368 (D5236/4/29 of 22/11/1368); Measham, D5236/4/23.

7. "Chaplain of Newton Solney" takes over from William de Measham & receives messuage and 1 bovate there from Wm. de Measham [PEC LXVII of 1354]; Thorold, Alfred de Solney confirms to him his house and 9 acres (PEC LXII of 1370), cf. Cox I (1874) 283, re Pinxton – also granted land at Newton 3/8/1375 (D5236/4/30); Neem, FF1055; Wm. de Newton, PEC CXXI; Bellowe & Taylor, PEC CLXXXVIII, D5236/8/5 of 7/10/1380 & PEC XXXIII of 8/12/1397. Adam de Bladon, PEC LXVIII; boat, Cox III (1877) 454; the list of rectors of Egginton in Cox IV (1878) 154 is acknowledged by its compiler as "imperfect". The de Alport 'chaplain' and 'rector of Newton' in J. 295 & 296 cannot belong to Newton Solney, which as a chapelry never had rectors.

8. Cal. Close Rolls 1389-1392,342-343 of 16/3/1391

9. Cox III (1877) 451; Pevsner (1978) 488; pictures: Mosley's view of Rock House and Rawlins' view in his MS in Derby Local Studies Library; font, etc., Cox II (1877) 452.

10. Lease: J. 1765 of 4/9/1528; sale: Carnarvon MSS, Highclere, Estate Papers, Vol. 21, 41-57, by permission of Rt. Hon. The Earl of Carnarvon.

11. 1588 lease, D5236/4/67 of 25th Nov.; re-letting, D5236/4/70 of 17/5/1591 & D5236/4/91 & '93 of

20/2/1610/11; relationships of Cure &c., BLG (1952) 582 & V. Cheshire 1580; Thacker, Cox III (1877) 431& his lease, D5236/4/96 of 29/9/1618; Recovery by Leigh, D5236/4/100 of 14/1/1627.

[12] Description, Cox, *op.cit.* 450; beam, *ibid.,* 452.

[13] *Cal. Cttee. for Compounding*, 2448-2450, 22/6/1652; committee report, Cox, *op. cit.* 45.

[14] Stipend, Every MS Ped.

[15] Carter brothers, Gunnis, R., *Biographical Dictionary of British Sculptors, 1660-1851* (London 1953) 84-86; timber canopy, Every MS Ped.; moved, Bulmer (1895) 789; chalice, DRO, D5236/32/25.

[16] Woodcock's appeal, D5236/32/40-42; tithes in trust, Every MS pedigree; stipendiary increase, Bagshaw (1846) 256 cf. White (1857) 369.

[17] Austin (1972) 128-129;dispute, D5236/32/83-85; organists, Vestry Minutes; musicians, DRO D5236 32/42; Leonard Haywood of Winshill officiated, 1923-1940; organ, Pounds (2000) 48.

[18] Wyrley, BL Harl. MS. 6592 f. 73b; effigies, Cox, *op. cit.*, 453 & Pevsner (1978) 488; marblers, Leland, *Itinerary* VII 24, cf. Camden (1789) II. 377

[19] Repair, Cox., *op. cit.*, 450.

[20] Hare at Repton: Censuses and directories to 1861/62. French, VCH *Staffs.* (2003) 121-122.

[21] White (1874) 249; Harrod (1870) 245.

[22] Chapel, White (1857) 370; Robinson, BLG (1952) 2181, Pevsner *passim*, DLC (4/1995) 37

[23] Pevsner, *passim* & Jansen, *passim*.

[24] Cost & donors: Bulmer (1895) 789; German services, WI (2000) 25

[25] Old vicarage, WI (2000) *loc,.cit.*; *Diocesan Year Book* (1979-1980) 74 & *Op. cit.* (1989-90) 142

*

Newton Solney:Main Street in the 1970s.

APPENDIX: PEDIGREES

Note: where there is more than one child, each generation is indented slightly and numbered differently, e.g. 1st generation = 1, second = (1), third = 1a and so on.

Abbreviations: b. = born; d. = died; dat. = dated (wills); *dsp* = died without issue; *dvp* = died in the lifetime of his father; Gent. = gentleman; marr. = married (followed by place where known); MI = monumental inscription; NS = Newton Solney; PRs = Parish Registers; pr. = proved (wills); yeo = yeoman. Abbreviations relating to sources will be found in the bibliography.

Sources are parish registers where not acknowledged in square brackets. Refer to bibliography for abbreviations relating to these.

The Every Pedigree is omitted as there is a diagrammatic outline pedigree in Chapter III, and for a full pedigree see the current (2003) *Burke's Peerage*, which was revised for the previous edition by the author with the assistance of the late Sir John Every and Sir Henry Every, Bt.

Note that the pedigrees are presented in the order in which they appear in Newton Solney history.

*

SOLNEY

Sources: various, as given in square brackets; spellings modernised throughout.

An unknown Norman father had issue:

ALFRED [ALURED] de SOLIGNY (I) attested a grant of Ranulph, Earl of Chester to the Abbey of St. Evroul, 1121/1125 [Barraclough (1988) No. 10]; he had been of age in 1093, and thus born no later than 1072. He had issue:

ALFRED DE SOLNEY (II) Witness to a Calke Charter of the Earl of Chester c. 1162/1170 [Barraclough (1988) No. 147] & (with John de Solney) to charter of Bordesley Abbey, gift of Combe, Warw., 1188/1189 [*ibid.* No. 206]. He was of Newton-on-Trent [cf. J. 1753], for which he paid his chief lord, the Earl of Chester 40/- [for a default 1185] and died 1204/5 [cf. witness to Barraclough (1988) No. 322, Bordesley Abbey re Combe again, dat. 1200/1204] and Nos. 337 & 338 re Great Tew and Olney. Alfred died c. 1205 having marr. Joan and had issue:

1. Ralph de Argosis,1204/5 [J. 1753] also de Suligny (cf. confirmation to Norton
   Priory 1207/1217 [Barraclough (1988) No.350])
2. Alfred de Solney (III), to whom Ralph conveyed a portion of his inheritance of the
   land which belonged to his father and mother [named] namely the Manor of
   "Neutona in Anglia" [J. 1753]. He was seised of a knight's fee in Upper Broughton,
   Notts. in 1211/1213 but was dead in or around 1230 [Barraclough (1988) 413]. He had issue:
   (1) Norman de Solney (Sir), witnessed a charter with his brother c. 1230 [Barracough (1988) 273]
       and to whom in 1230 the Prior of Repton released the park, mill and fishery at Newton . In
       1233 he held one and a half knight's fees in Derbyshire of the late Earl of Chester, which fee
       was assigned to William, Earl of Derby as part of his share in the Chester inheritance, along
       with service of Alfred in Leicestershire [*Cal. Close Rolls* 264]. By 1242/43 he held one
       knight's fee in Derbyshire of Earl of Derby and the same in Upper Broughton on each of which
       he paid scutage 40/- [Book of Fees, 994] He was a knight by 1244 [J.1757] and d. after 1257
       [PEC LIII] marr. (?) Juliana de Ulecotes [Statham, DAJ] and had issue:
       1a Thomas de Solney, probably *dspvp.* before 1248
       2a Alfred. son and heir of Norman in 1280, but presumably also *dspvp.* [D5236/4/5].
   (2) Alfred de Solney (IV) on whom see below

The younger son:

ALFRED DE SOLNEY (IV) (Sir) of Upper Broughton in Nottinghamshire (1 knight's fee) in his brother's lifetime, holding it in 1235 of the Earl of Chester; in 1242/43 he was holding it of the Earl of Arundel as co-heir of the Earl of Chester and it is referred to as 'Broughton Sulleney', i.e. Broughton Solney. By 1253, when he was serving the King in Gascony as Constable of the Gironde with a grant of £20 per annum, by which time he was also of Newton-on-Trent; he marr. Sybil daughter of John de Braytoft and was dead by 1262, when Sybil re-married Adam de St. Lo *jure uxoris* of Broughton Solney, Notts. [Throsby (1796) I. 103]. He had issue:

1. John de Solney (Sir) of Newton-on-Trent, living 1262, had Broughton Solney, Notts.
   settled on him, and in 1280 conveyed the manor to Sir Gervase Clifton with 8
   virgates of land which Adam de St. Lo and Sybil his wife had held in dower of
   John's inheritance [Throsby, *loc. cit.,* recording that Sir Gervase held half a
   fee in 1302, was Lord there in 1316 and his grandson Gervase held it in 1346].
   Also held a knight's fee at Raydon, Suffolk which he bequeathed to Sir Alfred (VI)
   at his death after 1280 and before 1293. He married – if he is indeed to be identified
   with '*Miles* de Newton Solney' - Margaret, daughter of Elias son of William son of Henry
   of Egginton of Egginton [PEC LXXII of 1311] but appears to have had no issue.
2. Alfred (V) de Solney (Sir), succ. his brother at Newton-on-Trent by c. 1272, when
   he illegally took a buck in the bailiwick of Alrewas, answering for it in 1282,
   In 1280 (by which time he had been knighted) he was a tenant of Burton Abbey at
   Findern or Mickleover and held a knight's fee at Newton of the King's brother, Edmund,
   He marr. Margery, daughter and ult. heiress of Odo de Hod[i]net (by Margery dau. (and
   ultimate coheiress) of Ralph le Poer of Pinxton, on which manor see J. 1862-1874, 1877)
   and left issue at his death:
   (1) Alfred de Solney (VI) born 1267, held a knight's fee at at Raydon, Suffolk of John de
       Vallibus, inherited from his uncle, which he settled on his son, John in 1293 [J. 1470]
       died 1302 [IPM 25 Edw. I No. 51]. Marr. Sybil, daughter and heiress of John de Or[re]by

of Orreby, Lincs., and had issue:

    1a John de Broughton of Upper Broughton, Notts., and Raydon, Suffolk, from 1293.

    2a Alfred de Solney (VII) on whom see below

    3a Geoffrey de Solney, paid poll tax £4 at Newton 1327.

        Perhaps father of

        1b Richard de Solney who witnessed a charter at Newton Solney in 1354 [PEC LII as Rico Sulny]; the year before (1353), he is described as 'of Newton Solney' and had a wife, Alice [PEC XIX]; he is referred to as and was still living in 1375, 1376 and 1379 [PEC, CLXXXVIII, LXXII & XVII]. He also had issue:

           1c [daughter and heiress] marr. [   ] Warde and had issue:

              1d Richard de Warde of Winshill heir of Richard de Solney 1375 [D5236/4/28]

  (2) William de Solney, clerk, curate of Newton Solney, given lands at Newton with a fishery at the confluence of the Trent and Dove 1274 [D5236/4/4], confirmed to him by Alfred de Solney (VII) 1304 J. 1758, confirmed FF519] and granted 10 acres at Newton in 1304 [PEC LXV of 1304] and 1316 [FF624]; paid poll tax in 1327 [see Chapter VII]. He may well have been the father of :

    1a William de Solney (II), Chaplain of Newton 1321 (if not identifiable with his father)

        Possibly father (or brother of):

        1b Richard de Solney, chaplain of Newton

  (3) John de Solney, clerk, presented to the living of South Normanton by Sir Alfred, presumably therefore, his father [alluded to in *Plea Rolls* 16 Edw. IV wherein Nicholas de Longford was claiming the patronage].

3. William de Solney, son of Alfred marr. Sibilla, daughter of Sir William Bagot of Bagot's Bromley, Staffs., before 1284 [PEC; *Feudary*, 1283-84]; living 1292/93 [PEC]

The second son,

ALFRED DE SONEY (VII) (Sir) of Newton-on-Trent, for which he paid 40/- to the chief lord 1302 [Feudal Aids, 251] b. 1287 as aged 30 in 1317 when he inherited a third of the lands of his kinsman John de Orreby of Oreby, Lincs., [Cal. IPM VI 71 and confirmed his grandfather's gift of land at Newton to his uncle William de Solney 11/6/1304 [J. 1758, confirmed FF519], knighted by 1305 [Burton Charter 289W]. He was in debt to the tune of £1000 to Robert de Holand, Lord Holand in 1320, but came to an arrangement that he should surrender the inheritance of the manor of Orreby to Lord Holand to cancel the debt, the record of which was lodged with the Prior of Repton [PEC XXI] d. c. 1346, marr. and had issue:

1. Alfred de Solney (VIII) on whom see below

2. William de Solney, paid poll tax £2 in 1327; quitclaims to Sir Alfred 1337 [D5236/4/19]; living 1342 [PEC CLV (w)] &1359 [PEC LXIII of 1359].

    Perhaps father of:

  (1) William Solney, witness of a grant by Sir John de Solney to Roger Saveney 7/1/1379 [D5236/4/18(ii)]

  (2) Nicholas Solney, witness of a grant by Sir John de Solney to Matilda Draper 29/9/1379 [D5236/4/18(i)]

3. Robert de Solney *f. Sir Alfred* 1347 [granted 10/- rent in Newton 16/6/1347, D5236/4/22] (d. in plague?)

1. Margaret, marr. Ralph de Longford of Longford and had issue (*inter alia*):

  (1) Nicholas de Longford of Longford who marr. Margaret (see below) dau. & co-heiress of Alfred de Solney (VIII) and had issue (see Longford)

2. Joan marr. as his second wife, William FitzHerbert of Norbury [DLSL MS6341, f. 99 r.], but *dsp.*

ALFRED DE SOLNEY (VIII) (Sir) of Newton-on-Trent, Pixton, Bilby & Ranby, Notts.[D5236/9/8 of 1348; father given as William f. Alfred f. Norman in DLSL MS 6341]. In 1326 he did homage for Basford, Notts,. which was his portion of the Orreby estates following the death of Simon de Orreby of that place 1326; paid 40/-for his knights fee at Newton which was his father's 1346 [*Feudal Aids*, i. 260], knighted by 1356 [J. 1863 & Burton Charter 524]; granted licence for an oratory within his manor of Cokeshale (Coggeshall?) for 2 years [Salt Arch. Soc. Vol. VIII (1907), Bishop's Register] and died 1379 [*Ibid.*, VII (1906) 44], having married Margaret [Elizabeth according to D5236/9 of 3/10/1348], daughter of Sir John Trussell of Cubblesdon, Staffs. [D5236/9/6] leaving issue:

1. Sir John de Solney on whom see below

1. Ermentrude (d. after 1396); she speaks, in an affadavit concerning a settlement between Sir Edmund Appleby and William Trussell, of Alfred de Solney as 'my brother' and confirms to him her right, title and claim in the Manor of Newton Solney [PEC LXVII] and again in a charter of 1380 [PEC XLVIII]; marr. (i) 1330 Robert Lathbury of Egginton (died 1360) and had issue [see LATHBURY]. She marr. (ii) 1356 John Folcher of Osmaston-by-Derby (he died before 1390) but had no further issue.

2. Agnes marr. 1348 (s his first wife) Sir Edmund de Appleby of Appleby Parva, their marriage settlement including the manors of Bilby and Ranby in Nottinghamshire, on condition that Edmund and Agnes and their heirs would waive all claim on that of Newton Solney [PEC XXXV of 1348, which reads as if John, Alfred's son, had not yet been born]. They had issue:

    (1) Margaret (widow 1428), marr. Nicholas de Longford of Longford, held fourth part of Manor of Newton in 1390 [J. 1761] also half the manor of Blackwell, property in Orreby [Orby] Lincs., and £4 – 6s – 8d annual rent in Willingham [D5236/9/13] and disputed another fourth part with John de Appleby in 1447 [J. 1763] and had issue [see LONGFORD of LONGFORD

    (2) Alice (d. after 1432), marr. (i) Robert Pype of Pype, Staffs., (ii) Sir Thomas Stafford and had issue [see also Chapter II]:

        1a Thomas de Stafford, dead sp by 1402, [D5236/9/15]; delivered seisin of half of Normanton & Pinxton with moiety of manor of Newton Solney & Blackwell, property in Orby & Willingham (Lincs.) [ibid.].

        2a John de Stafford (Rt. Revd.), Bishop of Bath & Wells, held a quarter of Newton Solney in 1431; quitclaims his share of the manor to William Lathbury & others 17/3/1439 [D5236/6/17] d. unm.

    (2) (Cont.) Alice Appleby marr. (iii) William Spernore

    Sir Edmund Appleby marr. (ii) and had further issue:

    (1) John de Appleby, disputed a fourth part of the Manor of Newton with Nicholas de Longford 1447 [J. 1763] and had issue

The only son:

JOHN DE SOLNEY (Sir) of Newton Solney and Pinxton, born after 1348 (?); leased half the manor of Newton to John Foucher & Ermentrude h. w. @ £22 5/5/1380 [D5236/4/33] dead by 1390, when Nicholas de Longford delivers seisin on a quarter of the manor to the Bishop of Coventry & Lichfield. [D5236/9/13], marr. (by 1380) Margaret, dau. of Robert Hastings, but *dsp.* 1392 when his holdings were divided into four moieties amongst his sisters and co-heiresses.

****

Pedigree II

LONGFORD

NICHOLAS de LONGFORD (Sir) was b. 1351 [IPM of his father 1373] of Longford, ktd. 1397 and living 1431. He was 6th in descent from Nigel de Longford (d. 1248) who married Cecilia daughter and co-heiress of Matthew de Hathersage and son of Oliver son of Nigel de Bupton. He, in turn was son of Nicholas fitz Nigel de Stafford (a younger son of Nigel de Gresley of the house of Stafford) by Margaret, daughter and co-heiress of Ralph son of Ercald of Longford and Bupton. His son was:

NICHOLAS de LONGFORD, marr. Margaret, daughter of Sir Edmund de Appleby of Appleby Magna, Leics., (by Agnes, daughter of Sir Alfred de Solney of Newton Solney and heiress of her brother Sir John de Solney, dsp. 1392) and heiress of her mother*. They had issue:

1. Nicholas de Longford (Sir), son & heir to half Newton Solney, the manor of Blackwell, property at Pinxton & South Normanton and land at Basford, Notts. 1/12/1412 [DRO D5236/9/18]. He *dvp* 1416 having marr. Joan, daughter of Sir Laurence Warren of Poynton, Cheshire, and had issue:

    (1) Sir Nicholas de Longford of Longford & Newton Solney, etc., succeeded by 10/10/1416 [DRO D5236/4/42], ktd. 1447 [J. 1763], awarded a quarter moiety of Newton in a dispute with John de Appleby of Appleby, 22/7/1447 [DRO D5236/4/38], marr. 1451 Margaret daughter of

Thomas Shaw of West Broughton and Culland [DRO D185B/Culland & DC B6, I8, K2, O8] but *dsp.* between 1474 and 1476.

(2) Sir Roger de Longford *dsp.* before 1498, having marr. Mary, dau. of Sir John de Melton [DLSL deed 597; DRO D185B; Indicted before a grand jury at Elvaston, (I) 1484]

(3) Sir Ralph de Longford, on whom see below.

(4) Edmund de Longford, living 1429, 1454 [I .1454]

(5) John de Longford, (Rev.) rector of North Wingfield, 1465 & 2/2/1474 [RLC 545; J. 1764] living at Longford Hall 1454 [I 1454], d. unm. 1475.

(6) Rowland de Longford [DLSL MS6341]

(1) Margaret marr. Humphrey de Bradbourne

(2) Joan marr. John, son & heir of Sir John Stanley

2. Henry de Longford of Longford, collector of rents at Longford and Ellastone and with brothers Alfred and Ralph in remainder to lands at Pinxton 28/9/1426 [RLC 580]; living 1430 [DLSL Deed 3303 & MS 6241]

3. Ralph de Longford living 1426 [DLSL MS 6341]

4. Alfred de Longford (Rev.), rector of Longford 18/11/1432 & 1/12/1434 [TC 330; RLC 163/164], took over a third of a sixth moiety of Newton Solney from Seth de Worsley [DRO D5236/4/44 & DLSL MS 6341]. d.unm.

5. Gervase de Longford of Pinxton 1426 [DLSL MS 6341], filiation etc. *Reliquary* VII (1867) 74-75 cf. V. Notts. 1569]. He marr. & had issue:

(1) Nicholas Longford [V. Notts. 1569; DLSL MS 6341], who marr. and had issue:
  1a George Langford [*sic*], acted as attorney to Sir Nicholas over property at Newton Solney 20/3/1458 [DRO D5236/4/46]
  2a Thomas Langford of Upton & Mansfield, Notts., marr.. Elizabeth dau. of Sir Thomas Low of Staffordshire and had issue, the Langfords of Mansfield, and Sutton-in-Ashfield, traceable to the present..

The third son:
RALPH de LONGFORD (Sir), of Longford, Newton Solney, Blackwell, Whitwell, Barlborough, Morton, Pilsley, North Wingfield, Duckmanton, Hathersage, South Normanton, Pinxton, Boythorpe, Killamarsh & Ellastone (Staffs.) [7/6/1513, IPM Rylands Library Charter (RLC) 242; ktd. by 1498 [DRO D5236/4/43; Culland I.1454], marr. Isabel, dau. of Sir Thomas Ferrers of Tamworth Castle and had issue:

1. Nicholas Longford, dvp. 1510 having marr. Margaret daughter of Sir Edmund Trafford and had issue:

(1) Sir Ralph Longford, on whom see below

(2) Nicholas Longford of St. Germans, Cornwall, recorded as a tenant at Longford 24/6/1536 [DLSL deed 15296] marr. and had issue:
  1a John Longford of St. German's Cornwall, 1589/92 [DLSL deed 3434] received a moiety of Newton Solney 4/2/1584 for £150 [D5236/4/65] which he later sold to Dr. Richard Taylor of London 25/3/1592 [D5236/4/72] living 25/2/1600 when holding the moiety jointly [D5236/4/78, 80]

2. Thomas Longford of Duckmanton, where he was granted land 14/1/1522 [RLC 552] granted a lease at Longford, 1536 [DLSL deed 15256].

3. John Longford, tenant of Sir Ralph Shirley at Shirley Manor House 31/5/1521 [RLC 552] also held at Hollington, Rodsley & Bupton 30/1/1538 [RLC 252]. He marr. and had issue:

(1) John Longford of Derby, later of Nottingham, marr. and had issue:
  1a Henry Longford np. St. Peter, Nottingham 8/4/1582
  2a John Longford, marr. St. Mary, Nottingham 20/8/21608 Dorothy Linacre and had issue:
    1a Anne bp. S.t Peter, Nottingham 20/10/1577 marr. there 2/5/1605 George Healey

4. Henry Longford of Newton Park 31/5/ 7 9/7/1521 [RLC 551-552], collector of rents at Longford & Ellastone 1494/95 [RLC 238]

6. William Longford living 31/5/1521 [RLC 552] marr. and had issue:
(1) Joan, marr. Sir Francis Gilbert *alias* Kniveton of Youlgreave both living 1569.

7. Richard Longford living 12/1/1523 [RLC 90]

1. Elizabeth marr. Sir Edmund Trafford (brother of the wife of Elizabeth's brother Nicholas) and had issue

2. Margery marr. Sir John Markham of Gotham, Notts.

3. Dorothy marr. Nicholas FitzHerbert of Norbury and had issue

Sir Nicholas's grandson:

RALPH LONGFORD (Sir) of Longford, Newton Solney, etc., d. 1544, having marr. before 6/3/1528 [RLC 245] Dorothy, daughter of Sir Anthony FitzHerbert of Norbury and had issue:

1. Nicholas Longford of Longford etc., b. 1530, held a great court at Newton Solney 2/5/1564 [DRO D5236/12/19]; held half manor there for 8/- plus the fishing in the river, which he sold to Nicholas Mosley and his wife Margaret for £143 – 6s – 8d (430 marks) in 1579 [D5236/4/63-64]. Later sold a moiety of the Newton estate to Hugh Beeston of the Strand, London 29/4/1592 [D5236/4/73] dsp .1610, having marr. Elizabeth, daughter of Ralph Okeover of Okeover, Staffs.

1. Maud marr. (i) Sir George Vernon of Haddon and marr. (ii) Francis Hastings of Cadbury, Somerset, leaving issue.

2. Elizabeth marr. Humphrey Dethick of Newhall

3. Margery, d. unmarr.

* She was not heiress of her brother John, who, as her half brother, was not heir to Agnes's portion of the Newton Solney estate.

*

Pedigree III

LATHBURY

Source: Visitations of Derbyshire 1569, 1611, amplified by charters etc (as noted).

HENRY de LATHBURY of Lathbury, Bucks, granted an exemption for life from juries, assizes etc. in recognition of having been made coroner against his will from H. de Malo Lacu, King's Clerk, his uncle [*Cal. Close Rolls* 1266-72]. His probable sons included

1. Robert de Lathbury, died 1311 *sp* leaving his brother John his heir.

2. John de Lathbury inherited lands from Robert 26/9/1311 [*Cal. Pat. Rolls* 17 Edward II, ii. 103]. He marr. and had issue (*inter alia*):

RALPH DE LATHBURY of Hargate and Egginton. He had an elder brother who inherited the Lathbury estate and a probable younger one, John de Lathbury, who was in 1312 a canon of the Abbey & Convent of Lavendon. Ralph was 'Chamberlain' (steward) to Ralph, 1st Lord Pipard of Linford, by whom these lands were granted 13/5/1300 and 1301 [DRO D5236/6/1-2; PEC XXXV, LXII, the latter dated Rotherfield Pipard 5/1301], Ralph probably came to Derbyshire in the Pipards' service. He died in 1315 [J. 1170, 1171] having marr. Margaret, a widow 1324, and had issue:

1. Ralph de Lathbury of Hargate, b. before 1308, also chamberlain to Ralph, Lord Pipard [J. 919], *dsp* 1326 [Salt Arch. Soc. Vol. V (1904) 99]; he marr. Margaret [widow, 1326 & 13/10/1340, (PEC LXXIV, LXXXIII; DRO 5236/6/5)], daughter of Sir John Giffard of Chillington, Staffordshire and had issue:

   (1) Ralph de Lathbury, *dvpsp* [J. 919; Tilney also refers to a Thomas de Lathbury in the period 1307/27, perhaps an uncle of this man]

2. ROBERT de Lathbury, see below

1. Matilda

The second son

ROBERT DE LATHBURY b. 1310, d. 1360, appointed collector of subsidy, Derbys., 1350, 1359; marr. 1330 Ermentrude (died after 1396), daughter of Sir Alfred and sister and co-heiress of Sir John de Solney of Newton Solney (who re-marr. John Folcher of Osmaston, (settlement 5/1376 [PEC XL]) who had died before 1390 [D5236/6/9]) and had issue:

1. ALFRED de Lathbury, on whom see below

2. Henry de Lathbury, living 1368 [J. 1178]

3. Ralph de Lathbury of Hardwick, Egginton, 1361 [J. 1202] marr. and had issue

   (1) Ralph de Lathbury, of Hardwick, son of Ralph in 1361 [J. 1202]

      perhaps father of:

      1a William Lathbury of Newton Solney, attorney (1423),

probably father of:
> 1b William Lathbury of Newton, attorney, executor of John Lathbury of
> Egginton and Newton (qv) 1439, attorney for John de Lathbury, jr.,
> 1434/35/35& 1438 [D5236/3/62; PEC LXVIII] witness to a charter
> concerning land at Egginton 1469 [J. 1185].
> *His descendant may have been*
> > 1c John Lathbury living 1527, [probably ancestor of the Lathburys of
> > Hoon, and Burton, Visit. Derby. 1611].

4. John de Lathbury (Rev), appointed to Shotteswell Warwickshire in 1368 [Lichfield
   Diocesan Register]
1. Beatrice, living 1376 [PEC XL]
2. Margaret marr. William Marshall of Sedsall in Doveridge, living 1376, when they
   were granted the rent from the holdings of Ermentrude and John Folcher in Newton
   Solney, Egginton etc. [PEC XL] and had issue:
   (1) John le Marshall, 1376 [PEC XL]
   (2) William le Marshall, 1376 [PEC XL]
   (1) Ermentrude, 1376 [PEC XL]
3. Agnes marr. Robert de Stanton of Radbourne [BL Shirley MSS, Add. MS 4928]

ALFRED DE LATHBURY (Sir) of Newton Solney & Egginton, living 1385, 1428 [J. 1284, 1934;
living 1405, FF1016]. On 25/12/1395 his mother released to him all her manors etc. which had been
Robert Lathbury his father's in Egginton, Heathhouses (i.e. Hargate), Ambaston, Thulston,
Chaddesden, Radbourne, Bearwardcote, Trusley, etc. [PEC XXIV]; he made settlements in 1424
(revised in 1428) of his lands on his grandson John, his son John by then having died, with provision
for dower, Reginald de Lathbury being chief nominee of the trust [PEC XLII, LI]. He marr. (i) before
1405, Alana, daughter and heiress of Ralph de Cadeby of Cadeby (Leics.) and in 1424 (ii) Margery. By
his first wife he had:

1. John Lathbury, of Newton Solney, where he and his 2nd wife were granted by Alfred 7 messuages
   and 180 acres plus a moiety of a mill at *Heathhouses* [FF1016], dvp about 1424 [PEC XLII], having
   marr. Joan, daughter of Henry Parr (marriage annulled 1399, on the grounds of adultery with Robert
   de Kythen ('formerly servant to Sir Alfred and related to…John (de Lathbury) in the fourth degree
   of kinship') [PEC LXXXII; D5236/10/7; DLSL deed 3258]) and marr. 1401 (ii) Elizabeth (died
   before 1422), daughter of Roger de Bradbourne of Bradbourne. By his first wife he had issue:
   1a JOHN Lathbury, see below
2. Ralph Lathbury, living 1419
3. Robert Lathbury of Cadeby *filius junior* of Alfred 1439 held a twentieth of a fee
   (90 acres) in Stockley [J. 1185; cf. DRO D5236/3/74]. In 1429 he granted John
   Lathbury son of John & Isabella his wife, land in Newton Solney which they (the
   grantees) had of the gift of W. de Lathbury [PEC no number]. Enfeoffed Isabella de
   Lathbury and her daughter Katherine with his lands 1439 [PEC]
4. Reginald Lathbury also of Cadeby 1420, 1422 [[J. 1280], 1428 [PEC LI]; marr. (as
   her first husband), Elizabeth, daughter of Sir Edmund Mulso (she marr. (ii)
   Baldwin Bugg and (iii) Sir Robert Milton) and had issue:
   (1) Alfred Lathbury, 1427
   (2) John Lathbury, 1427
   (3) Thomas Lathbury of Cadeby, Leics., will dat. 21/5/1470, marr. Margaret,
       widow, 1470.
   (1) Elizabeth, living 1427
1. Agnes marr. Robert Staunton of Staunton Harold, Leics. (they also jointly held half
   of the manor of Willington) and had issue, their line now represented by Earl
   Ferrers.

The eldest son:
JOHN LATHBURY 'of Newton Solney Esquire' in 1431 [*Feudal Aids,* i 308] and Egginton, took oath
of Allegiance 1429 [*Feud. Aids*] died 1438 [IPM; will dat. 20/8/1438, PEC LXVIII] holding half of
Newton (whereas Alfred had held only a quarter) & a quarter of a fee in Egginton [*Feud. Aids;* IPM].
He marr. Elizabeth de Mackworth. John de Lathbury re-married (ii) before 1425 Isabella Shatton [*sic;*
probably meant for Stretton; living a widow 1439 (will dat.): 'cousin to Isabella Franceys of Foremark'
PEC, and presumably formerly wife of Robert Franceys of Foremark] and had issue:
1. JOHN Lathbury, on whom see below
2. [   ] Lathbury (died before 1489), who marr. and had issue:
   (1) Anne marr. 5/10/1489 William son and heir of Richard Littleton

[D5236/10/14]

JOHN LATHBURY of Newton Solney and Egginton b. 1430/1 living 1439 [J. 1185, D5236/10/10], "senior" in 1454/1457 [J. 1764], dead by 1474 [Rylands Library, Manchester, Charter 545]; marr. (his cousin) Catherine, daughter of Robert Franceys of Foremark (by Isabella Stretton of Stretton-en-le-Field) and had issue:

JOHN LATHBURY of Newton Solney and Egginton 'junior' in 1467, inherited by 2/2/1474 [Rylands, *ibid.* and 547]; granted his capital mansion at Newton Solney to Sir Ralph Longford [PEC XLVII of 1500] living also in 1505 [D5236/4/47], but dead by 1509 [J. 1764; DLSL deed 3169], marr. Elizabeth (he must have married after 1489 for in that year he declared Anne Lathbury (qv), married 5/10/1489 to William, son and heir of Richard Littleton, to be his heiress apparent [settlement 3/10/1489, D5236/10/14]) and had issue:

1. Alfred Lathbury, dvp. 1485, bur. at Rugeley, marr. Joan (d. 1480) and had issue:
   (1) Anne, daughter and co-heiress, marr. (before 1508) Robert Leigh, son of
       Reginald Leigh of the family of Leigh of Adlington, Cheshire, and had issue
       [*see Pedigree IV,* LEIGH]
2. Ralph Lathbury living 1469 [D5236/15/19-20DLSL Deed 3169] & 1506 [PEC]
3. Henry Lathbury living 1469 [*ibid.*] attorney for his father 1505 [D5236/4/47] and
   in 1506[PEC]
4. Thomas Lathbury living 1469 [*ibid.*] and in 1506 [PEC]

NB There are some unplaced members of this family:

1. John Lathbury Esq., 'claims custody of his deeds' 1527 & in 1543 witnesses at Egginton [PEC no numbers]

2. Richard Lathbury, in fine re houses in Hilton and Hardwick-in-Egginton [FF 1550 &1563]. Held 2 houses in Hilton & Hardwick 1557 [PEC no number]

3. Francis Lathbury marr. Elizabeth before 1617 [Salt. Arch, Soc. Vol. VI (1905)]; robably in 1604 [final concord [Salt. Arch. Soc. Vol. IV (1903)]

4. William Lathbury d. by 1634 left issue:
   (1) Mary unmarr. 1635 [D5236/24/2]
   (2) Anne marr. William Holme of Burton-on-Trent, husbandman 1634
       {D5236/24/2 of 6/3/1634]

*

Pedigree IV

LEIGH OF EGGINTON

Sources: Visitations of Derbyshire 1569, 1611, of Cheshire 1580, charters [DRO D5236] and PRs.

ROBERT LEIGH of Adlington, Cheshire, sr., & South Normanton, Derbyshire, was 5th in descent from Sir John Leigh of Booths, Cheshire, second son of William Venables and Agnes, daughter and heiress of Richaerd de Leigh of Leigh, Cheshire, son of William son of Hamo de Leigh, first of Leigh. He d. 1415 [IPM 9/112/1415] having marr. (i) Isabel, daughter of John Savage of Clifton (who dsp) and marr. (ii) Isabel, daughter of Sir William Stanley of Hooton and by her had issue:
1. Henry Leigh, dvp having marr. and had issue:
   (1) Robert Leigh, on whom see below
2. William Leigh [filiation: 'f. Robert of Adlington senior', PEC XC of 1480]
3. Reginald Leigh of Mottram, Cheshire [filiation as above]
1. Isabel marr. Robert Holt
2. Blanche marr. Richard Lancaster of Rainhill, Lancs.,
3. Elizabeth, dead by 1480 [PEC XXI] having marr. Thomas Liversedge
4. Margaret marr. (i) John Moore of Park Hall & marr. (ii) Randle Hyde
5. Maud marr. John Mainwaring of Peover

6. Mrs. Pigot of Chetwynd, Salop.

ROBERT LEIGH of Adlington, yr., succeeded grandfather 1415, b. 1409/10 [D5236/10/8]; marr. Ellen dau. of Sir Robert Booth of Dunham and had issue:

1. Thomas Leigh of Adlington, Cheshire, of age 1480 [PEC XC] marr. Katherine
   dau. of Sir John Savage and had issue
2. Richard Leigh
3. Ranulph Leigh
4. John Leigh
5. William Leigh of Ingoldsby, Lincs., 1482 [PEC XXI, CV; bro. to Reginald, Jacob
   & Peter, to all of whom Reginald son of Robert Leigh of Adlington grants all his
   property in Derbyshire, probably to cover a minority]
6. Reginald Leigh on whom see below
7. Jacob Leigh (Rev.) rector of Rawston, Cheshire 1482 [PEC CV]
8. Peter Leigh, living 1482 [PEC XXI (as Piers) & CV]
1. Ellen [PEC XXI]
2. Agnes marr. Sir Andrew Brereton [PEC XXI]
3. Elizabeth [dead by 1480 PEC XXI]
4. Isabel marr. (i) Sir Lawrence Warren of Poynton and marr. (ii) Sir George Holford
   [PEC XXI]
5. Margaret marr. William Davenport of Bramhall [V. Cheshire 1580]

The sixth son:

REGINALD LEIGH of Annesley, Notts., [see Visit. Cheshire 1580; DLSL MS 6341]. He was of Bowdon, Wormhill and Whitfield, Derbys., confirmed to him by his father 1476 [D5236/5/20]. He had land at the Booths, Cheadle, and Kingsley, Staffs. confirmed to him by Richard Leigh of Adlington [where he is described as 'of Blackbrook esq.' PEC LXXXVII of 1492 – unless this is a nephew of this Reginald. He inherited Booths from Roger f. William Bradshaw 1489, *ibid.* XCVIII; it is possible this man is meant as there is another charter (PEC CI of 1503) wherein Reginald Leigh of Blackbrook and Robert his son confirm property in Hayfield to various people, probably in trust for dower; as both these charters descended to the Everys, it implies that these are the same Leighs; otherwise perhaps descendants of Reginald son of Robert of Adlington, the elder]. His will is dat. 1480 (PEC XXI), unless this is that of his uncle, qv. He had in illegitimate son:

1. James Leigh, living 1480 [PEC XXI]. It may be his widow, Mary, of Burton-on
   -Trent in 1508 who had a son:
   (1) Robert Leigh yeo. of Burton-up-on-Trent, where he was granted land by his
       mother 12/10/1508 [D5236/8/16]

He also marr. Anne daughter of Thomas Vernon, sister of Sir Richard Vernon of Haddon and had issue:

1. Robert Leigh.

And possibly

2. Roger Leigh of Clapham, Gent., merchant of the Staple, 1525 [PEC XXXV]

ROBERT LEIGH, living 1525 when party to a bond of £300 for wool from the Staple from Roger Leigh of Clapham, Surrey [PEC XXXV]; he held Blackbrook, land at Glossop, Chapel-en-le-Frith, Hope, Wormhill, Whitehall and Bowdon [IPM 6/11/1525 D5236/10/18] also *jure uxoris* of Egginton and Newton Solney [in dispute with John Lathbury over custody of "evidence concerning his inheritance" 30/1/1526/7 (D5236/15/19-20), arbitrated upon by Henry, Prior of Repton], having marr. Anne, daughter and of Alfred Lathbury (dvp.) and heiress of her grandfather John Lathbury of Egginton and Newton Solney and had issue:

1. William Leigh on whom see below
2. John Leigh marr. Elizabeth daughter of Robert Savage and had issue:
   (1) Elizabeth marr. Arthur Milward and had issue:
       1a James Milward of Egginton, in whom Sir Henry Leigh vested the manors of
          Egginton & Newton Solney 1632 (see below). He was ancestor of:
          1b J. Milward of Egginton, Gent., who sold a house and half an acre at
             Egginton to Sir John Every for £270 in 1767.
1. Elizabeth marr. Simon Starkey
2. Anne dsp.
3. Agnes

The elder son:

WILLIAM LEIGH of Newton Solney and Egginton b. 1512 d. 1546 [IPM of William Leigh of Newton Solney 18/10/1549, [Notts. RO, Mi 6/175/52 – or, could this be the youngest son?] marr. (i) (c. 1539)

Elizabeth Kniveton (by whom he seems to have had no issue) and marr. (ii) Dorothy ('of Newton Solney' d. c. 1563 D5236/4/51), daughter of Thomas Eyre of Highlow (who re-married Richard Needham of Snitterton) by whom he had issue:

1. Sir Thomas Leigh on whom see below
2. Ralph Leigh marr. Elizabeth, daughter of William Dethick of Newhall (sister to
    Anne, below) and had issue:
    (1) Humphrey Leigh living 1569
    (2) William Leigh living 1569
3. John Leigh, dsp.
4. William Leigh
1. Elizabeth marr. Matthew Kniveton of Bradley and had issue

THOMAS LEIGH (Sir) of Egginton and Newton Solney, ktd. after 1572 (when still 'Esq.' [DRO D5236/4/5]); granted a lease at Newton Solney to John Rennison 5/5/1563 DRO D5236/4/52; held manor of Blackbrook 5/10/1562 [D5236/10/19] he was also gtd. the manor of Newton Solney for life by Richard Needham of Snitterton and Dorothy his wife (Thomas's stepmother) @ £20 p. a. 6/11/1570 [DRO D5236/4/56]. He died 1591 having married (i) Anne (sister of Elizabeth, above) daughter of William Dethick of Newhall (who had a lease of the tithe barn yard and corn tithe for 20 yrs. from Repton Priory 1528 [J. 1765]. Marriage bond dated 27/10/1552 in which he made grants to tenants of capital messuages at Blackbrook (where 8/1/1583/4 he granted a 21 year lease on a messuage theretp John Carrington of Blackbrook [D5236/5/44]), Slackhall and Whitehaugh (D5236/5/26), leaving issue:

1. William Leigh, b. 1572, dvp. unmarr.
2. Sir Henry Leigh, on whom see below
3. Dionyius Leigh b. 1575, d. unm .vp.
1. Joan b. 1562
2. Mary, b. 1563 marr. Richard Fleetwood of Penwortham and had issue
3. Elizabeth, later Mrs. Babington [but NB Elizabeth Leigh marr. Egginton 5/6/1592
    Francis Coke]
4. Margery
5. Catherine, mar. Richard son of William Wharton [Catherine's husband is William
    in Visit. 1611]

Sir Thomas Leigh marr. (ii) Elizabeth dau. of Thomas Curzon of Croxall (who re-married Sir Francis Coke of Trusley; he died 1639 aged 78) and had further issue:

4. Thomas Leigh b. 1588
5. John Leigh b. 1590, Gent. in a bond for £100 with Sir henry 19/6/1627
    [D5236/15/31] marr. Elizabeth Rolfe (who died a widow 1672)
6. George Leigh bp. Egginton 15/8/1591, rector of Egginton 1616-1631, bur.
    Egginton 24/6/1631, marr. Elizabeth and had issue:
    (1) Thomas Leigh b. 1623
    (2) George Leigh b. 1625
    (3) John Leigh, b & d. 1631
    (1) Elizabeth (twin with Catherine)
    (2) Catherine (twin with Elizabeth, b. 1620)

Perhaps also father of:
7. Joseph Leigh (Rev.), marr. Sudbury 14/11/1622 Isabel Booth; rector of Egginton
    in succession to his cousin 1631-1640/1, d. 13/1/1640/1 bur. 24/1/1640/1 [or
    possibly a son or grandson of Thomas's first marriage]
1. Anne [PEC]

The eldest son:
HENRY LEIGH (Sir) of Egginton and Newton Solney, b. 1573/4, buys the Longford moiety of Newton Solney manorial estate 24/2/1602 for £4,582 [DRO D5236/4/83-85], ktd. between 1603 & 1608, sells land in north of county to Thomas Bagshaw of Ridge for £3005 20/11/1605 [D5236/5/60-61] and from his Egginton estates to Simon Every 2/2/1627/8 [DRO D5236/4/97] living 10/1/1632/3, when he vests the manors in his cousin once removed James Milward of Egginton [DRO D5236/4/101], marr. 6/7/1591 Catherine daughter of John Horton of Catton and had issue:

1. Mary
2. Anne (d. 1673) marr. (i) c. 1628, Sir Simon Every, 1st Bt. (1602-1647) by whom
    she had issue [see EVERY]. She marr. (ii) 2/6/1653 Lawrence Squibb of
    Winterbourne Whitchurch, Dorset.
3. Catherine

His will dated 16/3/1634 was proved by his widow in October 1635; he probably died in the latter year.

Pedigree V

FISHER

Source: Based on Pine, L. G. (ed.) *Burke's Landed Gentry* 17th edn. (London, 1952) 863-864, DRO Every deed D5236/18/1/8 and other sources noted in [brackets].

RALPH FISHER yeoman, of Foremark, b. c. 1520, died 1584/5; will pr. Lichfield 25/5/1585. Had issue (with a daughter Barbara, who married Thomas Thacker of Walton-by-Chesterfield, steward to Godfrey Foljambe (d. 1612) and left issue) a son:

JOHN FISHER of Foremark d. 1619 and married Helen (the widow Fisher of Newton Solney in 1662) by whom he had issue:

1. GABRIEL Fisher on whom see below
2. John Fisher b. 1605/6, of Lincoln College, Oxon. 1624-1627 & thereafter 1628-1631 at Cambridge where he obtained a MA in the latter year but died unmarried that autumn [NB, Tilley, J. (Derby Local Studies Library MS Tilley F) claims him as son of an intervening John]
3. William Fisher ('Mr.') of Newington Green, London, Newton Solney and Derby, bur. St. Werburgh, Derby 25/2/1693/4, having married Ann and had issue:
   (1) Thomas Fisher living 1693
   (1) Ann marr. Nathaniel Tench, of Low Leyton, Essex & Newton Solney, son of Henry Tench of Putney, where bp. 16/6/1631, made a will dat. 9/8/1706 [D5236/18/1/8] and died 2/4/1710 having had issue:
      1a Fisher Tench (Sir) of Low Leyton, HS Essex 1712, cr. Bt. 8/8/1715, sold property at Newton Solney to John Fisher; marr. Elizabeth dau. of Robert Bird and died 21/101736 leaving issue:
         1b Sir Nathaniel Tench, 2nd Bt. of Low Leyton b. 1697, d. unm. 2/6/1737
         1b Jane marr. Adam Soresby of Chesterfield, and dsp 18/5/1752.

1. Rachel, d. unmarr. 1665

GABRIEL FISHER of Foremark marr.1634, Elizabeth (died 1654) dau. of Randall Wade *alias* Bullock of Littleover and d. 1646 leaving issue:

1. THOMAS Fisher, see below
2. John Fisher Gent., living 1665/1701. Probably the John Fisher of Derby bur. St. Michael 19/4/1726, married Rebecca, bur. St. Michael, Derby 29/6/1722) & father of:
   (1) Thomas Fisher of Repton, Gent., married Elizabeth (b. 1698, d. 8/6/1735) daughter of Samuel Woodland of Leicester (by Mary his wife)
   (2) Joseph Fisher of Derby, later of bp. St. Michael, 7/9/1681 marr. St. Werburgh, Derby 5/4/1728 Sarah Brentnall of Repton
   (1) Mary bp. St. Michael, 22/12/1683 marr. there 15/8/1712 John Yates of Derby and had issue
   (2) Rebecca bp. St. Alkmund, Derby 17/4/1688 marr. St. Michael, 3/12/1705 Thomas Staples

THOMAS FISHER of Foremark, where he paid tax on 5 hearths in 1662 as "Mr., Fisher" suggesting that he enjoyed considerable status, perhaps, like his son, as steward or factor to the Foremark estate. He marr. 22/6/1659, Anne Payne (thought to be a relation of the Newton Solney Paynes, see Chapter III) and d. 1681 leaving issue:

1. John Fisher of Foremark, bp Foremark 2/8/1663 [PR]; educated at Repton School 1675, attorney & steward to 4th Earl of Chesterfield, to George Coke of Melbourne Hall and auditor to the Governors of Repton School. Acquired land at Newton Solney 1706 (which sold before 1719) He had his arms and crest confirmed by the College of Arms 15/9/1730. He marr.1686 Mary, dau. of Revd. Thomas Whelpdale of Ingleby (probably domestic chaplain to Sir Franceys Burdett of Foremark, 2nd Bt and d. 1731 having had issue:
   (1) John Fisher of Foremark, d. unm. 1748
   (2) Thomas Fisher, of Repton living 1745 marr. (i) Elizabeth, dau. of Samuel Woodland of Leicester and (ii) by 1730, Mary dau. of A. Wilmot of Kent but dsp. 1771
   (1) Mary d. unm. 1767

*

HOSKINS

Source: Based on the descent given in Sayer, M. J., in DAJ XCII (1972) & amplified by parish registers and other sources where noted.

JAMES HODSKINS of St. Budeaux, Devonshire, probably of Cornish descent, marr. Elizabeth and had issue:

ABRAHAM HODSKIN or HOSKINS (I) of Stafford, bp. St. Budeaux 31/10/1651 [IGI with filiation] d (aged 83 *sic*) 1732, Mayor of Stafford 1708, 1716 marr. Sarah and had issue (with two elder sons and four daughters):

1. RICHARD Hoskins, on whom see below
2. William Hoskins, of Isleworth, Middlesex, bp. St. Mary, Stafford, 11/8/1694, Equerry to HRH
   Frederick, Prince of Wales, died 1752, having marr. Elizabeth Stackhouse at All Hallows, London
   Wall, 7/4/1718) and had issue (with two daughters):
   (1) Abraham Hoskins of Shenstone Park, Staffs., marr. St. Philip, Birmingham, 2/2/1744 (his first
       cousin) Sarah (bp. Walsall 24/12/1722), dau. of Thomas Roe of Walsall.

RICHARD HOSKINS of Stafford, bp. St. Mary, Staffiord, 2/5/1684 marr. Jane and had (with a sister, who married in Burton before 1779) issue:

ABRAHAM HOSKINS (II) of Burton-upon-Trent, Stapenhill and Bladon Wood, Newton Solney, b. 1825, bp. St. Mary, Stafford, 18/9/1728, attorney, bailiff of the Manor of Burton, trustee of the Trent Navigation, and ppr. of the Burton Boat Co.; marr. Holy Trinity, Hull, 6/10/1757 Sarah (d. 8/5/1818 [MI St. Modwen, Burton]), dau. & coheir of Francis Haworth of Hull (a cadet of Haworth of Rawcliffe, Yorks., WR) by Ann, daughter of George Hayne of Burton and Ashbourne and died 274/1805 [MI St. Modwen, Burton; Will pr. 15/8/1805, PRO prob,. 11/1413]. With John Fowler, he took over the legal practice of Isaac Hawkins (whose daughter had married Sir Henry Harpur of Calke, Bt.), On Hoskins's death John Fowler, his partner's son and his own son-in-law took over the practice. Hoskins acquired Hanson Grange, Thorpe, from Sir John Every Bt. of Egginton 29/9/1772 [D5236/19/13] and left issue:

1. ABRAHAM Hoskins, on whom see below.
2. John Hoskins
3. Richard Hoskins
4. Francis Hoskins, bp. Burton, 22/6/1765, marr. St. Peter, Wolverhampton 13/2/1806 and had issue:
   (1) Elizabeth, bp. Burton, 2/4/1807 marr. Burton 5/5/1835 Robert Sherratt Tomlinson (bp.
       20/4/1806; Edlaston, Derbys., son of Thomas and Alice Tomlinson) of Burton upon Trent
1. Myrtilla marr. Burton 30/3/1799 Sir John Dickenson Fowler attorney and dep. steward of the manor
   of Burton (Ktd. 1815, d. 1839, son of her brother's partner John Fowler, attorney of Burton who
   retired 1802) [VCH *Staffordshire* IX (2003) 83-84, 87]. The elder Fowler was the Every family
   solicitor 1798-1812 [D5236/28/88]
2. Sarah marr. (2/1/1794) Michael Thomas Bass, the elder, who d. 9/3/1827 leaving
   issue [see Mosley (2003) I. 599, *sub* Burton, B.]
3. Mary marr. Burton 28/12/1799 Rev'd Hugh Jones, of Burton, curate of Stapenhill
   1824-1829, and of St. Modwen Burton, later of Tatenhill [VCH *Staffs.* IX (2003)
   216]
4. Ann, marr. Rev'd. John Blanchard
5. Elizabeth, d .unm.
6. Jane, d. unm.

ABRAHAM HOSKINS (III) of Burton-upon –Trent, attorney and of Bladen and Newton Park, Newton Solney, bp. Burton 14/12/1759; in 1786 appointed (with partner John Fowler & D P Coke) as trustees of the estate of Sir Henry Every, 9th Bt., a minor. From 1791 he owned a farm in Egginton which he exchanged as part of the Enclosure award with Every (then still under age) for 103 acres in Newton Solney in 1798 [recounted in confirmatory grant to Abraham Hoskins by Sir Henry 20/2/1829, DLSL Deed 5243]. This land was that east of and including the future site of Bladon Castle. He was 'noted for his greyhounds'; sold up 1837 and died at Woodside Villa, Uttoxeter 13/3/1842 [MI/NS; will pr. 24/12/1842, PRO prob. 11/1972] having marr. (i) Frances Somerville of Stafford (b. 1760, d. probably in childbirth 30/11/1798[MI/NS]), by whom he had issue:

1. Abraham Hoskins, b. 1792, d. unm. 10/8/1817.
2. Henry Hoskins, b. 1798, d. unm. 1/9/1824 [MI/NS]
1. Frances, b. c. 1797, marr. Henry Jackson, general manager of Bass's brewery, Burton.

Abraham Hoskins marr. (ii) Jane (b. 1784 d. 12/4/1852 [MI/NS]), dau. of Thomas Smith and had further issue:

2. Bartholomew Hoskins of Derby, later Turnditch, educated Repton from 1815 [Repton School Register], marr. Newton Solney 15/11/1834 Elizabeth Piddocke (probably a niece of the Elizabeth Piddocke who was mother to the Wilders brothers, see below) and had issue:
    (1) Abraham Hoskins, bp. Turnditch 1/7/1836 & at Newton Solney 23/1/1837
    (2) Henry Hoskins, bp. Turnditch 8/10/1837
    (3) Thomas Puiddock Hoskins bp. Turnditch 10/2/1839
    (1) Sarah Jane Elizabeth bp. Turnditch 29/12/1839

3. Capt. Francis Hoskins, bp. Newton Solney 16/8/1807, d. 1859, of Bladon House (i.e. probably Bladon Cottage), educ. Repton from 1815 [Repton School Register] marr. Mrs. Julia Brooks of Temple Houses, Portsmouth and had issue [career & issue from RIBA and Darlington Library]:
    (1) George Gordon Hoskins of Thornbeck House and later of Harewood Grove, Darlington, JP, FRIBA [career, RIBA Library] b. Birmingham 1837, he studied Architecture in London and Paris and was a pupil of W D Haskoll of Westminster. In 1864 he moved to Darlington, where his first domestic commission that year was probably 15 and 16 Westbrook Villas. He became ARIBA on the 3rd June 1867, proposed by P C Hardwick, Alfred Waterhouse and J P Pritchett,.and was based at Russell Street Buildings from 1867 to 1870. On 2/5/1870 Hoskins was elected FRIBA proposed by T Oliver, J P Pritchett and J Ross. He made useful contacts with Quaker families which lead to many commissions including Quaker houses at Woodburn and Elm Ridge, for John Pease in 1867. Extended Quaker connections outside the town led to commissions at the Temperance Hall at Hurworth, (1864), and the Victoria Hall in Sunderland, (1870). He gained the role of architect to the banking house of Backhouse after designing a manager's house added to the Backhouse Bank in 1867. Following this he designed branches in Sunderland (1868), Bishop Auckland (1870), Middlesbrough (1875), Thirsk (1877) and Barnard Castle (1878). His major work was the Middlesbrough Town Hall won in open competition in 1882. Alfred Waterhouse acted as assessor, and the Prince and Princess of Wales opened the building in 1889. He d. 1911, having marr. (i) Isabel Matilda (b. 1837, d. 1862) dau. of Joseph Robinson of Southend and marr. (ii) Annie, dau, and heiress of William Hudson of Brough, Yorkshire and had issue (with four daughters):
        1a [son] later an architect
        2a [son] later an architect
    (2) Walter Hamlet Hoskins ARIBA (1845-1921) of Darlington, whence he came with his mother and another brother to join G. G. Hoskins and to run a painting contracting business which did work on buildings designed by the firm.
    (3) [son] of Darlington, painting contractor.

4. George Hoskins, bp. Newton Solney 31/7/1808, d. infant 1809

5. William Hoskins, from 1834 an actor, of Melbourne, Australia, bp. Newton Solney 18/2/1816, from 1834 with Phelps' Shakespearean Company; encouraged Henry Irving; to Australia 1856 where appt. Mgr. of Theatre Royal, Ballarat, 1860. To New Zealand 1870s, retired to Melbourne in 1884, & died 23/9/1886 having marr. (1850) Julia Harland, singer.

6. Edward Hoskins, MD of Derby, later of Duffield House, Duffield , "eminent surgeon and Shakespearean scholar" [Bulmer,(1895); of him and his el. son, see also Watson (1991) 58] bp. Newton Solney 29/7/1817, died 21/9/1893, having marr. at St. Peter, Derby 13/8/1848 Florence Elizabeth dau. of Robert Hope of Derby and had issue:
    (1) Edward John Hadderton Hoskins, of Milford, of Duffield House, Duffield from 1893 and later of Belper, LRCP, LRCS, b. 30/10/1850, educ. Derby School, marr. Derby 11/9/1884 Rosalie Mary Iveson & d. 1917
    (2) Robert Hope Hoskins, of India. Born 1853, educ. Derby School, died 8/1899.
    (1) Eleanor Jane b. 1845 marr. Duffield 9/3/1871 Edward James Bury (b. 1833)

7. John Hoskins, bp. Newton Solney 25/6/1818, d. infant 1819

8. Horatio Hoskins, bp., 23/4/1820 at Newton Solney

9. Abraham Hoskins, bp. 17/11/1822, marr. (c. 1846) Ann [not corroborated].and d. 1913

2. Sophia, marr. at Newton Solney 1/12/1835 James Sutton of Shardlow JP, DL, b. 1800, (son of James Sutton of Shardlow Hall who died 1830 and Mary his wife), High Sheriff of Derbyshire 1842, d. 1868 [on these Suttons, see Fox-Davies (1910) 1553 & (1929) II. 1882 and had issue:

3. Charlotte bp. Newton Solney 1/8/1811 marr. Newton Solney 16/9/1834 Henry Wilders of Burton, brewer & partner of Thomas Wilders in the Burton Brewery Co.; b. Burton 25/8/1808, son of William Wilders of Burton and Elizabeth his wife, and had issue:

(1) George Henry Wilders, of Burton-upon-Trent, brewer, as the Burton Brewery Co., in receivership 1907, taken over by Worthingtons in 1915 and both by Bass in 1929 [VCH IX (2003) 47, 68, 80] bp. Uttoxeter 28/8/1840, marr. Annie Elizabeth and had issue:

    1a Evelyn Alice bp. Holy Trinity, Burton, 12/3/1873

    2a Rosa bp. Holy Trinity, Burton 20/8/1873 [*sic*]

(2) Albert Bartley Wilders, bp. Holy Trinity, Burton 17/7/1844

(3) William Henry Wilders, bp. Burton 14/6/1860

(1) Rosa, bp. Uttoxeter 16/1 & d. 2/2/1836

(2) Charlotte Victoria, bp. Uttoxeter 9/9/1838

(3) Mary Sophia, bp. Holy Trinity, Burton 26/5/1842

4. Frances marr. 3/4/1831 at Newton Solney, Henry Jackson

5. Jane bp. 27/8/1809 at Newton Solney, marr. 3/12/1833 at Newton Solney, William Wilders of The Cottage, Newton Solney 1835 (he was born at Burton 10/9/1800 and was brother of Henry and John) and had issue:

    (1) William Abraham Wilders bp. Newton Solney 27/11/1834

    (2) Edward Andrew Wilders bp. Newton Solney, 29/10/1837 & d. 11/3/1838

    (3) James Wilders bp. Newton Solney 28/7/1839 & d. 24/7/1841

    (1) Sarah Jane Elizabeth bp. Newton Solney 11/4/1836

6. Rosa bp. Newton Solney, 18/8/1810 marr. Newton Solney 30/8/1836 John Wilders (bp. Burton 3/12/1802, brother of William and Henry) but had no issue.

7. Eliza marr. Dr. Hyde [Wain (1976) II]

NB a Henry Hoskins, son of an Abraham (probably Rev'd Abraham Hoskins living 1786, Wain, *loc.cit.*) was educated Repton Sch. from 1814 [Repton School Register]

*

Pedigree VII

WORTHINGTON

Source: Townend, P (ed.) *Burke's Landed Gentry* (3 Vols. London 1965-72) III (1972) 978 and where noted.

WILLIAM WORTHINGTON of Burton-upon-Trent, brewer, b. 10/9/1764, marr. 28/7/1791 Martha, dua. of Henry Evans of Caldwell Hall d. 1825 having had issue:

1. WILLIAM Worthington, see below

1. Ann, marr. 17/8/1835 Revd. Roger Bass, second son of Michael Thomas Bass of Burton, brewer, sometime vicar of Austrey, Warw. He died 8/4/1844, leaving issue

The son:

WILLIAM WORTHINGTON of Burton-upon-Trent, JP, b. 16/2/1799, marr. 8/6/1824 Mary Anne (d. 24/4/1894) second dau. of Francis Calvert of Houndhill, Staffs., and in 1837 or shortly thereafter Lord Chesterfield's tenant of the Newton Park estate, Newton Solney. A brewer, he died 17/10./1871, leaving issue:

1. William Henry Worthington, b. Burton 28/8/1826, of Derwent Bank, Derby, JP first Mayor of Burton-upon-Trent. He died unmarr. 17/7/1894.

2. Calvert Worthington bp. Burton 7/10/1830, d. unm.arr. 11/1871

3. Francis (Frank) Worthington, drowned in Scotland, unmarr. 3/9/1872.

4. Albert Octavius Worthington, bp. Newton Solney 24/11/1844, of Maple Hayes and Pipe Hall, Staffordshire, who married and had issue (the Worthingtons of Kingston Russell).

1. Catherine, Elizabeth, marr. 21/7/1852 Col. Charles Denison Pedder of Kilburn Hall and had issue.

*

HOLBROOK

Source, Monumental inscriptions, Repton churchyard [MIs, recorded by Derbyshire family history Society, D119, D 120], Tachella (1902), Repton School Registers, and will of Rebecca Holbrook 6/2/1883 (private collection).

This family allegedly descend from:
JOSEPH HOLBROOK of London in 1703, also builder, later, of Repton Grange, allegedly Lord Mayor in c. 1703 [not noticed in the accepted list of Lords Mayor, however]. His descendant was:
FRANCIS HOLBROOK of Repton Grange, b. 1758 [perhaps, but not necessarily, the Francis, son of Francis, bp. Pentrich 20/3/1757] d. 30/3/1842 [MI D119, Repton] marr. Repton 20/2/1792, Rebecca Burton, b.1761, d.16/10/1841 [MI *ibid.*] and had issue:
1. Charles Holbrook of Nunsfield house, Boulton, & St. Peter's St., Derby, bp. Repton, 5/7/1796, educ. Repton 1810 onwards, lead merchant at Derby, St. Peter's St., marr. Mary Martha and had issue:
    (1) Mary Frances, bp. Alvaston 5/9/1830, marr. Mr. Ashworth and had issue:
    (2) Elizabeth, marr. William Charles Soresby of Shardlow, general carrier, and had issue:
        1a Charles Holbrook Soresby, b. 21/11/1852, educ. Derby School & Repton 1866-67; of 205, Uttoxeter New Road, Derby, later (1902) of Nunsfield House and in 1908 of The Firs, Shardlow.
        2a Walter James Soresby, b. 7/4/1854, educ Derby School & then Repton from 1866.
        1a Elizabeth (probably died young)
        2a Frances Beatrice, marr. (1889) Henry Freckleton Gadsby (d. 1902), Town Clerk of Derby 1879-1902, of The Mayor's Parlour, Tenant St., Derby (son of Alderman John Gadsby (1818-1883), Mayor of Derby in 1858) and had
            issue.
        3a Mary Elizabeth, Mrs. Ashworth
    (3) Rebecca, of Repton, d.unm. 1883, will dat. 6/2/1883.
2. FRANCIS Holbrook on whom see below
1. Mary b. 1794, d. unm. 5/5/1857
2. Elizabeth, b. 1797/8, d. unm. 1/3/1877
3. Rebecca, b. 1804, d. unm. 8/11/1895
The elder son:
FRANCIS HOLBROOK of Repton Grange, tanner, later of Bladon Castle, b. 25/5/1801, d. 14/8/1882 marr. Marianne (b. 1811, d. 2/3/1900) and had issue:
1. Francis William Holbrooke of Bladon Castle b. 10/1836, d. 20/12/1882, marr. Emma Georgina (b. 1830, d. 10/12/1928) and had issue:
    (1) Francis George Seymour Holbrooke of Bladon Castle, b. 1865, d. 13/12/1937, principal legatee of Rebecca, marr. Elizabeth (b. 1886, d. 7/11/1938)
1. Mary Frances, marr. Mr. Hancock (she had d. by 1883)
2. [daughter] marr. William John Drewry (1842-1901) of Burton, solicitor.

*

SALT

Source: Michael Day's notes, Directories & VCH Staffordshire

THOMAS SALT of Burton–upon-Trent, said to have been son of a doctor from Abbott's Bromley, b. 1777, marr. Burton 1804, Susannah, daughter of Rev'd. William Dawson, curate of St. Modwen, Burton (1738-1772; by Susannah, daughter of Leonard Fosbrooke of Shardlow Hall, High Sheriff of Derbyshire 1725, d. 1762) died 1813 and has issue:
1. THOMAS FOSBROOKE Salt on whom see below
2. William Dawson Salt
1. Susannah
2. Mary Sophia
3. Laura

4. Frances

THOMAS FOSBROOKE SALT of Stapenhill b. 1808, took over his father's brewery 1829, becoming T. Salt & Sons, in partnership with Henry Wardle MP (son of Francis Wardle of Highfield, Winshill) who died 1892. The brewery was sold to Bass 1927. [VCH IX (2003) 71] He marr. 1839 Mary Frances Atkinson of Huddersfield, and died 1864 leaving issue:

1. Thomas Fosbrooke Salt, b. 1842, succeeded his father in 1864, marr. 1867 Sophia Warbreck
2. Edward Dawson Salt, of Rock House, b. 1844, living in Newton Solney 1904; a director of Salt & Sons., marr. (1863) Jane Lampard (b. 1842)
3. William Cecil Salt, bp. Burton 1/7/1845, later a director of the brewery c. 1864
4. Charles John Sellack Salt, b. 1852
5. George Atkinson Salt, b. 1854
1. Mary Ellen b. 1840 marr. her father's partner, Henry Wardle of Highfield, Stapenhill MP (L) S. Derbyshire 1885-1892; died 1892 and had issue
2. Clara, b. 1846
3. Susanne Margaret, b. 1848
4. Marion Emma, b. 1850
5. Frances, b. 1851

*

PEDIGREE X

RATCLIFF

Source: Michael Day's Notes, Fox-Davies, A. C., *Armorial Families* (2. Vols., London 1929) II. 1622 & where noted.

JOHN RATCLIFF, b. 1759; was a commercial traveller for Bass, when in 1797 he was made a partner with a 25% share, renewed in 1830; marr. (i) Burton 17/4/1780 Martha Dawson (d. 27.5.1785) and whom he had issue:

1. James Ratcliff of Burton, marr. and had issue:
    (1) Mary Anne, marr. Burton 13/9/1836 John Wright of Tamworth solicitor, (a descendant of the Wrights of Eyam and Great Longstone) and had issue, two sons and four daughters.
2. SAMUEL Ratcliff, on whom see below.
1. Martha

John Ratcliff married (ii) at Aston-on-Trent 23/1/1791 Elizabeth Somerfield and had further issue:

2. Ann b. c. 1795, marr. Repton 22/2/1827 Thomas Allsopp of The Mount, Newton Solney (1782-1855) and had issue:
    (1) William Allsopp, dvp unmarr.

He died 16/1/1835. The second son:

SAMUEL RATCLIFF bp. Burton 19/2/1783; built Cliff House, Newton Solney 1860; a brewer and a partner holding a three sixteenth share of Bass, died 5/4/1861 having marr. 25/10/1813 at St. Peter, Derby, Sarah Tunley, and left issue:

1. John Ratcliff bp. Burton 26/1/1814 marr. Northwood-by-Stoke, 1857 Anne Crewe and had issue:
    (1) John Ratcliff bp. Burton 13/31863, educ. Repton 1877-1882
2. James Ratcliff of Burton, bp. Burton 6/9/1815, marr. Mary Coxon and had issue:
    (1) Stephen Coxon Ratcliff, bp. Burton 21/3/1841
    (2) James Ratcliff bp. Burton Holy Trinity 26/7/1843
    (1) Sarah Ann bp. Burton 2/2/1840
    (2) Mary Parkes, bp. Burton 7/8/1842
3. Samuel Ratcliff of Burton, bp. Burton 21/4/1819, marr. Harriett, and had issue:
    (1) Samuel Ratcliff, bp. Burton 16/11/1853
    (2) John Ratcliff, bp. Holy Trinity, Burton 15/2/1860
    (3) Charles Robert Ratcliff, bp. Holy Trinity, Burton 10/7/1863
    (1) Harriett Sarah, bp. Holy Trinity, Burton 25/10/1854

(2) Helen Rose, bp. Burton 13/10/1856

(3) Alice Emma, bp. Burton, 16/6/1856 [*sic*]

(4) Margaret Martha, bp. Holy Trinity, Burton, 3/9/1861

4. Edwin Ratcliff, bp. Burton 2/3/1821

5. Frederic Ratcliff, of Cliffe House, Newton Solney, bp. Burton, 23/9/1825, living 1871, d. umn.

6. Capt. Richard Henry Ratcliff, JP, bp. Burton 27/8/1830, partner in Bass 1863, Capt. Leicestershire Yeomanry, of Orgreave Hall, Staffs., and Stanford Hall, Leics., d. 1902, having marr. in 1894 Caroline Christina, 3rd dau, of Vaughan Henning Vaughan-Lee of Dillington Park, Som. (d. 1882, by Clara Elizabeth, dau. of George Moore of Appleby Hall, Appleby Parva, Derbys.) who re-marr. (1908) Horace Ogilvie Peacock of Stanford Hall) [Walford (1909) 859] and had issue:

(1) Kathleen Joan, living unmarr. 1909

7. William Henry Ratcliff, bp. Burton 23/8/1833

8. Robert Ratcliff, bp. Burton 13/10/1837 of Stapenhill to 1877, later (1879) of Newton Park, who with his brother Richard built Burton's first Baths 1872-3 and later paid for the addition of Turkish Baths. A director of Bass he d. 1912 [will adm. 3/2/1913, estate valued at £968,413 – 13s – 8d] having marr. 18/7/1866 at Burton, Emily (1836-1916), dau. of Thomas Payne of Burton-upon-Trent (b. Newton Solney 1/1803, son of Peter Payne of Newton and Hannah) and had issue:

(1) Col. Robert Frederick Ratcliff of Newton Park, CMG (1916), VD, BA, JP, DL, of Newton Park; also of Clatford Mills, Upper Clatford, Andover, Hants., Chittlehampton, Devonshire and Dundonnell, Ross & Cromarty, bp. Burton 24/4/1867 educ. Rossall, & Jesus Coll. Cantab., Lt. Col. cmdg. 6th North Staffordshire Regt. TA 1900-1924, a director of Bass, MP (Liberal Unionist) Burton 1902-1918, High Sheriff Derbys. 1929, member Brooks's & Devonshire Clubs; d. unm. 1943 at the York Hotel, Derby [will pr. 29/5/1943 estate valued at £844,527 – 8s – 4d]

(2) Richard Ratcliff, b. 1872, presumed died young

(3) Lewis Sidney Ratcliff, b. 1875, presumed died young

(4) Percy William Ratcliff of Newton Park, b. 1877, educ. Rossall & Clare Coll. Cantab., later a director of Bass; member Flyfishers' Club; dsp 21/2/1955 having marr. 1921 Olive Margaret, dau. of Alderman Francis Gilbert Thompson of Burton-upon-Trent (cllr. Burton 1926-1949; alderman 1949-1958). [will pr. 5/5/1955, estate valued at £1,079,894 – 8s – 4d; on his career and that of R. F. Ratcliff, cf. Kelly, *Handbook* (1939) 1527]. Mrs. Ratlcliff was from 1956 of The Cedars, Newton Solney, and d. 11/5/1971 [will pr. 26/5/1971, estate valued at £915,321 – 0s – 0d]

(1) Emily Ada bp. Burton 5/12/1868

(2) Laura Maria, bp. Burton 9/11/1870

1. Martha, bp. Burton 10/5/1817

2. Sarah, bp. Burton 15/1/1824, later of Cliff House, Newton Solney

3. Emma, bp. Burton 2/11/1827, later of Cliff House, Newton Solney

*

Pedigree XI

GRETTON

Source: Mosley, C (ed.) *Burke's Peerage, Baronetage, etc.,* 3 Vols. (London 2003) II. 1660, amplified by PRs and other sources as noted.

RICHARD GRETTON of Uttoxeter marr. Ellen and had issue:

1. THOMAS see below

2. John Gretton, bp. Uttoxeter 15/12/1695 marr. Elizabeth and had issue:

(1) William Gretton bp. Uttoxeter 1/11/1734 marr. Uttoxeter 3/1/1766 Mary Watson and had issue:

1a Richard Gretton bp. Uttoxeter 7/6/1768

2a William Gretton, bp. Uttoxeter 12/4/1772

1a Elizabeth bp. Uttoxeter 7/11/1766

2a Jane bp. Uttoxeter 28/7/1769

3a Abigail Lander bp. Uttoxeter 7/8/1773

4a Sarah bp. Uttoxeter 21/2/1776

3. Richard Gretton, bp. Uttoxeter -/7/1698 marr. Ellen and had issue:

  (1) John Gretton, bp,. Uttoxeter 21/3/1719

1. Ellen bp. Uttoxeter 23/3/1689

THOMAS GRETTON of Uttoxeter, bp. there 4/6/1688 marr. Wirksworth 28/8/1718 Mary (b. 1697) dau. of Joseph [or Elisha] Hodgkinson of Wirksworth and had issue:

1. THOMAS Gretton, see below

2. John Gretton, bp. Uttoxeter 18/2/1726, d. 12/7/1730

3. Richard Gretton, bp. Uttoxeter bp. 3/6/1731, marr. Rolleston-on-Dove 29/10/1765 his cousin Elizabeth (bp. 10/1/1743) dau. of John & Sarah Powis of Rolleston (John was bp. Newton Solney 30/5/1714, son of Walter of Newton Solney and Mary Jobey, who marr. Burton 20/1/1712; Walter was the son of John Powis of Rolleston where he was bp. 12/8/1688). They were later of later of Burton-upon-Trent and had issue:

  (1) Benjamin Gretton, bp. Burton 7/6/1781 marr. Burton 13/9/1808 Tominson [*sic*] Smith and had issue:

    1a Sarah, bp. Burton 17/10/1808

  (2) Joseph Gretton, bp. Burton 21/9/1788

  (1) Anne, bp. Burton, 2/10/1774

  (2) Rebecca bp. Burton 8/9/1776

  (3) Sarah, bp. Burton 31/12/1779 marr. Burton 3/12/1802 Joseph (bp. 6/2/1774) son of Joseph & Ann Upton of Hanbury

1. Mary bp. Uttoxeter, 19/5/1720

2. Elizabeth, bp. Uttoxeter 6/6/1736 marr. Uttoxeter 4/12/1766 Edward Cope

THOMAS GRETTON of Burton-upon-Trent, bp. Uttoxeter 12/9/1723 marr. Burton 24/10/1764 his cousin Sarah (bp. Burton 5/10/1737), dau. of Thomas Powis of Newton Solney (who was bp. there 1/6/1722, son of Walter & Mary, on whom see above) and had issue:

1. THOMAS Gretton see below

2. Joseph Gretton, bp. Burton 25/10/1778, marr. Burton 28/1/1801 Sarah Walker and had issue:

  (1) Joseph Gretton of Clay Mills, Stretton, coal dealer, marr. Burton 28/9/1829 Mary Tooby and had issue:

    1a Joseph Gretton, bp. Burton 17/11/1831

    2a Thomas Gretton, bp Burton 7/11/1833

   3a John Gretton bp. Burton 30/9/1838

   1a Jane, bp. Burton 11/7/1830

   2a Frances of Horninglow Street, Burton, bp. Burton 17/9/1834, living unmarr. 1897

  (2) William Gretton of Clay Mills, Stretton, schoolmaster there 1834

  (1) Sarah, bp. Burton 29/11/1801 marr. Burton 18/4/1825 Samuel Dooley

  (2) Anne, bp. Burton 8/5/1814, marr. Burton 8/5/1832 Thomas Hardy

3. William Gretton, landlord of the *Carpenters' Arms* inn, New Street, Burton, bp. Burton 22/6/1788, marr. Burton 23/3/1811 Hannah Ward and had issue:

  (1) John Ward Gretton, bp. Burton 24/4/1825

  (1) Sarah, bp. Burton 16/5/1811 marr. 12/4/1837 her kinsman James (bp. Burton 23/6/1816) son of Edward Upton & Sarah Watson (who were marr. Burton 8/2/1814; Edward was son of William & Sarah Upton of Hanbury) and had issue

  (2) Jane, Bp. Burton 13/9/1812

  (3) Hannah, bp. Burton 3/7/1814

  (4) Anne, bp. Burton 21/1/1819

  (5) Mary Elizabeth, bp. Burton 4/2/1821

  (6) Emma, bp. Burton 1/10/1829

  (7) Esther Jane, bp. Burton 12/4/1835

1. Anne, bp. Burton 7/3/1781

2. Hannah, bp. Burton 22/6/1783

The elder son:

THOMAS GRETTON of Burton-upon-Trent bp. there 30/8/1765 marr. Burton 18/8/1790 Sarah (bp. 7/8/1774) dau. of William Bath of Church Gresley, Derbys., and had issue:
1. JOHN Gretton, see below
2. Francis Gretton bp. Burton 25/5/1797, landlord of the New Inn , Horninglow, 1834, of Burton, marr. Hannah and had issue:
   (1) Francis Gretton, bp. Burton 16/12/1826, marr. Sarah and had issue:
      1a Robert John Gretton bp. Burton 5/10/1859
   (2) John Gretton bp. Burton 10/4/1830
   (3) Thomas Gretton, bp. Burton 6/12/1842, marr. Burton 3/2/1866 Mary Heath
   (1) Elizabeth, bp. Holy Trinity, Burton, 10/2/1828
   (2) Mary Anne bp. Burton 6/10/1831, d. 12/10/1837
   (3) Alice bp. Burton 5/5/1844
3. Thomas Gretton, bp. Burton 19/10/1800. Burton 17/11/1825 Mary Taylor and had issue:
   (1) Thomas Gretton bp. Burton 4/3/1827, marr. Mary and had issue:
      1a Samuel Gretton, bp. Burton 8/5/1864
      1a Fanny bp. Burton 26/3/1854
      2a Jane bp. Nurton 2/11/1862
   (2) John Gretton bp. Burton 2/2/1833
   (1) Anne bp. Burton 2/7/1829
   (2) Ellen bp Burton 27/2/1831
1. Sarah bp. Burton 21/8/1803

JOHN GRETTON of High St., Burton-upon-Trent, brewer (eg. 1846/57) and (from 1860) Bladon House, Winshill, b. 0/6/1793, d. 30/12/1867 marr. Burton 10/7/1832 Mary dau. of James Sutton of Shardlow and had issue:
1. JOHN Gretton, see below
2. Frederick Gretton, bp. Burton 17/4/1839
1. Mary bp. Burton 10/7/1833
2. Clara, bp. Burton 30/8/1843

JOHN GRETTON of Bladon House and from 1894 Stapleford Park, Leics., JP, DL, b. 27/7/1836 d. 2/10/1899 having marr. 27/6/1866 Marianne Louisa, dau. of Major John Richard Molyneux of Brook House, Compton, Surrey and had issue:
1. JOHN Gretton, on whom see below
2. Hugh Frederic Gretton (Col.), b. 12/5/1869, d. unmarr. 19/7/1928, of Bladon House (from 1894) and Donington Hall, Leics.
3. Rupert Harold Gretton (Capt. Beds. Regt.), b. 1886, KIA Ypres 18/12/1915 unmarr.
1. Katherine, marr. 18/10/1903 Sir John Burgoyne, 10th Bt., of Sutton Park, but d. unmarr.
2 Alice, d. unmr. 7/1892
3. Christine Rose d. unmarr. 22/12/1966
4. Muriel Elise, d. unmar. 5/1962

The eldest son,
JOHN GRETTON (Col.), cr. 27/11/1944 1st Lord Gretton of Stapleford Park, PC, CBE (1919) DL, JP, OStJ, VD, TD, MP (S. Derbys. 1895-1906, Rutland 19007-1918 & Burton-upon-Trent 1918-1943), b. 1/9/1867 d. 2/6/1947 having marr. Hon. Maude Evelyn de Moleyns, dau. of 4th Lord Ventry and had issue:
1. JOHN FREDERIC Gretton, see below
1. Kathleen Fanny (Hon.) d. 3/5/1976, marr. 9/4/1929 Brig. Sir Henry Robert Floyd, 5th Bt., CB, CBE and had issue.
2. Mary Catherine Hersey (Hon.) d. 6/2/1972 marr. 19/7/1933, Capt. Edward William Brook and had issue.

The only son:
JOHN FREDERIC GRETTON, 2nd Lord Gretton, OBE, MP, b. 15/8/1902, d. 26/3/1982 marr. 6/5/1930 Anna Helena Margaret, fau. of Capt. Henri Leoffler of London and had issue:
1. JOHN HENRIK Gretton, see below
2. Anthony David Erik Gretton (Hon.), b. 25/7/1945 d. unmarr. 13/11/1982
1. Mary Anne Maude Sigrid (Hon.) b. 5/2/1939 marr. 1956 Thomas Henry Wragg of Hinckley, Leics.
2. Elizabeth Margaret (Hon.) b. 25/5/1945 marr. 12/10/1968 Christopher Mark Meynell son of Revd. Mark Meynell, MA of Leamington Hastings, Warw.

The only son:
JOHN HENRIK GRETTON, 3rd Lord Gretton, b. 9/2/1941, d. 1989, marr. 17/10/1970 Jennifer Ann, dau. of Edmund Moore of York and had issue:
1. JOHN LYSANDER Gretton, see below
1. Sarah Margaret (Hon.), b. 7/12/1971 marr. 3/7/1999 John, son of Simon Biddulph of
   Rodmarton, Gloucs. and has issue.
The only son:
JOHN LYSANDER GRETTON, 4th Lord Gretton, b. 17.5.1975, marr. 2006 Sarah, dau. of Alfred Altard of Malta GC and has issue:
1. John Frederick Druce Gretton (Hon.), b. 9/6/2008
1. Eloise Victoria Anne (Hon.), b. 09/12/09.

*

Sunnyside Cottages: 18th century sundial   *[M. Craven]*

BIBLIOGRAPHY

*Abbreviations to be found in the footnotes are listed to the right in **bold**.*

Manuscript Sources:
Challenor, J., Pedigrees from the Heralds' Visitations of 1569 and 1611, amplified
      locally, 1613, DLSL MS 6341.
Day, M. J., MS notes dated 9/12/1999 on the more recent history of Newton Solney and
      Newton Park, in the possession of his family.
Every, E. M., Narrative MS pedigree of the Every family (private collection, by kind
      permission of Sir Henry Every, Bt., DL)   **Every Ped.**
Every MSS Derbyshire RO D5236.
Every MSS (private collection) by kind permission of Sir Henry Every Bt., DL   **PEC + No.**
Manchester University, John Rylands Library, Crutchley MSS, Longford Charters
                                                                         RLC + No.
Melbourne Hall MSS by kind permission of Lord Ralph Kerr, DL Nottinghamshire Archives
Rawlins, R. R., *A Critical Examination and Survey of the Parish Churches and chapels in the
      County of Derby* (3 vols., MS, 1843) in DLSL
Staffordshire & Stoke-on-Trent Archives, Lichfield, Talbot & Co. MSS

Printed Sources:
Askey, M., *Henry Isaac Stevens of Derby, architect, (1907-1873)* unpublished doctoral
      thesis, de Montfort Univ. (Leics., 1994)
Austin, M .R., *The Church in Derbyshire in 1823-4: The Parochial Visitation of Samuel
      Butler, Archdeacon of Derby* DRS V for 1979 (Kendall 1972)
Bagshaw, S. *Directory of Derbyshire* (Sheffield 1846)
Barraclough, G. (ed.) *The Charters of the Anglo-Norman Earls of Chester c. 1071-1237*
      Lancashire & Cheshire Record Society, Vol. CXXVI (1988)
Beard, G., *Craftsmen and Interior Decoration in England, 1660-1820* (London 1981)
Biddle, M. & Kolbye-Biddle, B, *The Repton Stone* in *Anglo-Saxon England* XIV (1985) 233
      -292
Bigsby, R., *Historical and Topographical Description of Repton* (Derby 1854)
Blome, R., *Britannia,* (London 1673)
Bolland, A. K. (ed.), *Repton School Register* 3rd suppl. to 3rd edn. (London, 1957)
Bridgeman, C. G. O., *The Will of Wulfric Spot,* in William Salt's Staffordshire Collections
      (1916)
Brighton, T., *Royalists & Roundheads in Derbyshire* (Bakewell 1981)
Britton, J., & Brayley, E. W., *The Beauties of England & Wales* Vol. III (London
      1802).
Bulmer, T., *Directory of Derbyshire* (London 1895)
Burke, Sir B. & A. P., *Burke's Colonial Gentry* (2 Vols., London, 1891/1895)
Burke, Sir J., *Burke's Commoners* 4 Vols. (London 1833-1838)   **BLG + date**
Burke, Sir J. & J. B., *Burke's Dormant & Extinct Baronetcies* (1st Edn., London, 1838)
Burke, J. B., 2nd. edn., rev. Burke, Sir B., *General Armory* (London 1884)
Camden, W., *Britannia,* rev. edn., by Gough, R. (London 1789)
Cameron, K., *The Place Names of Derbyshire* English Place-Name Society Vol.
      XXIX, 3 Vols. (Cambridge 1959)
Cameron, K., *English Place Names* (London 1961)
Cokayne, G. E. *see* GEC
Colvin, Sir H., *Biographical Dictionary of British Architects 1600-1840* (3rd edn. New Haven
      & London 1995 & 4th edn., 2008)
Cox, J. C., *Notes on the Churches of Derbyshire,* 4 vols., (Chesterfield, & London,
      1874-79)

Craven, M., *The Derby Town House* (Derby 1987)

Craven, M., *A Derbyshire Armory,* Derbyshire Record Society Vol. XVII (Chesterfield 1991)

Craven, M., *Keene's Derby* (Derby 1993)

Craven, M., & Stanley, M. F., *The Derbyshire Country House,* 2 Vols., 3rd edn. (Ashbourne 2001)

Darlington, R. R., *The Cartulary of Darley Abbey* (Kendal 1945) **DC + no.**

Davies D. P., *A View of Derbyshire* (Derby 1811)

Dictionary of National Biography, compact edn., 2 Vols. (Oxford 1975) **DNB**

Dugdale, Sir W. (ed. Caley, J., & Ellis, H.), *Monasticon Anglicanum* 6 vols. (London 1817-1830)

Edwards, B., *Transport in Derby* (Derby 1993)

Edwards, D. G., *Derbyshire Hearth Tax Assessments 1662-1670* Derbyshire Record Society, Vol. VII (Chesterfield 1982)

Ekwall, E., *The Oxford Dictionary of Place Names* 3rd Rev. edn., (Oxford 1951)

Ellis, S., *The Jervis Newton Park Hotel* (1997)

Emery, A., *Greater Medieval Houses of England and Wales 1300-1500,* (3 Vols. Cambridge 1996-2006), Vol. II (2000)

Farey, J., *A General View of the Agriculture and Minerals of Derbyshire* 3 vols. (London, 1811/13/16)

Finberg, H. P. R., *Roman and Saxon Withington* University of Leicester, Dept. of English Local History, *Occasional Paper No. 8* (Leicester 1957)

Fletcher, W. G. D., *Leicestershire Pedigrees and Royal Descents* (Leicester 1887)

Foster, J., *Baronetage* (London 1882)

Fox-Davies, A. C., *Armorial Families* (London 1910) & 2 Vols (London, 1929)

Fraser, W., *Field Names in South Derbyshire* (Ipswich, 1947)

Garratt, H. J. H., *Derbyshire Feet of Fines, 1323-1540* Derbyshire Record Society Vol. XI (Chesterfield 1985) **FF + no.**

GEC et al *The Complete Peerage,* 2nd edn. (ed. Gibbs, V., et al), 14 vols. (London, 1910 -1998) **CP + vol.**

Gelling, M., *Place Names in the Landscape* (London 1993)

German, J., *The Newton Park Estate,* Sale Catalogue (Burton 1956)

Glover, S., *Gazetteer of Derbyshire for 1827* (Derby 1829)

Glover, S., *History and Gazetteer of the County of Derby,* 2nd edn., 2 vols., (Derby 1831/1833)

HMSO, *Return of Owners of Land 1873,* 2 Vols (London 1875)

Hanks, P. & Hodges, F., *A Dictionary of Surnames* (Oxford 1996)

Hart, C. R., *The Early Charters of Northern England and the North Midlands* (Leicester, 1975)

Headley, G. & Meulenkamp, W., *Follies* (London 1986)

Heath, J. *Derby & District Motor 'Bus Proprietors and their Services Prior to 1930* (Castle Donington, 1985)

Heath, P., *Hoskins' Derbyshire Elysium* (Swadlincote 2005)

Higham, N., *The Death of Anglo-Saxon England* (Stroud 1997)

Hipkins, F. C., *Repton and its Neighbourhood* (Repton 1899)

Humphery-Smith, C. R., *Anglo-Norman Armory* (London 1973)

Hunter, J., ed. Clay, J. W., *Familiae Minorum Gentium* Harleian Society Vol. XXXVII-XL, 4 Vols. (London, 1894-97) **FMG + vol.**

Hutton, W., *History and Antiquities of the Borough of Derby* (Derby 1791)

Ireland, G. (transcr.) & Squibb G. D. (ed.), *Dugdale's Nottinghamshire and Derbyshire Visitation Papers* Harl. Soc. NS Vol. 6 (London 1987)

James, J. W., *Rhygfarch's Life of David* (Cardiff 1967)

Jansen, F. C. T., *The Church of St. Mary, Newton Solney* (rev. edn., Derby 1989)

Jeayes, I. H. & Deanesley M., *The Charters of Burton Abbey,* Staffordshire Record Society (Kendal 1937) **BC + No.**

Jeayes, I. H., *Derbyshire Charters* (London 1906) **J + no.**

Keats-Rohan, K. S. B. *Domesday Descendants* 2 Vols. (Woodbridge 1999, 2002)
Kelly's Directory of Derbyshire (London, 1888, 1891, 1903, 1908, 1926, 1932, 1936 & 1941)
Kelly's Handbook of the Titled, Official, and Landed Classes (London 1939)
King's College, London *Prosopography of Anglo-Saxon England* (2 Vols. London 2005, 2007)   **PASE**
Kirby, D. P., *The Earliest English Kings* (London 1991)
Lawson, Sir C., *Hardinges of History* (London 1910)
Leland, J., *Itinerary* Ed. Chandler, J. (Sutton 1993),
Le Neve, P (ed. Marshall, G. W.) *Pedigrees of the Knights Created by King Charles II, James II, William III, Queen Mary II and Anne* Harleian society Vol. VIII (London 1873).
Liddiard. R.. (ed.), *The Medieval Park, New Perspectives* (Macclesfield, 2007)
Lloyd, Sir J. E. & Jenkins, R. T., *Dictionary of Welsh Biography Down to 1940* (Oxford 1959)   **DWB**
Lysons, S. & D., *Magna Britannia,* 6 Vols. (London, 1806-1822)
        Vol. I Pt. 1, *Bedfordshire* (London 1806, rev. 1813)
        Vol. V, *Derbyshire* (London, 1817)
McKenna, J., *Clockmakers & Watchmakers of Central England* (Mayfield 2002)
McManus, P. A., *One Man's Scotland* (Derby 2002)
Moore, D., *British Clockmakers and Watchmakers Apprentice Records* (Mayfield 2003)
Morgan, P. (ed.) *Domesday Book* Vol. 22 *Leicestershire* (Chichester 1979) – **DB *Leics.***
Mosley, C. (ed.) *Burke's Peerage* 107th Edn., 3 Vols. (London 2003) – **BP + date**
Newton Solney Womens' Institute, *Newton Solney Remebered 1900-2000* (Burton-upon -Trent, 2000)
Nichols, J., *History and Antiquities of the County of Leicester* 4 Vols. in 8 (Leicester 1795-1811)
Owen, C., *The Greatest Brewery in the World: A History of Bassm, Ratcliff & Gretton* Derbyshire Record Society Vol. XIX (Chesterfield 1992)
Owen, C., *Illustrated History of Burton-upon-Trent* (Derby 1994)
Pain, W., *The Practical Builder or, Workman's General Assistant* (London 1787)
Papworth, J. W., *Ordinary of British Armorials* (London 1874)
Parker, C. & Wood, S., *Domesday Book ,* Vol. 28, *Nottinghamshire* (Chichester 1977)
                                                                          DB *Notts.*
Pevsner, Sir N. & Williamson, E., *The Buildings of England, Derbyshire* 2nd edn., (London,1978)
Pevsner, Sir N., *The Buildings of England, Staffordshire* (London 1974)
Pilkington, J., *A View of the Present State of Derbyshire* 2 Vols. (Derby 1789)
Pine, L. G., *Burke's Landed Gentry* (London 1952)   **BLG + date**
Pirie-Gordon, H., *Burke's Landed Gentry* (London 1937)   **BLG + date**
Pounds, D. P. W., *My First 22 Years* (Quebec 2001)
Rietstap, J. B., *Armorial General* (Gouda, 1861)
Repton Charters DAJ (1932) 64-89   **RC + No.**
Robinson, J. M., *Georgian Model Farms 1700-1846* (Oxford 1983)
Roffe, D., *Domesday Derbyshire* (Matlock 1986)
Roffe, D., *Domesday: the Inquest and the Book* (Oxford 2000)
Saltman, A. (Ed.) , *The Cartulary of Dale Abbey* Derbyshire Record Series, II (London, 1967)   **Dale + no.**
Saltman, A. (ed.) *The Cartulary of Tutbury Priory* Historic Manuscripts Commission, Staffordshire Record Society 4th Series, IV (London 1962)   **Tutbury + no.**
Saltman, A. (Ed.), *The Kniveton Leiger* Derbyshire Record Series VII (London 1977)
Saltman, A., *The Cartulary of the Wakebridge Chantries at Crich* Derbyshire Record Series VI (Kendal 1976)
Saunders, E. J., *A Biographical Dictionary of English Wrought Iron Smiths in the Seventeenth and Eighteenth Centuries* in *Journal* of the Walpole Society (London 2005) 237 - 384.

Sawyer, P. H., *Charters of Burton Abbey* (Oxford 1975)

Simpson, R., *Notes Towards a History of Derby,* 3 Vols. (Derby 1826)

Somerville, Sir R., *Office Holders in the Duchy and County Palatine of Lancaster from 1603* (London & Chichester, 1972)

Squibb, G. D. (Ed.) *Dugdale's Nottinghamshire and Derbyshire Visitation Papers 1662-1667* Harleian Society, NS VI (London 1987)

Stenton, D. M. (ed.) *The Great Roll of the Pipe for the Second Year of King Richard I to the Third year of King John AD1189 to 1201* Pipe Roll Society (PRS) New Series, Vol. 10, (London 1930)

Stenton, Sir F. M., *Anglo-Saxon England,* Vol. 3 of the Oxford History of England, 3rd Edn., (Oxford, 1971)

Stone, B., *Derbyshire in the Civil War* (Cromford 1992)

Tachella, B., *Derby School Registers* (Derby 1902)

Taylor, C., *Village and Farmstead* (London 1983)

Thoroton, J., ed., Throsby, J. *History and Antiquities of Nottinghamshire* 4 Vols., (London 1792)

Tilley, J., *The Old Hall, Manors and Families of Derbyshire* 4 Vols. (Derby 1894 -1902)

Todd, M., *The Coritani* (Leicester 1973)

Townend, P. & Montgomery-Massingberd, H., *Burke's Landed Gentry* 3 Vols. (London 1965-1972)   **BLG + date + vol.**

Turbutt, G., *A History of Derbyshire,* 4 Vols. (Cardiff, 1999)

Turner, S., *Aspects of the Development of public Assembly in the Danelaw* York University occasional paper (York 2000)

Universal British Directory (London 1791)   **UBD**

VCH *Staffordshire* IX (2003)

Wain, H. J., *The History of Newton Solney,* 8 pt. series of weekly articles in *Burton Mail,* 10/5 - 1/7/1976.

Walford, E., *County Families of the United Kingdom* (London 1883)

White, W., *Directory of Staffordshire* (Sheffield, 1834)

White, C. N., *Directory of Derby and its Environs* (Sheffield 1874)

White, F., *Directory of Derbyshire* (Sheffield 1857)

White, F., *Directory of Staffordshire* (Sheffield 1851)

Whitwell, J. B., *The Coritani* in BAR British Series No. 99 (Oxford 1982)

Williams, A., Smyth, A. P. & Kirby, D. P., *A Biographical Dictionary of Dark Age Britain* (London 1991)

Wiltshire, M. & Woore, S., *The Medieval Parks of Derbyshire* (Ashbourne 2009)

Wood, S., *Domesday Book:* Vol. 27, *Derbyshire* (Chichester, 1978)   **DB**

Woolley, W. (ed. Glover, C., & Riden, P), *History of Derbyshire,* Derbyshire Record Society Vol. VI, original MS of c. 1714, (Chesterfield 1981)

Wright, S., *The Derbyshire Gentry in the Fifteenth Century* Derbyshire Record Society Vol. VIII (Chesterfield 1983)

Periodicals & Journals

Architectural History Journal of the Society of Architectural Historians (from 1957)

Branch News of the Derbyshire Family History Society (From 1971)   **BN/DFHS**

Derby Mercury 1732-1928   **DM + date**

Derbyshire Archaeological Journal Derbyshire Archaeological Society's journal, from 1878   **DAJ + vol + date**

Derbyshire Life & Countryside, esp,. Vol. XXXI No. 1 (1/1966) 45-51; XXXI No.8 (8/1966) 57-59, Sinar, J., Vol. XLVI no. 4 (4/1981) 50-51 & Christian, R. C., in Vol. LV, no. 1, (1/1990) 38-41.   **DLC = date**

Derbyshire Miscellany (From 2/1956)
Reliquary Ed. LL. Jewitt (1860-1892),
Salt Archaeological Society's Journal, New Series from 1900
Staffordshire History

D. Misc
Reliquary

*

Hawfield Lane, photographed just where is crosses from Winshill into Newton   [*M. Craven*]

INDEX

Notes:

1. *Where a page number is given in bold, e.g.* **90**, *this indicates an illustration of the subject in question is included in that page.*

2. *Where the same first name is shared between two or more members of the same family, they are distinguished by the use of a superscript digit: e.g. Solney family: Alfred[1], Alfred[2], Alfred[3], etc.*